ENGINEERING CONTRACTS

ENGINEERING CONTRACTS
A Practical Guide

Engineering Contracts: A Practical Guide is a new title in the **McGraw-Hill International Series in Civil Engineering**

ENGINEERING CONTRACTS
A Practical Guide

John G. Betty

McGRAW-HILL BOOK COMPANY

London · New York · St Louis · San Francisco · Auckland
Bogotá · Caracas · Lisbon · Madrid · Mexico
Milan · Montreal · New Delhi · Panama · Paris · San Juan
São Paulo · Singapore · Sydney · Tokyo · Toronto

Published by
McGRAW-HILL Book Company Europe
Shoppenhangers Road · Maidenhead · Berkshire · SL6 2QL · England
Tel 0628 23432; Fax 0628 770224

British Library Cataloguing in Publication Data
Betty, John G.
  Engineering Contracts: Practical Guide. –
  (McGraw-Hill International Series in Civil Engineering)
  I. Title II. Series
  624

  ISBN 0-07-707779-2

Library of Congress Cataloging-in-Publication Data

Betty, John G. (John Galtress)
  Engineering contracts: a practical guide/John G. Betty.
    p.   cm. — (McGraw-Hill international series in civil
  engineering)
  Includes index.
  ISBN 0-07-707779-2
  1. Engineering contracts.   I. Title.   II. Series.
TA180.B48 1993
620′.0068—dc20   92-37010
                                                                CIP

12345 CUP 96543

Typeset by Alden Multimedia, Northampton
and printed and bound in Great Britain at the University Press,
Cambridge

CONTENTS

PREFACE

This is a book primarily for engineers, particularly engineers who are called upon to take the leading role in the procurement process for an engineering enterprise.

There are, of course, situations where the leading role is taken by a member of another profession, in which case the engineer plays a supporting role. A typical example is in large domestic or commercial building projects where an architect is often responsible for the documentation and tendering procedures. The engineer's role is then usually confined to the preparation of the design, specification, and drawings for the engineering components of the work.

Having overall responsibility for a project means that the engineer undertakes or supervises the preparation of the documents which define the requirements for the work; inviting, receiving, and evaluating tenders; and finally negotiating an agreement to perform the obligations under a contract. Success demands more than just technical competence. Many skills are required, not the least of which is the art of documentation.

The contract-by-tender system is fundamental to the engineering industry. Unfortunately, many engineering faculties pay insufficient attention to the importance of adopting and following logical and consistent procedures during tendering and to the art of writing technical documents.

The lack of training in documentation may be compounded by inadequate schooling in the English language.

Consequently, many young engineers enter the profession deficient in spelling and grammar and lacking the skills of letter and report writing, a poor basis for drafting documents for contract purposes. Furthermore, newly qualified engineers, no doubt well trained in the theory of design and construction, are often left to their own devices when asked to negotiate a contract. At best, they may receive a hurried briefing from a more senior colleague, or they may be told to follow procedures adopted for an earlier project. These, in turn, could well have been prepared by someone equally ill-equipped for the task. And so the errors are compounded.

To redress these inadequacies, this book aims to guide the engineer through the entire tender procedure, step by step, from the initial concept of a project to the signing of the contract agreement. The author is convinced that if more attention is paid to the preparation of the contract documents and to the adoption of a meticulous approach to tendering procedures, many of the difficulties and disputes arising during the implementation stage of a contract could be avoided.

In Part I the background to the development and planning of a proposed engineering enterprise is first described and the role and responsibility of the professional engineer defined. The function of contracts in engineering is discussed, the law of contract is summarized, and the documents required to substantiate a contract are explained. In Part II the procedures to be followed during the tendering process are outlined and the function of the various documents described. Finally, in Part III the preparation of the individual documents is explained in detail.

It is important for engineers to appreciate that hard and fast rules do not always apply in engineering. It is unfortunate that many engineers tend to look upon their function as finding unique 'solutions' to neatly defined 'problems'. This no doubt stems from their early introduction at school to the mathematical and physical sciences. They should avoid using the words 'problem' and 'solution' and instead should consider their task as a series of often overlapping challenges to each of which there can be a number of possible responses. The art of engineering and the skill of the engineer is in selecting the most appropriate response under the circumstances.

The suggestions made in this book should not be regarded as 'hard and fast solutions'. Data presented and recommendations made are for information and guidance only and are not intended for use without independent investigation on the part of the engineer. Each project should be considered on its own merit and the engineer is expected to use common sense and prudence in adopting or adapting these to the particular situation. Discussion of the legal issues involved and the associated case law is outside the scope and purpose of this book. Independent legal advice should be sought when required.

Definitions

The following definitions have been used in this book:

party   An individual, a group of individuals or a corporation who is a signatory to a legal agreement.

contract   An agreement enforceable at law. (The term is discussed in more detail in Chapter 2 – 'The Role of Contracts in the Project'.)

Owner   The *party* (see above) who ultimately pays for the *work under the Contract* and who will accordingly 'own' the *Works*. In contracts involving site work this usually means the owner of the property on which the work under the contract is carried out.

Principal   The principal party to the Contract who invites tenders, negotiates the Contract and eventually signs the Agreement. The Principal may or may not be the Owner, depending upon circumstances.

Contractor   The second party to the Contract, who undertakes to perform the work or to supply goods or services under the Contract.

work under the Contract   All work which the *Contractor* is required to perform under the Contract: this includes all authorized variations, temporary work, making good defects, and the use of constructional plant and equipment.

Works The whole of the work performed in accordance with the Contract and which, on completion, is to be handed over to the Principal.

Engineer The professional engineer delegated to act in a technical capacity on behalf of the Principal during the Tender or Negotiating stage. The Engineer may be an employee of the Owner, or of the Principal, or of any other party engaged to act on behalf of the Owner or Principal.

Superintendent The individual delegated to act in a supervisory and administrative capacity on behalf of the Principal during the implementation of the Contract. The Superintendent may or may not be the Engineer, depending upon circumstances.

Variations in Terminology

Many terms used in engineering contracts have meanings which can differ according to local practice and the particular type of engineering. The terms used to identify the parties mentioned in a contract are prime examples. 'Employer', 'Owner', 'Principal', 'Proprietor', and 'Purchaser' are all used to refer to the first party to the Contract, while 'Contractor', 'Fabricator', 'Manufacturer', 'Subcontractor', and 'Vendor' are frequently used to refer to the second party. Whichever term is adopted in a particular case is usually determined by the nature of the contract.

In legal terminology, one of the definitions of 'Principal' is 'the person initiating an action'. It is a generic term applicable in all types of contract to the party inviting offers to perform a contract. Similarly, the party who contracts to supply goods or services, or to undertake work under the contract, is usually referred to as the 'Contractor'. Accordingly, the terms 'Principal' and 'Contractor' are used in this book to refer to the two parties to the contract, while 'Owner' refers to the party who ultimately 'owns' the Works.

The term 'Engineer' is often used to identify the Principal's representative in both the tender and the implementation stages of a project. In this book, separate terms ('Engineer' and 'Superintendent') are deliberately used for each stage to facilitate the explanation and discussion of the different responsibilites and duties. During the tender stage, the Principal's representative should, and most probably will, be a professionally qualified engineer. During the implementation stage, the duties of the Principal's representative could be, and often are, performed by a person with other qualifications. In most cases, however, the Engineer and the Superintendent are the same person.

Consistency in terminology takes precedence over geographical variations. Obviously, the terms used in any pre-printed, standard form of

Contract Conditions should determine their use for all relevant documents. In every case, the terms must be clearly defined in the Contract.

In this book, 'work under the Contract' and 'Works' are used to distinguish between work which the Contractor will be required to carry out (including any work of a temporary nature) and the final Works which are to be handed over to the Principal on completion.

In accordance with usual practice, terms beginning with an upper-case letter refer to the particular application as defined above. When printed with a lower-case initial letter, the generic or dictionary meaning applies. This convention should be adopted when preparing documents for a contract.

Other terms used in this book are defined as they arise and are listed in the Glossary.

PART
ONE

THE FUNCTION OF CONTRACTS
IN ENGINEERING

THE ORGANIZATION OF AN ENGINEERING PROJECT

1.1 THE PLANNING AND MANAGEMENT OF A PROJECT

In today's commercial and industrial environment, a large proportion of capital investment is for facilities containing a significant engineering component. This could include investment in plant or equipment, in the construction of buildings for commercial purposes, or in infrastructure or facilities for the manufacture, storage, or handling of goods and materials. Any proposal for this type of investment would normally be subjected to a detailed cost–benefit evaluation by the Owner, and management is turning increasingly to professional engineers for assistance in this evaluation.

As a result, engineers have developed skills and expertise in the planning and management of the early stages of such projects. Although the Engineer (who has been given the task of initiating the implementation of a project) may not have been directly associated with the decision-making, it is important that there is an understanding of the factors involved. It is to be hoped that when making a decision whether or not to proceed with such an investment, the Owner has followed a structured decision path taking into account the following five elements:

3

- Corporate planning
- Conceptual design
- Project planning
- Design and documentation
- Project management

Whether the project comprises, on the one hand, the purchase of a single item of plant or equipment for installation on an existing site, or, on the other, the construction of a large, multi-discipline facility on a completely new site, the process to be followed should be basically the same, with the necessary modifications for a particular situation.

Corporate Planning

Most large organizations have carefully planned corporate strategies for their operations and future development, and any proposed capital expenditure would have to be examined to ensure conformity with those strategies. This appraisal would take into account:

- Acquisition strategy
- Evaluation of existing assets
- Market research
- Financial modelling
- Cost–Benefit analysis
- Availability and source of funds

If this appraisal confirms that the proposal is in conformity with the corporate strategy, the next stage is to undertake a conceptual design study and prepare preliminary cost estimates; these will form the basis of any decision to proceed.

Conceptual Design Study

Before an engineering enterprise can be countenanced, its feasibility must first be established. This usually requires input by a number of professionals including accountants, economists, market analysts, architects and quantity surveyors, as well as engineers. They will examine all the factors affecting its viability so that a decision can be made whether or not to proceed with the project.

Conceptual Design encompasses the preliminary design and cost estimate for the work to the degree required to determine the feasibility and viability of the project. This stage of the design process is usually undertaken by the

Owner, using either in-house resources or the services of a consultant; in a 'turnkey' type of contract it may form part of the Contractor's responsibility.

The study would investigate and compare the various design options available including the possibility and advantages of using new technology. If the choice of the preferred option cannot be readily determined, it may be necessary to expand the investigation until a choice can be made.

The Conceptual Design study comprises a number of distinct steps:

- Defining the task and ascertaining the constraints
- Identifying a variety of solutions which may be considered in any way to be practicable
- Obtaining all information and data readily available on the potential solutions
- Identifying the nature and extent of additional data and information required for the final design
- Identifying and preparing preliminary calculations of all external loads and forces to be taken into account in the final design of the Works
- Undertaking preliminary designs and estimates for comparative purposes on the options identified
- Reviewing the options and selecting one (or more) which seems most likely to produce the best final result

Although preparing the cost estimates necessarily requires making many assumptions in regard to matters which time does not permit to be fully investigated, in many cases this preliminary estimate can be closer to the final cost than the more detailed estimate made when the design has been completed.

The Engineer should be alert to the danger of assuming that the final estimate has allowed for everything required; insufficient allowance may not have been made for contingencies which will certainly arise during the execution of the work.

Having established the viability of the project, the next stage is to prepare a Project Plan.

Project Planning

The *Project Plan* establishes the framework within which the corporate objectives are to be achieved and forms the basis for transforming initial concepts into practical and economic realities.

This stage is to determine the parameters within which the work is to be designed and operated. Primarily it should be an engineering responsibility; otherwise difficulties could arise in the implementation stage in trying to devise engineering solutions to meet corporate requirements.

Project Planning may include an examination of the proposed site and an assessment of the effect of the work on the environment. At the same time a decision will need to be made on the procedure to be followed in undertaking the work; this procedure usually involves obtaining firm quotations for the construction, fabrication, or purchase of the facility and entering into a contract for its implementation.

The ability to identify key issues is the basis for all sound planning and decision-making. The factors to be considered when developing the Project Plan include:

- Identification of critical decision points
- Evaluation of time, cost, and risk
- Programming and logistics
- Procurement of services
- Contractual arrangements
- Operations planning
- Environmental issues

It is essential to prepare a viable Project Plan before undertaking the next stage – the design and documentation of the work to be undertaken.

Design and Documentation

Design is the detailed formulation of the requirements for the execution of the work; *documentation* is the preparation of the documents required for tendering and implementation purposes. The prime function of this book is to describe the procedures and to provide guidelines for the Engineer.

Those responsible for these aspects will need to establish good quality control to ensure proper coordination between the parameters established in the conceptual and planning stages and their incorporation in the design and documentation. The engineer responsible for the documentation (the Engineer) is well placed to take the lead in this coordination; careful cross-checking with the designer and the drawing office at all stages will be essential if errors, duplications, and omissions are to be avoided.

When an engineering project runs into trouble or is deficient in some respect, the cause is more likely to be a failure in documentation or communication rather than a failure in design. The fundamental principle in the documentation of an engineering contract is first to define clearly the work to be performed. Then, having identified all the risks and responsibilities, to allocate them clearly and unequivocally to one or other of the parties to the Contract. Trouble is inevitable if the parties involved do not know precisely what is expected of them or where responsibility lies. All too often, disputes have arisen because the Engineer has ignored such matters or has been unwilling to make necessary decisions in regard to them.

Project Management

The prime function of *Project Management* is to monitor and control time and money. Many engineers see Project Management as an activity confined to the control and supervision of the actual implementation of the project. However, an effective management system should be incorporated into the project as soon as the decision has been made to proceed. To be truly effective, Project Management should be carried out by individuals who are not otherwise involved in the project. A practicable Project Management system can be of value not only to corporate management but also to the Engineer.

Tasks involved in a functional Project Management system include:

- Monitoring the programme
- Controlling the expenditure
- Expediting and coordinating
- Supervision and quality control
- Reporting on progress and expenditure

If the Engineer has established effective coordination systems, the work of the Project Management team will be principally a monitoring and reporting function. The Engineer should not rely on the Project Management system to control the design and documentation; this is the Engineer's responsibility.

1.2. THE DEVELOPMENT OF THE PROJECT PLAN

In developing the Project Plan, the Owner is first faced with making a number of important decisions concerning the manner in which the project will be handled. These decisions will materially effect the procedures to be followed in the implementation of the project. The first question is fundamental:

> Is the whole of the work, including the design and installation/construction (as appropriate), to be carried out using the Owner's own expertise and resources, or are other parties to be involved?

The answer to this question will, of course, depend upon the 'in-house' expertise and resources available to the Owner. If the first option is chosen, the question of negotiating contracts does not arise and the procedure to be followed is outside the scope of this book.

In following the second course, commercial prudence would suggest that the Owner enters into firmly binding contracts with each party engaged to carry out work not undertaken by the Owner.

This leads to the next question:

Does the Owner prefer to employ a single party to take all the responsibility, leaving the Owner 'at arm's length' from the work, or does the Owner want to be more closely involved with the implementation of the project?

If the answer is that the Owner prefers to hand over the whole of the project to another party, the most practical course of action is for the Owner to enter into a written agreement with a contractor to undertake the work on a 'turnkey' basis. This agreement should clearly define the Contractor's obligations under the Contract and the rights and responsibilities of both parties.

A *Turnkey Contract* is one in which the Contractor assumes complete responsibility for the project. This may include the whole of the design, supply, construction/installation, supervision, quality control, and management of the work. The Contractor may even be required to locate and purchase a site and arrange finance for the Owner. Such a contract is all-embracing and gives full responsibility to the Contractor. On completion of the work, the Contractor hands over the completed and fully commissioned Works to the Owner.

If a Turnkey Contract is negotiated, the work is handled entirely with the Contractor's own resources, or other contractors are engaged to undertake various parts of the work. In the latter case, the Turnkey Contractor becomes the Principal when dealing with these other contractors.

The alternative is for the Owner to negotiate directly with contractors to undertake the work. This will require the Owner to become the Principal and thus to assume responsibility for (a) the design and documentation and (b) the supervision and the administration of the contracts during the performance of the work. This then raises two more questions:

Are the resources available to the Principal sufficient to handle the design, documentation, and supervision of the work without outside assistance?

If outside assistance is required, to what extent is it needed and where is this help to be obtained?

In considering these questions, the Principal's involvement should be looked at as being divided into two stages:

A. *The tender or negotiation stage.* Preparing the designs and documents required to define the extent of the work under each Contract and the terms and conditions under which it is to be carried out, inviting and receiving tenders, negotiating contract(s), and arranging for the Agreement to be signed.

B. *The contract or implementation stage.* Administering the Contract(s), supervising the work to its completion and seeing that the terms and conditions of the Contract(s) are carried out to the satisfaction of both parties to the Contract(s).

The choices open to the Principal are:

1. Undertake both Stage A and Stage B entirely with 'in-house' resources.
2. Engage an independent organization to carry out those parts of Stage A and Stage B considered outside the expertise or capacity of the Principal's 'in-house' resources.
3. Engage an independent organization to carry out the whole of the work comprised under both Stage A and Stage B.

If outside assistance is required, the Principal would be well advised to turn to a professional consulting engineering organization specializing in the particular field of expertise required. The procedures for selecting and appointing a Consulting Engineer are well documented by the various national associations for professional Consulting Engineers.

These associations are affiliated under the international body Fédération Internationale des Ingénieurs-Conseils (FIDIC). A list of them is given in Appendix B.

A decision path diagram outlining the above steps is shown in Fig. 1.1.

The duties and responsibilities of the Consulting Engineer must be clearly specified by the Principal when making the appointment. This is particularly important where the Principal wishes to retain responsibility for some aspects of the work. In this situation, the interface between the areas of responsibility between the Principal and the Consulting Engineer must be clearly defined so that there can be no misunderstanding as to the obligations of each party.

The next step is to determine how the conceptual design can be translated into an effective working design. This then raises the next question:

What is the extent of design required and who is to be responsible for this work?

There could be two types of design to be considered, depending upon the nature of the project:

1. *Process Design* is the design of a production process itself as opposed to the design of the components of the system. It is applicable to the design of production installations such as oil refineries, chemical plants and food-

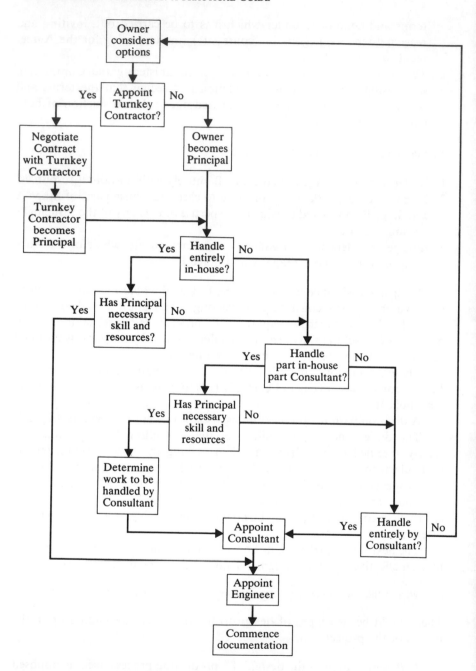

Figure 1.1 Decision path diagram.

processing facilities and is normally a highly skilled and specialized field of activity.

Process design frequently involves the use of highly confidential or patented information and is usually undertaken by or on behalf of the Principal by firms or organizations possessing expertise in the particular field. Alternatively, it can form part of the Contract if the work comes within the area of expertise of the Contractor.

2. *Detailed Design* is the design of the components of the project and comprises two parts. The first part is the preparation of the design to the extent of detail accepted in normal contracting practice. This can be undertaken by the Principal in-house or by a Consulting Engineer engaged by the Principal. Alternatively, this part of the design can be included in the work under the Contract and it then becomes the responsibility of the Contractor.

The second part is to complete the design to the extent of detail required for actual fabrication or construction. This part includes the preparation of such designs as shop drawings for the fabrication of machinery, structural steelwork, and timberwork, reinforcement bending schedules, pipe and conduit layouts, wiring diagrams, and the like. Such design is normally included in the work under the Contract and is then the responsibility of the Contractor.

At this stage the Principal will have been identified and responsibilities for various aspects of the design allocated. The task then becomes a matter of determining the contractual procedures to be adopted and preparing the documents required for tendering and contract purposes.

The Project Plan, in effect, becomes the brief for the Engineer. It should be a written document clearly defining what the Engineer is to do and what is the Engineer's responsibility, duty and authority. The matters covered should include, but not necessarily be restricted to, the following:

- Identification and description of the preferred design option (or options) with an outline of the reasons for the choice
- A clear direction as to who is to be responsible for the design
- An indication of the preferred contractual procedures
- The nature, extent and reliability of the data on which the conceptual design has been based.

While the Project Plan should be as precise as possible, the Engineer should be given enough latitude to be able to make further investigations and suggest modifications to the Plan.

It is at this point that the Engineer should be appointed.

1.3 THE ROLE AND RESPONSIBILITY OF THE ENGINEER

What is an Engineer?

The modern English word 'engineer' most probably evolved from an earlier word 'enginer' meaning a contriver or schemer. It derived from 'engin' meaning skill or device by the addition of the agential suffix '-er'. The word is of Latin origin and entered the English language through the French spoken by the Norman invaders. Niccolo Machiavelli could be described as an 'enginer'.

The following quotations illustrate the use of these words by early English authors:

'A man hath sapiences thre, Memorie, engin and intellect also.'

Chaucer, *Canterbury Tales*

'For 'tis the sport to haue the enginer
Hoist with his own petar.'

Shakespeare, *Hamlet*, III. iv. 206

(A petar or petard was an explosive-filled canister used to blow in the doors or gates of a fortification.)

In the second quotation, it is interesting to note the connection between 'enginer' and military operations. Initially, engineering was a military function and it was not until the eighteenth century that the term 'civil engineering' was introduced to differentiate its application to the community at large from its military application. As a result of the Industrial Revolution in England in the latter half of the eighteenth century, specialized fields of engineering such as mining, mechanical, and electrical began to be recognized and the term 'civil engineering' contracted to its present meaning.

The use of the term 'engineer' to refer to a machinery attendant is relatively modern, although in the USA locomotive engine drivers have been referred to as 'engineers' since the early nineteenth century. Apart from this, the connection between 'engines' and 'engineers' is casual.

The probable etymology of the word 'engineer' is shown in Fig. 1.2. It is clear that, by definition, an engineer is primarily an adviser, a planner, and an inventor.

In this book, the term is used to refer to a professional engineer, who is usually defined as an academically qualified person who uses professed knowledge and experience in the application of the art and science of engineering.

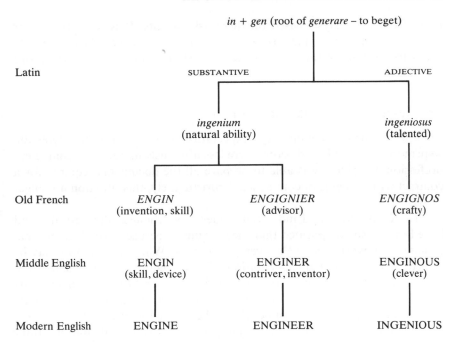

in + *gen* (root of *generare* – to beget)

Latin	SUBSTANTIVE		ADJECTIVE
	ingenium (natural ability)		*ingeniosus* (talented)
Old French	*ENGIN* (invention, skill)	*ENGIGNIER* (advisor)	*ENGIGNOS* (crafty)
Middle English	ENGIN (skill, device)	ENGINER (contriver, inventor)	ENGINOUS (clever)
Modern English	ENGINE	ENGINEER	INGENIOUS

Figure 1.2 Etymology of 'engineer'.

The Art of Engineering

Engineering is the art and science of planning, designing and accomplishing the fabrication of machinery and works for the use and benefit of the community at large.

It is important to appreciate that engineering is an art as much as it is a science. A science can be taught in the lecture room and in the laboratory; an art must be learnt by practice and observation. A hundred years ago, the science of engineering was taught at the technical college while the art was acquired by the system of 'pupilage', where the student engineer was 'apprenticed' to a more senior and experienced practitioner. The situation today is different. The newly qualified engineer, imbued with the enthusiasm and impatience of youth, and with the ink scarcely dry on the degree or diploma, is tossed straight into the practice of engineering with little opportunity to acquire an insight into the art.

All engineering decisions, whether in design or in construction, are based on probabilities and empirical assessments. The art lies in using experience, creativity and intuition to produce an economical, practical, and aesthetic result from an analysis based on these assessments. It is not possible for engineers to give an unqualified guarantee of performance. The community needs to be made aware of this fact and should modify its expectations accordingly.

The Responsibility of the Engineer

In the past, when the community's expectations of the engineering profession were more reasonable and people were less litigiously minded, the competent professional engineer was able to prepare all the documents required for a contract with a degree of confidence. Unfortunately, this situation no longer exists.

The contracting and industrial scenes have changed dramatically and have become so complicated that they require expertise beyond the normal training and experience of the average engineer. While the engineer may be skilled in design and documentation of the technical requirements of a project, the preparation of the so-called 'legal' or 'up front' documents (Conditions of Tendering, Conditions of Contract, Invitation to Tenderers, and the like) has become a minefield, to be entered with trepidation.

Legal interpretation of court judgements, government and statutory authority regulations, insurance, industrial relations, and environmental issues are a few of the pitfalls awaiting the Engineer. The growing tendency of the community to view every misfortune as a source of financial windfall has created a hostile environment, not only for engineers but for professionals generally. The strength of common law lies in its capacity to change; however, a weakness lies in its capacity to change with little regard to logic.

Prudent engineers should be aware of the dangers of stepping into fields which lie outside their competence. Whether an engineer is a sole practitioner or an employee, this awareness should lead to the practice of referring such non-technical documents to persons with expertise in such fields. Whether the expert or the engineer, after receiving appropriate advice, actually undertakes the drafting, is immaterial to the overall responsibility for the document. This still must remain in the hands of the engineer.

THE ROLE OF CONTRACTS IN THE PROJECT

2.1 THE FUNCTION OF AN ENGINEERING CONTRACT

What Is an Engineering Contract?

An *Engineering Contract* is a mutual agreement negotiated between two parties for the purpose of undertaking, on a commercial basis, certain clearly specified engineering work.

Who Are the Parties to an Engineering Contract?

In accordance with the definitions adopted in this book, the parties to the Contract are the Principal and the Contractor. The Principal is the party who wants the work done and is prepared to pay for it and the Contractor is the party who agrees to undertake the work in return for payment.

What Are Negotiations?

Negotiations are the spoken and written transactions between the Principal and the Contractor leading to the contract agreement to undertake the work or to supply goods and/or services under the contract.

How Is a Contract Negotiated?

Negotiations for a contract are begun by the Principal inviting an offer or a proposal to undertake the work under a contract from one or more suitably qualified individuals or corporations. The formal offer made by a contractor in response to such an invitation is referred to as a *tender*.

Where one party only is invited to submit a tender, the agreement may be reached by direct negotiation. Where two or more parties are invited, the agreement is usually reached by a competitive tendering process in which tenders are invited and evaluated in accordance with clearly defined provisions.

Reaching the final agreement may be a lengthy procedure, during which the negotiating parties prepare and exchange documents setting out their respective requirements, offers and counter offers. These documents must be carefully and meticulously prepared so as to avoid misunderstandings and misinterpretations which could lead to disputes during the contract stage.

How Is the Existence of a Contract Demonstrated?

To ensure that the finally negotiated agreement is enforceable at law, the Contract should be clearly 'evidenced' by writing down the agreed terms and conditions under an *Instrument of Agreement*, to be signed by the parties to the Contract.

The legal aspects of the procedure have been outlined in Sec. 2.2 – 'The Law of Contract'.

2.2 THE LAW OF CONTRACT

Anyone involved in preparing documents which are intended to be used in the negotiation and formation of an engineering contract inevitably encounters a situation which requires some knowledge of contract law. While one may have little or no legal training, an overall understanding of the law in this matter is advisable, if only to be aware of the necessity of obtaining professional advice when the limit of one's legal knowledge is reached.

This brief discussion of the law of contract is appropriate to English common law, which forms the basis of the legal systems of most English-speaking Commonwealth countries. While the law may differ in detail between such countries, the basic principles enunciated will generally apply. Within each country the law may change from time to time – what is law today may not be law tomorrow. Therefore, it is not practicable to give an exhaustive review of current contract law in each English-speaking country and, for a more complete understanding of the current local legal position, the reader is advised to consult a lawyer or an appropriate textbook dealing with the legal aspects of contract law.

Origins of Contract Law

Contract law is the product of commercial civilization. The legal enforcement of promises made by an individual became necessary with the evolution of a barter economy into a market economy. In communities based on a barter economy, most transactions were completed by both sides at the same time in a single operation. If a dispute over the transaction subsequently arose, such primitive societies had other means of enforcing the commitments of individuals. These were usually based on kinship ties or the authority of the established religion. Even when a transaction did not involve an exchange of goods, security for a debt usually took the form of pledging property such as land or slaves or even the person of one of the parties to the agreement.

By the sixth century AD, Roman Law recognized various types of contracts and agreements, but the concept was lost with the collapse of the Roman Empire. With the development of market economies in Western Europe in the twelfth and thirteenth centuries, the procedures evolved for a barter economy became impracticable when promises for the future exchange of goods or provision of services were involved.

Informal agreements, not enforceable at law, were adopted by the merchants and it soon became necessary to establish courts. These were initially administered by the merchants themselves to regulate and enforce the informal and flexible procedures used.

This led to the development of contract law within the established legal system and it was at this point that two diverging practices emerged. In England, contractual problems were dealt with under the common law through the actions of debt and covenant. On the Continent, civil law evolved from the classical Roman Law, influenced by the canon law of the Church.

Definition of a Contract

The simplest definition of a *contract* is that it is a promise enforceable at law. The promise may be to do something or not to do something. By extension, the term 'contract' has also come to refer to the written document in which the terms of the promise are written down.

In a commercial sense, a contract is a mutual agreement enforceable at law between two or more parties that something shall be done or not done by either or both parties. By implication, both parties thereby accept certain responsibilities and in return receive certain benefits.

Classification of Contracts

Traditionally there are two main classes of contracts, namely:

- Formal contracts
- Simple contracts

A *formal contract*, also referred to as a *contract under seal*, is a deed whose validity depends solely upon its form. In legal terms, *form* refers to the manner in which the agreement is expressed. A *deed* is an instrument in writing and must be signed 'under seal' by the party executing the deed and attested by a witness who is not a party to the contract. It is not necessary for a party executing the deed to actually place a seal on the document, provided that the deed states that it is signed 'under seal'. However, since a corporation does not have a signature, it can only execute a deed by affixing its common seal in the manner prescribed in its articles of association.

The party executing the deed must then hand or deliver the signed deed to the other party – 'signed, sealed, and delivered as a deed'.

A *simple contract*, on the other hand, does not have to be in any particular form. It can be made verbally or in writing or partly in both.

In practice, there are only a few differences between formal contracts and simple contracts in writing.

The first difference is that, to be enforceable, a simple contract must be supported by *consideration*. Consideration is an inducement to enter into a legally enforceable agreement. It can be either a detriment incurred by one party or a benefit received by the other party. Thus, the party seeking to enforce the agreement must have paid, or promised to pay, some money, parted with some goods, or forgone some benefit.

The second difference concerns the period during which action can be taken under the contract. This period can vary, depending upon the jurisdiction under which the contract is established, but generally it is longer for formal contracts than it is for simple contracts.

In an engineering situation, a formal contract therefore gives the Principal greater protection.

The third difference is that a contract under seal creates an *estoppel*. This is a rule of law which precludes a party from later claiming that a statement expressed in the contract is incorrect, especially if others may have been led to rely or act upon that statement.

Corporations

A *corporation* is a legally created artificial body. It has a legal existence quite apart from the individual persons who comprise it, and, by virtue of this separate existence, it can only enter into a contract through an agent. This limitation requires that a corporation can only enter into a legally binding contract under its seal, although it is generally accepted that, in respect of everyday matters of minor importance, the signature of its agent is sufficient.

However, under many jurisdictions, a contract which, if made between individual persons, would be required to be made in writing and signed by the parties, may be made in writing on behalf of a corporation and signed by an authorized person, such authority being either expressed or implied.

Formal Instrument of Agreement

Sometimes the parties to a simple contract later execute and substitute a formal Instrument of Agreement. This written agreement identifies the parties by name and registered address, states the date of the agreement and sets out the terms and conditions of the contract, frequently by reference to annotated, annexed documents. It is the form of the agreement primarily established by the manner of signing which determines whether it is a simple or formal contract.

If both parties sign as individuals, without the presence of witnesses, the agreement becomes evidence in writing of a simple contract. If either of the parties is a corporation, the individual signing on its behalf must be its authorized agent. However, the document may be signed by affixing the corporation's common seal in accordance with its articles of association. The fact that a seal is affixed does not necessarily make it a formal contract.

If, on the other hand, the instrument of agreement states that it is a deed and that it is signed, sealed, and delivered by the parties in the presence of attesting witnesses, it becomes a formal agreement. In this instance the agreement cannot be signed by the corporation's agent and the common seal must be affixed in the proper manner.

If the parties to a simple contract later execute and substitute a formal deed in its place, the formal deed takes precedence. The simple contract ceases to exist provided that the formal deed is signed by the same parties and that it covers the same matters. In legal terms this is known as a *merger*.

This situation frequently arises in engineering contracts. Contracts are negotiated and agreed upon, either verbally or in writing, and the parties later execute a formal Instrument of Agreement, possibly some time after work under the contract has commenced.

There are four basic requirements to be satisfied to form a valid contract, whether it is a simple or a formal one:

• The intention by both parties to form an enforceable contract must be demonstrable.

- The consent of both parties must be genuine.
- The legality of the agreement must be objective.
- Both parties must have the legal capacity to form an agreement.

Intention It must be clear that the parties intended to create a legally binding agreement. There can be no contract unless the parties' intention to enter into an agreement enforceable at law can be demonstrated. Where such an agreement can be shown, usually it will be accepted that the parties intended to create such an undertaking.

In an engineering context, where one party has invited bids and another party has made an offer, the intention to enter into an agreement will be assumed and, for this to be challenged, the onus of proof will rest with the party seeking to dispute the intention.

Genuine consent For a contract to be valid, the consent of the parties must be genuine. Consent obtained under duress or by undue influence can make a contract invalid at the application of the weaker or injured party. A consent obtained by fraud or misrepresentation or through a mistake in facts is not genuine, although it does not necessarily follow that a court will hold that the contract is invalid.

Legality of purpose A contract may be held to be illegal by common law or by statute. Contracts deemed illegal by common law rarely arise in engineering situations.

Agreements to commit a crime or to hinder the administration of justice or to injure public services or to defraud the revenue or to attempt corruption are examples of actions illegal at common law. However, illegality by statute commonly arises in engineering contracts. A contract may be legally entered into, yet its performance may be in breach of a statute or regulation. Such a contract will be void and unenforceable at law and neither party can claim relief under it.

Legal capacity Not all persons can enter into a legally binding agreement. Infants and persons deemed incapable of rational action such as those who are insane or under the influence of alcohol or narcotics cannot legally enter into a valid contract. The law also takes into account the general incapacity of bankrupts and persons in legal custody. The peculiar standing of artificial bodies such as corporations, already referred to, must also be considered.

Elements of a Simple Contract

In addition to the four basic requirements previously listed, the two main elements which are required to comprise a valid simple contract are:

- An offer and an acceptance
- A valuable consideration

Offer and acceptance A contract is formed when an offer is made by one party to another party and is unconditionally accepted by the second party. The keyword is 'unconditional'. A qualified acceptance does not form a contract but constitutes a counter-offer. This in turn requires an unconditional acceptance of the counter-offer by the first party before a contract exists. Offers and counter-offers may continue to be exchanged until an unconditional acceptance is made and then, and only then, will a contract be constituted.

An offer and an acceptance do not have to be made in writing, but can be made orally or implied by conduct. For example, a hand raised at an auction is a case of implied acceptance by conduct. In an engineering situation, if, with the knowledge of the Owner, the Contractor who has made an offer starts work on a job, it would be held that the offer had been accepted if the Owner was in a position to object and did not do so.

Adequate communication is also essential for legal validity. The fact that a party takes, or fails to take, some action which would otherwise amount to an implied acceptance of an offer does not form a contract, unless the offer has been properly communicated.

Where there is an agreement and it can be demonstrated that both parties were aware that their actions could be construed as forming a contract, a legally binding contract would be held to exist.

It is important to distinguish between an offer and a willingness to trade. It is generally accepted that displaying an item for sale with a price tag does not constitute an offer but is held to be a willingness to trade.

Under English common law, an invitation to tender is not an offer but an indication of a willingness to trade. However, in Canada this precept has been overturned by the Supreme Court of Canada in the landmark Ron Engineering case (*R.* v. *Ron Engineering and Construction (Eastern) Ltd* (1981)). Primarily the case concerned the right of a tenderer to withdraw a bid without penalty when the tenderer discovered an error in pricing. The Court held that, once tenders had been submitted, a unilateral contract imposing obligations on both parties came into existence for the duration of the tender period.

Valuable consideration In an engineering contract, the money paid by the

Principal to the Contractor is the consideration given by the Principal to the Contractor. In return, the work performed or the equipment supplied by the Contractor for the Principal is the consideration given by the Contractor to the Principal.

In earlier times, a nominal consideration, such as a single coin or a peppercorn, was held to be sufficient but today the courts require that the consideration be significant, although not necessarily equal in value to what is received.

Rights and Liabilities Under a Contract

The two principal elements to be considered under this heading are:

- Privity
- Assignment

Privity Privity of contract means the legal relationship and mutual interest which exists between the parties to a contract. The word 'privity' itself implies that the relationship is private and concerns only the parties to the contract. Only the parties to a contract can acquire rights or incur liabilities under it. Two parties to a contract cannot make a third party liable under the contract unless the third party is also a party to the contract.

Although no right of action under the contract can exist against a third party who is not a party to the contract, such a third party can be liable under tort if the third party, without justification, induces a party to the contract to commit a breach of existing obligations. The word *tort* means injury or wrong. In a legal sense the word is used to describe a breach of a duty imposed by the law whereby a party acquires a right of action for damages resulting from an alleged injury or wrong.

The implications of this in engineering contracts is that the two parties to a contract (the Principal and the Contractor) cannot agree to make a third party (such as the Superintendent or Consulting Engineer) liable under the contract. But if such a third party, without sufficient justification, induces either or both of them to breach the terms of the contract, the third party can be held to be liable under tort.

Assignment An assignment occurs when one of the parties to a contract substitutes another party in its place as a party to the contract for all or some of the purposes of the contract. Many engineering contracts include a clause specifically denying either party the right to assign unilaterally all or part of the contract. However, since a contract is an agreement, the parties can mutually agree to an assignment.

Discharging a Contract

A contract is said to be *discharged* when it is completed or otherwise terminated. A contract may be discharged by:

- Performance of its provisions
- Agreement between the parties
- Operation of the law
- Frustration or
- Fundamental breach

Discharge by performance When the parties to a contract fulfil all their obligations in strict accordance with the provisions of the contract, the contract is said to be discharged by performance.

Discharge by agreement Since a contract is an agreement between two or more parties, it may be discharged by a further agreement between the parties. Such a further agreement may cancel the original contract by mutual consent, or it may vary the terms of the original agreement by a substituted agreement.

Discharge by operation of law A contract may be discharged by operation of the law independently of the wishes of the parties to the agreement. A contract may be discharged if it is held to be illegal by common law or by statute or if one of the parties becomes bankrupt.

Discharge by frustration The term *frustration* is used to describe the situation which arises when, without default of either party to an agreement, a contractual obligation has become incapable of performance. It can occur when the circumstances under which the performance required become radically different from those which were envisaged by the contract. Frustration must have the effect of frustrating the performance of the whole of the contract and not merely some of its terms. Frustration cannot be claimed because some or all of the work under the contract has become more difficult or more costly. Frustration is sometimes referred to as *force majeure*. In the context of engineering contracts, frustration has been rare to date, but it may become more common in the future as the amount of legislation affecting development and construction increases.

Examples of frustration include the destruction by fire of a building wherein the work under the contract was to be performed or the *resumption* (see Glossary) by the government of the land whereon the work was to be carried out.

Discharge by fundamental breach Every breach of contract will entitle the injured party to sue for damages but not every such breach will have the effect of discharging the contract. Whether or not a particular breach is a *fundamental breach* giving grounds for the injured party to terminate the contract is a matter of determining whether the breach amounts to a repudiation or whether it merely amounts to a breach of certain provisions of the contract.

A repudiation usually arises when an impossible situation is created by one party to the contract either before the contract is due for performance or during the performance of the contract. A party to a contract cannot terminate the contract by unilaterally repudiating the obligations under the contract. If a party attempts to repudiate its obligations under the contract, there are two courses open to the injured party – either accept the repudiation and sue for damages or ignore the repudiation, reaffirm the contract and then sue for damages.

It is rare for a party to breach the contract by a complete repudiation of the whole of the work under the contract. A breach in performance usually involves a breach of certain obligations under the contract.

The law acknowledges that the terms of a contract may not all have the same importance. It distinguishes between what are called *conditions* and what are called *warranties*. A *condition* is a term in the contract which is of such basic importance that a breach goes to the root of the contract and gives the injured party the right to treat the contract as terminated. A *warranty*, on the other hand, refers to a term in the contract which is subsidiary to the main purpose of the contract and its breach merely gives the right to sue for damages.

Whether or not a breach of a condition is to be treated as terminating the contract is at the option of the injured party. If the injured party does not elect to treat the breach as terminating the contract then the condition is considered to be at the same level as a warranty.

Remedies for Breach of Contract

Any breach of a contract will entitle the injured party to sue for damages, whether or not the particular breach is considered to be grounds for treating the contract as discharged.

In assessing a claim for damages, it is first necessary to determine the grounds upon which the claim is made and then to assess the amount of compensation. The injured party usually will be awarded such damages naturally arising from the breach. In assessing the amount of the damages, the courts usually place the injured party, in a financial sense, in the same position as they would have been had the contract been discharged by performance, provided that the injured party had taken all reasonable steps to mitigate the loss caused by the breach.

2.3 TYPES OF CONTRACTS

Classification of Contracts

Contracts for any particular engineering project can be classified in the first instance as either *Main Contracts* (sometimes referred to as *Head Contracts*) or as *Subcontracts*. The essential difference is that a Main Contract is directly between the Principal and a Main Contractor, whereas a Subcontract is between a Main Contractor and another contractor, referred to as a Sub-contractor.

Engineering contracts, whether Main Contracts or Subcontracts, can be further described in a number of ways, each of which depends upon a particular characteristic or feature.

The three most commonly used characteristics for this purpose are:

- The method by which the Contractor is selected
- The method by which payment for the work under the Contract is evaluated
- The method by which responsibility for the technical and administrative aspects of the work is allocated

There are a number of options under each of these headings which can apply to any contract, and the contract can be defined by selecting the appropriate option from each. However, using three terms to describe a contract can be unwieldy and it is usual to select one, or at the most two, of the most significant characteristics.

Subcontracts can further be classified in a number of ways, depending upon procedures laid down in the Contract.

Classification by the Method of Selecting the Contractor

The Principal has two options when selecting the Contractor:

- By a competitive tendering procedure
- By direct negotiation with a selected contractor

A *Competitively Tendered Contract* is one where an agreement is reached between the Principal and a Contractor following a formal competitive tendering procedure in which a number of tenderers are invited to submit bids against a common set of tender enquiry documents. This is the most widely used form of engineering contract and is suitable for engineering projects where the nature and extent of the work under the Contract can be clearly identified.

A *Negotiated Contract* is one where the Principal negotiates directly with a contractor to arrive at a mutually satisfactory agreement to undertake the work. This form of contract is suitable for work of a highly specialized nature or where there is a limited number of contractors experienced in the work required or where the nature of the work cannot be precisely defined.

A contract can sometimes be negotiated by a combination of these methods. For example, tenders can be invited from a shortlist of suitable contractors for that part of the work under the contract which can be precisely defined, and an agreement negotiated for the whole of the work with the contractor who submits the most attractive offer.

Classification by the Method of Payment for the Work

The method of payment is of such importance, particularly to the Contractor, that contracts are often classified solely by the method of payment.

There are four basic methods of payment used in engineering contracts:

- By Lump Sum
- By Schedule of Rates
- By Part Lump Sum, Part Schedule of Rates
- By Cost Plus

The Lump Sum and the Schedule of Rates may be either 'fixed' or 'subject to cost adjustment' as specified in the Contract. In a 'fixed-price' contract, the Contractor accepts responsibility for all fluctuations in costs and charges due to escalation, delays and other reasons and no additional payment will be made to cover such costs. In a contract 'subject to cost adjustment', provision may be made for additional payments due to fluctuations in wages and conditions or for the cost of delays outside the Contractor's control.

In a *Lump Sum Contract* (also known as a *Stipulated Price Contract*) the Contractor is paid the amount nominated in the Contract for the work as agreed with the Principal when negotiating the Contract. This amount may, of course, be increased or decreased owing to additions to or deletions from the scope of the work under the Contract in accordance with the terms of the agreement. This type of contract is commonly used where the nature and extent of the work can be precisely defined when the Contract is negotiated.

In a *Schedule of Rates Contract* the Contractor is paid for the work actually done at pre-agreed unit rates. This type of payment is also known as 'payment by *quantum meruit*'. In this type of contract it is important that the items in the Schedule of Rates or the Priced Bill of Quantities cover the whole of the work and that the method of measurement of quantities is clearly defined. Schedule of Rates Contracts are generally used where the nature and extent of the work can be accurately defined but the quantity of work cannot.

Some contracts combine the two methods of payment. Part of the work under the Contract may be covered by a lump sum and part of it paid for under a Schedule of Rates. This type of contract is referred to as a *Part Lump Sum, Part Schedule of Rates Contract*. Strictly speaking, the inclusion of a Provisional Sum for some particular item or work in a Lump Sum Contract makes the Contract a Part Lump Sum Part Schedule of Rates Contract.

In a *Cost Plus Contract* (also known as a *Cost Reimbursement Contract*) the Contractor is reimbursed the actual costs incurred in carrying out the work under the Contract plus a fee to cover overhead costs and profit. The fee can be one of the following:

- A fixed sum
- A fixed sum with a profit-sharing arrangement
- A fixed sum with a bonus arrangement
- A fixed fee with a sliding-scale adjustment
- A percentage of the costs

A Cost Plus Contract may also have a guaranteed ceiling price nominated.

The main use for a Cost Plus Contract is where the nature, extent or quantity of the work cannot be accurately defined when negotiating the Contract.

Classification by Technical and Administrative Responsibility

The implementation of an engineering project involves a number of separate tasks, the responsibility for which must be established clearly from the outset.
These tasks are:

- Project Management and Coordination
- Engineering – Design: Conceptual
  : Process (if applicable)
  : Detailed
  – Documentation
- Construction/Installation/Supply

- Procurement
- Supervision
- Construction or Supply and/or Installation
- Contract Administration

Engineering contracts can be classified by the manner in which these responsibilities are allocated. There are a number of classifications under this method, the principal ones being:

- Engineering (only) Contract
- Engineering/Procurement Contract
- Construction/Supply/Installation Contract
- Engineering/Procurement/Construction Contract
- Construction Management Contract
- Turnkey Contract

Engineering (only) contract This type of contract is usually between the Principal and a Consulting Engineer, the negotiation for which is outside the scope of this book. However, where Process Design is involved it may be that a contractor is engaged to carry out the design and documentation.

Engineering/procurement contract This type of contract includes Procurement in addition to the Engineering. Procurement comprises three parts – Purchasing, Expediting, and Inspection and Quality Control.

A definition of the work comprised under these three parts is given in Sec. 11.3 – 'The Specification Format'.

Construction/supply/installation contract In this type of contract it is the Contractor's responsibility to carry out the work under the Contract in accordance with designs, specifications, and other details provided by the Principal. In some cases, such as in process and industrial projects, the Contractor may be required to undertake all or part of the design.

The Principal is responsible for all the other tasks; these may be carried out on the Principal's behalf by one or more specialist consultants. The agreements between the Principal and these specialist consultants is outside the scope of this book, and the engineer is referred to publications on the subject issued by the various professional consultant associations.

Engineering/procurement/construction contract This type of contract combines the work described above for Engineering/Procurement and for Construction/Installation/Supply contracts.

Construction management contract In this type of contract the Contractor undertakes the responsibility for coordinating the work under the Contract by a number of other contractors selected in consultation with the Principal. The Principal, usually with the assistance of consultants, prepares the designs and supplies the drawings and specifications for the various contracts which are then handed over to the Contractor to invite tenders. The Principal plays a significant part in both the negotiation with and the selection of the other contractors, and provides the overall project management. The Contractor is paid a fee for this work, the payments to the other contractors being made, or provided to the Contractor for payment, by the Principal. This type of contract is a form of 'cost plus' contract and the Contractor is usually confined to a predetermined and agreed budget. It is usually associated with the 'fast track' method of construction.

A *Turnkey Contract* is one in which the Contractor assumes complete responsibility for the project and, in effect, becomes the Principal.

Subcontracts

In most cases the Contractor will not undertake the whole of the work of a major project entirely from within the Contractor's own resources. The Contractor usually divides the work up into a number of elements and enters into separate agreements with *subcontractors* to carry out some of the work directly for the Contractor. The Contractor, of course, may undertake some of these elements using the Contractor's own resources and workstaff.

Although such a procedure is at the Contractor's option, it is usual for the Contract to specify that any such subcontract agreements must be approved by the Principal. It is not always practicable to require tenderers to nominate their subcontractors in their tenders. Contractors usually have their own stable of subcontractors on whom they call when preparing a tender, but many like to keep their options open until after they have been awarded a contract.

A more practicable approach is for the Enquiry Documents to require tenderers to nominate those areas of work which the tenderer intends to subcontract and for the Principal to approve or reject the subcontractor eventually nominated by the Contractor.

Sometimes the Principal has very definite ideas on subcontracts. The Principal has three options to choose from in such cases:

- Designated Subcontracts
- Selected Subcontracts
- Nominated Subcontracts

Which of these options the Principal wishes to adopt must be set out in the Enquiry Documents.

A *Designated Subcontractor* is one named in the Enquiry Documents to carry out certain work or to supply certain items or services, the nature and extent of which are clearly described in the documents and which the Contractor can be reasonably expected to price and allow for at the time of tendering. It is up to the Contractor to negotiate with the designated subcontractor before submitting the tender. As the Contractor knows right from the beginning who the subcontractor is, there can be no right of objection to the designation once an agreement has been reached with the Principal.

The Principal must, of course, accept responsibility for default by a Designated Subcontractor. In the event of a Designated Subcontractor defaulting, the Principal must nominate another subcontractor and be liable to the Main Contractor for any additional costs incurred as a result of the default.

Examples of work carried out as Designated Subcontracts include piling, specialized coatings and the supply of certain mechanical and electrical equipment.

A *Selected Subcontractor* is one selected by the Contractor from a restricted list of approved subcontractors nominated by the Principal and included in the Enquiry Documents. As long as the work is carried out by one of the selected subcontractors on the list, the Principal must approve the subcontractor. As with a Designated Subcontractor, the Main Contractor must negotiate with the subcontractor and be responsible for the work.

The Principal accepts no responsibility for default by a Selected Contractor. In the event of a Selected Subcontractor defaulting, it is the Main Contractor's responsibility to negotiate with one of the other subcontractors on the list to complete the work.

A *Nominated Subcontractor* is one selected by the Principal without reference to the Main Contractor. As a general rule, the work carried out by a Nominated Subcontractor is covered by a Provisional Sum in the Contract.

Frequently, the Principal independently invites tenders for the work under the subcontract, negotiates a subcontract and directs the Main Contractor to enter into a subcontract with the Nominated Subcontractor selected on terms and conditions negotiated by the Principal. As with Designated Subcontractors, the Principal accepts responsibility for nominating a new subcontractor in the event of the Nominated Subcontractor defaulting and is liable for any resulting costs.

In each of the above situations, notwithstanding the approval of the subcontractor by the Principal, the Main Contractor is entirely responsible for seeing that the subcontractor undertakes the work under the subcontract and fulfils the terms of the Contract.

2.4 DOCUMENTS FOR ENGINEERING CONTRACTS

The following is an outline of the central role documents play in the negotiations leading to the formation of an engineering contract.

There are three distinct stages in the negotiations leading to the final agreement:

1. The Invitation to Tender
2. The Submission and Receipt of an Offer
3. The Consideration and Acceptance of the Offer

The first stage is begun by the Principal inviting one or more parties to submit offers to undertake the work; the second involves the response from any or all of these parties (referred to as *tenderers*); the third comprises negotiations with some of the tenderers leading to a contract between the Principal and one of the tenderers.

Each stage of the negotiations may require a number of separate documents. The purpose of each stage determines what documents are required and how they are to be presented. Some documents will be common to all three stages; others pertinent to only one or two.

Giving a suitable title to each group of documents is most important. A proper understanding of their purpose enables the selection of an appropriate title to identify each clearly. Unfortunately, the various documents required at each stage are often given titles carelessly, with consequent ambiguity and imprecision.

Ambiguity may be both cause and effect of imprecise thinking. Sometimes, little effort is made to distinguish by title the function and purpose of these sets of documents. Terms such as 'Tender Documents', 'Contract Documents', and 'Specification' are often used loosely for any, or even all the documents, and then quite inconsistently applied. In some cases, terminology can vary from country to country.

Such carelessness can lead to confusion and misunderstanding. To avoid these problems, it is recommended that particular attention be paid both to the purpose of each stage of the procedure and to the nomenclature used to identify the relative sets of documents.

In the interest of consistency, the following terminology is recommended and has been adopted in this book:

Tender Enquiry Documents (usually abbreviated to *Enquiry Documents*) comprise the documents involved in the first stage – the Invitation to Tender. They include all the documents which are issued to tenderers and which prescribe the Principal's requirements for the preparation and submission of bids and the performance of the work under the Contract.

Tender Documents are those involved in the second stage – the 'Submission and Receipt of an Offer'. They are all those which comprise a tenderer's offer; they form the actual tender to be submitted.

Contract Documents are those involved in the third stage – the 'Consideration and Acceptance of an Offer'. They comprise all the documents referred to in the contract agreement; they must incorporate ALL AMENDMENTS to the Enquiry Documents and Tender Documents arising from negotiations before the signing of the Contract.

The following chapters provide guidelines for the preparation and presentation of the the various documents required at each stage of the tendering procedure.

PART
TWO

OUTLINE OF THE TENDERING PROCESS

THREE

THE ENQUIRY DOCUMENTS

3.1 FUNCTION OF THE ENQUIRY DOCUMENTS

The Enquiry Documents inform the tenderers of the nature, extent, and detailed requirements of the work under the proposed Contract and the contractual obligations which will govern the performance of the Contract. They will also define the procedures to be followed when preparing and submitting tenders and the basis upon which tenders will be evaluated.

The Enquiry Documents are prepared by the Principal and are issued to tenderers under cover of a formal invitation to submit a tender. A set of Enquiry Documents is normally made up of three parts, each part comprising a number of individual documents to serve a specific purpose:

1. *Requirements for Tendering*. Three documents, which specifically cover the tendering procedures, make up this part:

   - The Invitation to Tender
   - The Instructions to Tenderers
   - The Content of Tender

2. *Contract Documents for Tendering*. This part comprises three groups of

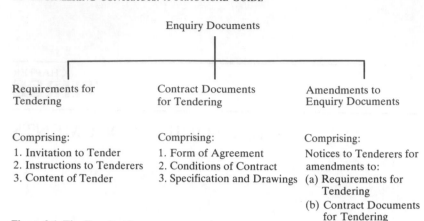

Figure 3.1 The Enquiry Documents.

documents prepared by or on behalf of the Principal and which are intended to form the basis for the final Contract:

- The Form of Agreement
- The Conditions of Contract
- The Specification and Drawings

3. *Amendments to the Enquiry Documents.* These documents are those issued during the *Tender Period* – the period between the issue of the Enquiry Documents and the opening of tenders. During this period it may be necessary to amend or supplement one or more of the Enquiry Documents and all tenderers are informed of any such changes by a Notice to Tenderers.

The hierarchy of the documents and the relationship between the various parts are shown in Fig. 3.1.

3.2 CONTRACT IDENTIFICATION

Each contract should be given a name or title by which it can be identified. For practical reasons, this name or title should be as concise as possible with the minimum number of words required to identify the work. The identification should also include the name of the Principal or Owner and the location; e.g.

Black Stump Shire Council
Bridge over Rocky Creek,
Black Stump, Queensland

Acme Manufacturing Company
Factory Air Conditioning System,
Taunton, Somerset

If the project is divided into a number of separate contracts, then the title should distinguish the particular contract:

Black Stump Shire Council
Piling for Bridge over Rocky Creek,
Black Stump, Queensland

Black Stump Shire Council
Earthworks for Bridge over Rocky Creek,
Black Stump, Queensland

Black Stump Shire Council
Superstructure for Bridge over Rocky Creek,
Black Stump, Queensland

The Contract should also be given a reference number. This will be important during the contract administration stage, particularly if there are a number of separate contracts for the same project. The sorting and filing of correspondence, invoices, and certificates will be made easier by the use of a discrete reference number.

The Owner/Principal may also have definite requirements in regard to reference numbers and this point should be verified. These requirements may be accommodated if they do not interfere with the Principal's standard computer procedure(s). The Contractor may also have a numbering system. There should be no reason why all these individual requirements cannot be met.

3.3 REQUIREMENTS FOR TENDERING

The purpose of the Requirements for Tendering is to inform tenderers of the Principal's requirements regarding the preparation and submission of tenders. Once tenders have been submitted and evaluated, the documents comprising the Requirements for Tendering have no further relevance and, as they will not form part of the Contract, they should not contain any matter relating to the performance of the Contract.

The following is a brief outline of the three documents comprising this part.

The Invitation to Tender

The *Invitation to Tender* is a formal request to tenderers to submit an offer or a proposal to undertake the work under the Contract. Its function is to advise prospective tenderers of the proposed contract and provide enough information to enable them to decide whether or not the work falls within their area of competence and interest.

The form the Invitation will take will depend upon the method used for inviting tenders. Where an Open Tendering procedure is being followed, the invitation is usually in the form of a public notice in the classified advertisements section of one or more appropriate publications.

Where tenders are being invited from Nominated or Pre-Qualified Tenderers, the Invitation may be in the form of a letter individually addressed to each tenderer. If this approach is adopted, the text of each individual letter must be identical. Failure to do so may lay the Principal open to an accusation of being unfair and possibly to a claim for damages from an unsuccessful tenderer.

The Invitation to Tender should briefly set out the following information:

- Project identification
- A formal invitation to tender
- Outline of the work
- Location of the work
- Who is involved
- The type of contract
- Programme of the work
- Closing time, date and place for receiving tenders
- Procedure for opening tenders (if applicable)
- A request for the tenderer to confirm that the invitation will be either accepted or declined.

Recommendations for the preparation of the Invitation to Tender are given in Sec. 9.1 – 'Preparing the Invitation to Tender'.

Instructions to Tenderers

The *Instructions to Tenderers*, together with its complementary document, the Content of Tender, contains all the provisions relating specifically to the preparation and submission of tenders.

The prime function of the Instructions to Tenderers is to ensure that a tenderer is told exactly what to do when submitting a tender. A detailed Instructions to Tenderers is, of course, only required when the selection of the Contractor is to be the result of a formal tendering procedure. Where the Contract is directly negotiated with a single tenderer, it is not necessary to prepare the Instructions to Tenderers to the same detail. However, in such a situation it is prudent to advise the tenderer in writing exactly what is required, rather than relying solely on a verbal request.

It is most important to understand the purpose underlying the function and operation of the Instructions to Tenderers. Even though it will not form part of the finally negotiated Contract, the listing of all the essential requirements makes this document just as important as any other document which may eventually be incorporated in the Contract.

For ease of reference the various instructions should be set out so that related matters are grouped together. The following is a suggested grouping and order:

- The Tender Enquiry Documents
- The Instructions for the Preparation of Tenders
- The Conditions of Tendering
- Commercial Requirements
- Site Data
- Miscellaneous information

Recommendations for the preparation of the Instructions to Tenderers are set out in Sec. 9.2 – 'Instructions to Tenderers'.

Content of Tender

It must be made clear to tenderers precisely what is required to be included in their tenders. This is the function of the *Content of Tender*, which supplements the Instructions to Tenderers in that it specifically reiterates what is required to be included in tenders.

This document comprises a listing of all the forms, schedules and supporting statements required to be completed and submitted by tenderers. A statement at the head of the list should make it clear that failure to complete any form or schedule or to submit a required statement may make the tender non-conforming. Blank *pro-formas* of all the forms, schedules and statements required to be returned by tenderers with their tenders, beginning with the Tender Form, should be attached to the Content of Tender. These schedules, forms and statements, together with the Tender Enquiry Documents by reference, comprise the tenderer's formal proposal in response to the Invitation to Tender.

Many tenderers are reluctant to commit themselves any more than they believe necessary and they will, with justification, provide no more than the amount of detail requested. Therefore, the required information listed in the Content of Tender and detailed in the forms and schedules must be carefully selected to ensure that all tenders are in sufficient detail to enable them to be properly and fairly evaluated. The preparation of the forms and schedules must be such that they can be easily understood by tenderers, with no excuse left for the omission of important information or the misinterpretation of the requirements.

Tenderers should only be required to respond to matters which are directly related to the work under the Contract. This will enable the tenders to be thoroughly evaluated and compared and the most appropriate tender selected for possible further investigation. Requiring insufficient or unsuitable information may lead to the need to solicit further details after the close of tenders. This may not only delay the procedure of selection but, most importantly, it will imply a lack of experience on the part of the Engineer responsible for drafting the Enquiry Documents. It is the responsibility of the Engineer to see that the Enquiry Documents make it clear exactly what information tenderers are to provide in their tenders.

A list of the various forms, schedules, and statements for inclusion in the Enquiry Documents together with guidelines for their preparation is given in Sec. 9.4 – 'Forms, Schedules and Statements for Tendering'.

3.4 CONTRACT DOCUMENTS FOR TENDERING

This group of documents tells tenderers exactly what has to be done, how the work is to be carried out and the terms and conditions under which the Contract is to be performed. During the tender stage, these documents may be considered to be provisional as they may require amendment before being incorporated in the formal Contract in accordance with any Notices to Tenderers issued or any changes arising from negotiations leading to the final agreement.

Form of Agreement

If it is intended that the parties to the Contract are to complete a formal Instrument of Agreement (referred to hereafter as the *Agreement*) this should be made clear in the Instructions to Tenderers and a draft Form of Agreement included with this part of the Tender Enquiry Documents.

The Form of Agreement should provide spaces for including the following:

- Date of the Agreement
- Name and address of both parties to the Agreement
- Name and identifying number of the Contract and/or a brief description of the work under the Contract

- Schedule of the documents deemed to form part of the Agreement identified by title and mark and including reference to all annexures, appendixes and schedules attached to those documents.
- Positions for the signatures of the parties and witnesses and for the affixing of seals (if appropriate)

Sample Forms of Agreement are included in many standard General Conditions of Contract. One of these forms may be used as a model for preparing the Agreement; alternatively the draft Form of Agreement included in Appendix A can be used, either as shown or modified to suit the particular application.

Some forms of Agreement provide spaces for including the Contract Price and the Completion Period or Date. However, since these terms can sometimes be complicated, it is often better to cover these matters elsewhere in the Contract Documents.

The final Agreement may differ in detail from the form issued with the Enquiry Documents. This will depend upon any modifications negotiated in reaching the final agreed terms of the Contract.

Conditions of Contract

The *Conditions of Contract* define the 'rules' under which the Contract will be administered. These rules set out the basic provisions regarding the rights and obligations of the parties to the Contract and the actions to be taken if various eventualities arise during the performance of the work under the Contract. These Conditions of Contract are distinctly different from the requirements regarding the technical details of the work which are described in the *Specification* and the *Drawings*

The clear definition both of the nature of these rights and obligations and of their limitations is so important and can have such far-reaching legal consequences that Conditions of Contract should be drawn up, or at least reviewed, by experts in the legal profession.

The absence of any formal Conditions of Contract would not abrogate what would otherwise be a legal contract. This may be the case for a contract for the supply of an off-the-shelf item of plant or equipment. However, in most cases, it is important to document all the terms and conditions under which the Contract is to be performed. It is dangerous to rely purely on spoken accords in contractual matters. The nature and extent of the Conditions of Contract will depend on such factors as the size and complexity of the work to be performed and an assessment of the situations and conditions which may be encountered.

To overcome the daunting task of having to prepare a fresh set of

Conditions for each new contract, many professional engineering institutions and standards associations have prepared and published model or standard forms of Conditions of Contract known as *Standard* or *General Conditions of Contract*. In this book these standard forms of Conditions of Contract are referred to as *General Conditions*. These General Conditions are kept continuously under review and new editions incorporating amendments published periodically.

In addition, many government, semi-government and statutory authorities, as well as many large commercial organizations, have created their own General Conditions tailored to suit their own particular needs.

The main benefit from using well-known General Conditions is that tenderers will already be familiar with their provisions. In most cases they will be comfortable with the prospect of signing a contract based on their terms and will be more concerned with what changes or amendments have been made to the standard conditions.

However, no two engineering contracts are exactly the same. Not only do the requirements for work in the respective engineering disciplines (civil, structural, mechanical, electrical and chemical) differ, but the very diversity of engineering contracts makes it virtually impracticable to prepare a universally acceptable standard Conditions of Contract.

In some cases, General Conditions prepared by the various national organizations are discipline-oriented. For example, the Institution of Civil Engineers, London, has a standard 'Conditions of Contract for Works of Civil Engineering Construction', while the Institution of Mechanical Engineers and the Institution of Electrical Engineers, London, have jointly produced a 'Model Form of General Conditions of Contract' for mechanical and electrical engineering work. In other cases, national standards associations, such as the Standards Association of Australia, have issued different sets of General Conditions of Contract to cover the requirements of the various disciplines in engineering. However, difficulties can arise when using such General Conditions in contracts involving multi-discipline work.

Because of the diverse nature of engineering work, it is recognized that any one set of General Conditions is unlikely to satisfy all the requirements of a particular contract. For practical reasons, therefore, most General Conditions comprise only those conditions which may be regarded as universally applicable and are usually printed in a format which will enable them to be included as they stand in the Contract Documents.

The Engineer is thus faced with deciding which General Conditions is most appropriate for the work and what amendments, if necessary, may be required. Owing to the immensity of the task and the time and cost involved, the alternative of preparing a unique Conditions of Contract is not normally a viable option. Whichever General Conditions is selected, there will always be certain conditions which vary according to the circumstances of the work under the Contract. There are two ways of including this information in the Contract Documents.

1. Where the information to be included is a simple statement or numerical or similar data such as monetary amounts, percentages, periods of time or dates, many General Conditions include an appendix or annexure in the shape of a form to be completed by the Engineer which details the requirements and is included in the Enquiry Documents. In this book the term *Annexure* is used for this form.

2. Where the additional information requires a more detailed explanation, or where clauses in the General Conditions require amendment or deletion, these conditions are usually set out in clauses in a supplementary document.

This document is variously entitled 'Conditions of Particular Application', 'Special Conditions' or 'Supplementary Conditions'. The name 'Special Conditions' should be avoided if possible as it may be interpreted to imply that the provisions therein are 'special' and have precedence over provisions of the General Conditions. In this book, the term *Supplementary Conditions of Contract* is employed (referred to hereafter as *Supplementary Conditions*).

An outline of the major points to watch in selecting a General Conditions is given in Chapter 10 – 'The Conditions of Contract', together with guidelines for the completion of the Annexure and the preparation of a Supplementary Conditions.

The Specification and the Drawings

The *Specification* and the *Drawings* describe in detail the work to be performed and the engineering aspects of the facility or equipment to be purchased, fabricated, constructed or installed under the Contract. Collectively, they are sometimes referred to as the *Technical Requirements*. In this role, they are complementary to the Conditions of Contract which deal with the rights and duties of the parties to the Contract.

Depending upon the nature of the Contract, the Specification and Drawings may cover both off-site activities such as design, quality and supply of materials, fabrication of components and workmanship and on-site activities such as construction, installation and commissioning through to acceptance testing.

Basically, the Specification prescribes those matters which are best described in words while the Drawings delineate those items which are best shown in a graphical form. They therefore complement each other.

The Specification describes the technical scope and engineering requirements for the work, while the drawings are used to show details such as form, size, quantity, location, physical constraints, and the arrangement of objects and components. For contracts involving installation or construction, details of physical conditions at the Site at the time of tendering are usually set out on the Drawings.

Because of the nature of their respective roles, the Specification, as issued with the Enquiry Documents, will be incorporated in the Contract Documents and used in the performance of the work under the Contract with little, if any, amendment. The Drawings, on the other hand, which concentrate on the extent and form of the work, can be amended or supplemented during the course of the Contract without affecting the scope of the work. The price could, of course, be affected if an amendment varies the scope or quality of the work.

It is advisable to avoid, as far as possible, the duplication of material in both the Specification and the Drawings. This may not always be possible, but the Engineer must be aware of the possibility of errors arising from duplication and take particular care when checking the documents.

The Specification and Drawings issued with the Enquiry Documents must be in sufficient detail to enable tenderers to prepare and submit firm offers for the work. The amount of detail provided will depend largely upon the type of contract.

Where the design is provided by the Principal, the Specification and Drawings must be complete in every detail so that the Contractor can supply the goods or construct the Works without further basic design on the Contractor's part.

Where the design is provided by the Contractor, the Specification and Drawings must clearly define the parameters within which the Contractor must work in designing and undertaking the work under the Contract. It is important to ensure that the documents provide all the information known to the Principal and which might not be readily available to the Contractor. It is also important to make clear the purpose and function of the Works so that, when completed, they will be fit for their intended use. Notwithstanding any review or approval by the Principal of the Contractor's design, the Contractor remains totally responsible for the design and performance of the Works.

If the design is provided by the Principal, the Contractor will have to do no more than carry out the work in accordance with the Specification and the Drawings in a competent manner, even if the Works turns out to be unfit for the intended use.

The Specification and the Drawings are the documents most widely referred to during the currency of the Contract. In legal terms they are of equal importance to the other documents evidencing the Contract but which are rarely consulted once work starts unless some administrative difficulty or dispute arises. These other documents, such as the Conditions of Contract, are more relevant to the administrative and managerial staff of the Contractor and the Principal.

The Specification and the Drawings will be in daily use by the workers and their supervisors and by suppliers, all seeking direction and clarification. These people may come from widely differing backgrounds and have varying capacities for comprehending written English. In many cases, English may not be their mother tongue. The Specification must, therefore, be written in quite explicit but simple language.

Although all the Contract Documents may be bound initially in a single volume, the Specification and the Drawings will almost certainly be copied and issued separately to members of the Contractor's supervisory and operative workforce. The other components of the Contract Documents (such as the Agreement and the Conditions of Contract) may contain commercially sensitive information which the Contractor and the Principal may prefer to be restricted to their senior administrative staff. In any case, such information would be of little concern to, and may even confuse, the operative workforce.

Recommendations for preparing and compiling the Specification and the Drawings are outlined in Chapter 11 – 'The Specification and the Drawings'.

3.5 REVIEWING THE ENQUIRY DOCUMENTS

When the drafting of all the documents required for tendering has been completed, before final printing and issue to tenderers, they should be subject to a final review. Each document should have been checked independently for content, typographical errors, omissions, and duplications, but this final review is to ensure that the documents comprise a coherent package. Matters often necessarily left to the last minute are sometimes overlooked. Points which should be checked in this final review include:

- Are all the documents correctly titled and identified?
- Are all pages included and in their correct place?
- Is the time, date and place for the receipt of tenders correctly stated *in one place only*?
- Have blank copies of all the schedules and forms required to be completed and returned by tenderers been included, and do they cover all the statements and data required?
- Has the Annexure attached to the General Conditions been correctly completed?

- Have all the accompanying documents, such as annexures and appendixes, referred to in the documents, been included?
- Have all the drawings listed in the Schedule of Drawings been included and are they marked 'For Tender Purposes Only'?

Only when the Engineer is completely satisfied with the composition and presentation of all the documents should they be printed, collated and bound for issue to tenderers.

3.6 AMENDMENTS TO THE ENQUIRY DOCUMENTS

Notices to Tenderers

During the Tender Period it may be necessary to correct or amend one or more of the Enquiry Documents. This can arise from queries raised by tenderers, the discovery of errors or omissions in the documents or amendments due to changed circumstances. Any such amendments should be in writing and issued to all tenderers as a *Notice to Tenderers*.

Preparing a Notice to Tenderers

As stated earlier, a Notice to Tenderers forms part of the Enquiry Documents and must be prepared and distributed with the same care and attention as was given to the Enquiry Documents initially issued to tenderers. It may be issued as a letter, or, preferably, as a separate and suitably endorsed notice.

It should have the words 'Notice to Tenderers' at the head and notices should be consecutively numbered and dated. The particular Contract should be clearly identified by name and, if appropriate, by number. A draft format for a Notice to Tenderers is given in Appendix A.

Amendments should be complete in themselves, and tenderers should not be expected to appreciate the implications and decide whether or not other changes to the referenced document or to other documents are required. If an amendment affects a document in more than one place or if other documents are affected, each and every place where changes are required should be identified. Amendments to documents must be clear and unambiguous and tenderers should be left in no doubt as to what is to be amended or corrected.

If the amendment involves the issue of a new or amended Drawing, a separate Notice to Tenderers should accompany the new or amended Drawing and describe the amendment. Amended Drawings should have the amendment noted above the title block and, if practicable, the amendment should be encircled and marked in pencil on the tracing before printing.

If the Instructions for Tendering require tenderers to endorse their tenders by confirming receipt of each Notice received, identified by number and date of issue, a statement to this effect should be included in the Notice. It is also advisable to include a receipt slip with each Notice which should be signed by each tenderer and returned to the Engineer. This may remove a possible cause of embarrassment in the event of a Notice going astray.

If possible, the issue of amendments late in the tender period should be avoided. If a need for a late amendment arises, consideration should be given to extending the tender period if the amendment is of sufficient importance. It should be remembered that changes of a minor nature may be more easily dealt with as a variation after the tender has been accepted or negotiated before acceptance of the tender.

FOUR

THE ENQUIRY

4.1 METHODS OF TENDERING

Tender Options

A *contractor* is a firm or individual who supplies goods or services or who undertakes erection, installation or construction work as a commercial business.

There are four basic methods used for inviting tenders from contractors. These are:

- Unrestricted Tendering – Openly Invited Tenderers
  – Pre-registered Tenderers
- Restricted Tendering – Nominated Tenderers
  – Pre-qualified Tenderers

Unrestricted tendering is not generally favoured for major contracts as it can attract a large number of enquiries, some of which may not be really serious, or are from firms or individuals which investigation will reveal as being unsuitable. As a result, the Principal can be involved in an unnecessary expenditure of time and money. On a major project, the cost of preparing, recording and issuing each set of the Enquiry Documents can be considerable.

Making a non-refundable charge for the Enquiry Documents can defray the cost to some extent and it does tend to discourage such contractors. (See Sec. 4.2 – subsection 'Charging for Enquiry Documents'.)

Many reputable and otherwise suitable contractors are reluctant to spend much time and money on unrestricted tendering as it is felt that the competition would be too great and there is a real possibility of an unrealistically low bid being submitted and accepted. Consequently, if such a contractor does bother to tender at all, the tender may not be as thoroughly investigated and as keenly priced as it would have been if the field had been smaller and limited to other experienced contractors.

Restricted tendering is usually the preferred option where:

- The cost of preparing a tender is likely to be significant.
- The invitation to tender involves a substantial pre-tender design element or where tenderers are specifically permitted to offer design alternatives.
- It is desired to exclude from the outset tenderers who may not be technically or financially competent.
- The nature of the project requires the mobilization of significant labour, plant, and material resources, involving heavy financing costs.

It should be kept in mind that where tenders are sought from nominated or pre-qualified tenderers, to accept other than the lowest conforming tender could leave the Principal open to an accusation of impropriety and a possible claim for damages.

Openly Invited Tenderers

In this method, contractors are invited by public advertisement to submit tenders for the work.

This method is widely used for the smaller type of contract, and an openly advertised call for bids may attract a good offer from a tenderer who may have been overlooked if one of the other procedures had been adopted.

Openly invited tendering is more or less obligatory for many government and some statutory authorities. For these organizations, openly invited tendering is still the preferred procedure, but the alternative of pre-registration of tenderers is becoming more widely adopted.

Pre-registered Tenderers

In this procedure, contractors are invited, usually by public advertisement, to apply for registration as tenderers. An alternative to this is not to publish an advertisement, but instead to send a written invitation to known and reputable contractors to pre-register. All registrants will automatically be issued with Enquiry Documents and invited to tender.

The advantages of pre-registration over open tendering are that:

- It indicates the extent of interest by contractors in tendering for the work.
- It enables a more accurate assessment to be made of the number of sets of documents required.
- It does tend to discourage tenderers who are not really serious about submitting a tender.

As with openly invited tenders, making a charge for the Enquiry Documents will also help to discourage casual enquiries and contribute towards defraying costs. The main disadvantage of the procedure is that it still does not allow the weeding out of unsuitable contractors at an early enough stage.

Nominated Tenderers

Many of the problems encountered with unrestricted tendering can be overcome by inviting a selected number of suitable contractors to submit bids. The problem is who to invite?

Contractors who have previously been pre-qualified or whose good past performance is well known are obvious candidates for inclusion in the list of nominated tenderers. The size and complexity of the project will largely dictate the number of tenders to be sought. In the case of contracts for the supply of specialist services or equipment where the number of potential tenderers is limited and they are well known, or where the nature of the work limits the field, there is little problem. It is where the number of potential bidders is large that it is sometimes difficult to make a selection.

The preparation of a list of potential tenderers from one person's knowledge or previous experience or from hearsay may result in the omission of qualified and competent contractors who would otherwise prove suitable but who are not well known to the person preparing the list.

On smaller projects or where time is limited, inviting bids from a list of selected tenderers may be the only practicable way.

Pre-qualified Tenderers

In this procedure, contractors are invited by public advertisement to apply for pre-qualification as tenderers. From an analysis and evaluation of the applications, a comparatively short list is prepared of suitably qualified tenderers who will be invited to submit bids.

It is important to appreciate the difference between 'Pre-registration' and 'Pre-qualification'. The object of Pre-registration is simply to find out who is interested in tendering without knowing beforehand their qualifications or capacity to do the work. Pre-qualification involves a screening process to determine which of those who have indicated an interest in tendering are capable of doing the job.

Pre-qualification is a time-consuming and painstaking operation if it is carried out correctly, but in the long term it is possibly the best procedure for large and complex projects.

The advantage of pre-qualification is that tenders are sought only from contractors who have already been checked as having the requisite resources and capability and are in a position to perform the work satisfactorily.

The main disadvantage is that it requires a comparatively long lead time and this must be taken into account when planning the overall project timetable.

Some major organizations with continuing or extensive works programmes have standing lists of pre-qualified tenderers. Sometimes these contractors are given a rating and advised accordingly. Advertised invitations to tender would then nominate which rating tenderers must have in order to apply for Enquiry Documents. This procedure can substantially accelerate the process. It is, of course, only suitable for organizations who are inviting tenders on a regular basis. Contractors who have previously been pre-qualified for earlier projects may not need to be required to pre-qualify again.

Selecting the Appropriate Option

In choosing which method to use, the following factors should be considered:

- The Owner's or Principal's policy
- The type and size of the contract
- The current tendering climate
- The overall project budget and timetable

Whichever is chosen, each step in the procedure must be fully documented and all discussions with tenderers recorded.

Collusion in Tendering

Engineers have always been aware of the possibility of collusion between tenderers to the detriment of the party inviting tenders (the Principal). Until recently, evidence of such practices has been largely anecdotal, although occasional isolated instances have been made public.

This situation changed dramatically during the 1991 Building Royal Commission established by the New South Wales State Government. The Terms of Reference were initially aimed at investigating allegations of stand-over tactics, intimidation and blackmail by some persons engaged in the building industry and witnesses gave evidence of some startling and un-savoury practices common in the industry. What was unforeseen was the emergence of evidence of widespread collusion between contractors during tendering.

The Commissioner's Report, handed down in May 1992, found that there were entrenched collusive tendering malpractices by construction con-tractors and their company associations. Collusive tendering was charac-terized by 'unsuccessful tenderers' fees', 'cover tenders' and 'special fees'.

An 'unsuccessful tenderers' fee' is an amount included in the tender sum to be distributed by the successful tenderer to the unsuccessful tenderers, ostensibly to help defray the costs of tendering.

A 'cover tender' is a tender submitted by a selected tenderer which is really non-competitive, as it has been priced to lose. The price is usually obtained from a rival tenderer and often does not involve an independent assessment of the price.

'Special fees' were paid by the successful tenderer to the contractors' industry associations and formed a substantial proportion of the revenue of these associations. As with the 'unsuccessful tenderers' fees', these arrange-ments were not made known to clients, including both state and federal government departments.

What was most disquieting, and possibly illegal, was that:

• The existence of these 'fees' within the Tender Sum was not revealed to the Principal.
• The amount of the 'fee' often bore little or no relation to actual tendering or other costs.
• The contractors' industry associations named in the Report appeared both to approve and to participate in the distribution of the 'fees'.
• Many of the witnesses could see no harm in the practice.

Although the Commissioner was investigating the building industry in New South Wales, the Report says that 'the analysis of the material suggests that collusive tendering extends to civil engineering projects'. Furthermore, the contractors and associations named were nationally based and there is every reason to believe that the practice is widespread, not only in other States and Territories of the Commonwealth, but probably overseas. Some of the con-tractors named in the hearing were UK-registered firms.

Dealing with Collusion

There is no question that the cost to a contractor of responding to an invitation to tender can be substantial. Owing to the increasing complexity of today's engineering projects, Enquiry Documents often impose excessive and unrealistic demands upon tenderers. Furthermore, owners sometimes invite tenders with hastily prepared documents for the sole purpose of 'testing the market' or of obtaining a 'realistic estimate' at the feasibility study stage. Engineers should appreciate that such requirements and practices often encourage contractors to adopt an unethical and unsatisfactory approach to the tender procedure.

It would not be difficult for a contractor to spend up to one per cent of the Tender Sum on preparing a tender, particularly if a significant design component was involved. Not only do tenderers have to allow for the possibility of having to deal with industrial action by the trades unions, but the need to comply with the demands of complex government regulations and environmental issues, coupled with the increasing requirement to use high technology, has led to ever-increasing tendering costs. Allowing for the ratio of unsuccessful to successful tenders, it can readily be seen that tendering costs form a significant portion of a contractor's overheads.

To be effective, collusion would have to involve all tenderers. In the cases quoted before the NSW Royal Commission, the apparent approval and cooperation by the contractors' industrial associations no doubt made this easier. In a Schedule of Rates tender or one where a Priced Bill of Quantities is required, it would be difficult to hide an 'unsuccessful tenderers' fee' unless all tenderers agreed where to 'bury the body'. Concealment would be easier in a Lump Sum tender, but the use of a Schedule of Prices for Tendering would help to show up any obvious overpricing.

One way to reduce, if not eliminate, these practices is to use a more sophisticated pre-qualification procedure to select a limited number of nominated tenderers (probably three) who would then be paid a fee by the Principal to prepare tenders. Some major organizations who invite tenders frequently are already using this technique.

4.2 GUIDELINES FOR TENDERING

Notices and Advertisements

Tender notices and advertisements should be published in the appropriate classified advertisement columns of suitable newspapers and journals. The particular circumstances of the project usually dictate the amount of publicity to be given to the advertisement.

For urban work, if the work is of a conventional nature and suitable for the average general contractor, it is usually sufficient to advertise in the appropriate newspaper in the town or city involved. For major work, advertisements should be placed in newspapers nationally and in all nearby towns and cities where major contractors are likely to be found.

If the work is to be carried out in a country area, additional advertisements may be placed in local regional newspapers to attract competent local contractors.

Nationally published trade journals should not be overlooked. Some of these journals try to list all projects currently out to tender, picking up the advertisements from the daily newspapers. However, they are often pleased to receive an advance copy of the advertisement which they may publish in an abbreviated form without charge.

Charging for Enquiry Documents

A charge may be made for supplying the Enquiry Documents. The charge can be either non-refundable or refundable on receipt of a 'bona fide' tender – that is, a genuine tender.

The question of whether or not to make a charge for the Enquiry Documents is a matter to be decided by the Principal. The Principal is usually the one who has to bear the cost of printing and issuing the documents.

If the prime purpose of making the charge is to discourage contractors who are not really interested in submitting a genuine tender, the charge can be refundable. If, on the other hand, the prime purpose is to defray the cost of preparing and issuing the enquiry documents, the charge can be non-refundable.

Where a refundable charge is made, the handling of the deposit, accounting for it, and refunding the amount when a tender is received are costly and time-consuming and impose an additional burden on the Principal's (or the Consulting Engineer's) accounting staff.

There are three ways of charging for Enquiry Documents. These are:

- A charge is made for the first set issued to each tenderer and is refundable on receipt of a 'bona fide' tender; a non-refundable charge is made for any additional sets of the Documents requested by a tenderer.
- No charge is made for the first set issued to each tenderer, but a non-refundable charge is made for any additional sets of the Documents requested by a tenderer.
- A non-refundable charge is made for all sets of the Documents supplied.

The first option would be suitable for unrestricted tendering, whether from openly invited tenderers or from pre-registered tenderers where the

Principal is prepared to bear the cost of supplying a reasonable number of Enquiry Documents. However, it should be appreciated that this option only increases contractors' overheads; ultimately this must be paid for in higher tender sums.

The second option is suitable for restricted tendering, whether nominated or pre-qualified, and where the Principal is prepared to bear the cost of supplying a reasonable number of Enquiry Documents. However, a recent tendency has been to apply the third method to all types of tenders, and it now seems to be the preferred option.

If a charge is set for supplying Enquiry Documents, it should be realistic and should be:

- Sufficient to cover the cost of printing and handling the documents
- High enough to discourage the non-serious tenderer
- Low enough not to discourage a genuine tenderer

Not only should the charge cover the cost of plan and document printing, but it should also include the cost of collating, binding and handling. An allowance should be made for wastage and losses; a reasonable surcharge for these costs would be 10 to 25 per cent of the net cost.

Where possible, tenderers should be required to collect the documents, cash in hand, at the nominated place of issue rather than having the Engineer arrange delivery and having to send out an invoice. The same situation should apply to supplying extra copies of the documents required by a tenderer.

Fixing the Tender Period

The length of the tender period will largely depend on the type of the contract, the nature of the work, the scope and quality of the documentation and the size and complexity of the investigations involved.

The following suggested tender periods are offered as a guide only. The actual period will depend upon the Engineer's assessment of the situation:

Design by the Principal:
Normal conventional projects   3–4 weeks
Projects involving obtaining quotations from specialist suppliers 6–8 weeks
Projects involving obtaining quotations from overseas   10–12 weeks
Design by Contractor   14–16 weeks

Since the time budgeted for design and documentation is often found to be inadequate, the Engineer can be pressed to reduce the tender period to make up time in order to keep the overall project schedule on target. If this temptation is not resisted, it will almost certainly be regretted later. It is essential to give tenderers adequate time to price their bids. Hurriedly prepared tenders may contain mistakes, or the tenderer may have to guess some items, usually overestimating in the process. Having once decided on a realistic tender period, it should be adhered to strictly.

4.3 PROCEDURES FOR INVITING TENDERS

Openly Invited Tenders

The aim of this procedure is to invite all interested contractors to submit tenders.

The invitation to tender should be advertised sufficiently far in advance of the planned contract award date to allow ample time for tenderers to prepare their offers and for the review of tenders by the Engineer. It should be kept in mind that it will be necessary to allow sufficient time for tenderers to see and respond to the advertisements, and that extended investigations may have to be made into previously unknown and possibly unsuitable tenderers.

The advertisement should be concise but clear and should contain sufficient information to enable average contractors to assess whether or not they would be interested in tendering. The advertisement should contain:

● A heading – 'Invitation to Tender'
● The name of the Principal (or the Consulting Engineer) as a subheading
● The project title and location
● An outline of the work under the Contract
● Nature of the Contract (e.g. Lump Sum, Schedule of Rates)
● Where Enquiry Documents can be inspected and obtained
● Whether or not there is a charge for the Enquiry Documents and details of the charge
● How, when, and where tenders are to be submitted
● The name and address of the Principal or of the Consulting Engineer under whose authority the advertisement is issued

Inviting Pre-registration of Tenderers

The aim of this procedure is to determine in advance the number of contractors who intend to take out enquiry documents and at the same time to discourage unsuitable tenderers from wasting both the Engineer's time and their own. This is the preferred option where tenders are publicly advertised and is now widely accepted by many government and statutory authorities.

As the procedure requires a longer time than is needed for open tendering, the invitation to pre-register should be published about four weeks before and the register should be closed one week before the scheduled date for the issue of the Enquiry Documents.

The advertisement should contain:

- A heading – 'Pre-registration of Tenderers'
- The name of the Principal (or the Consulting Engineer) as a subheading
- The project title and location
- An outline of work under the Contract
- The nature of the Contract (e.g. Lump Sum, Schedule of Rates)
- The planned dates for the issue of the Enquiry Documents, submission of tenders, award of Contract, and completion of the work
- An invitation to potential contractors to pre-register as tenderers
- Instructions for applying for pre-registration including details of information to be submitted with each application
- The name and address of the Principal or of the Consulting Engineer under whose authority the advertisement is issued

Since this procedure is pre-registration and not pre-qualification, the contractor need only indicate a wish to receive Enquiry Documents and the contractor's name and address. However, by asking the applicants to provide some additional information about themselves, casual enquirers can be discouraged. Applicants could be asked to provide the following information:

- The contractor's name, postal address, registered address and telephone, telex, and fax numbers
- The name and authority of contact person
- A description of the applicant or the applicant's firm, including the type and nature of work normally undertaken
- A brief outline of the applicant's experience in similar work

A register should then be prepared, listing all the applicants.

If any of the applicants are obviously unsuitable, it may be appropriate to make a discreet attempt to have their applications withdrawn. If this is successful, a letter should be sent to the applicants confirming the withdrawal. If an applicant still wishes to continue after such an approach, the application will have to be accepted and nothing further can be done until a tender is received.

Preparing a List of Nominated Tenderers

The aim of this procedure is to select tenderers based on past experience and present knowledge, of the Principal (and of the Engineer), concerning the various contractors nominated.

This procedure is frequently the only practical way of obtaining tenders where time is short or where the specialized nature of the work limits the number of potential bidders. It should otherwise only be used for smaller projects where the effort involved in the other options discussed could not be warranted. As pointed out previously, the main danger is overlooking otherwise acceptable tenderers.

Consequently, it is essential to make thorough enquiries to identify suitable contractors. Frequently, the Principal may have firm opinions. Reliance should not be made solely on the knowledge and experience of the person preparing the list of tenderers.

Having prepared a list of potential tenderers, the next step is to ascertain if the tenderers selected are in a position to tender and, if successful, to undertake the work. If time is short, a telephone call may be acceptable, but it is preferable to make the enquiry in writing.

The procedure should be initiated three or four weeks before the scheduled date for the issue of the Enquiry Documents. This should give adequate time for the enquiries to be sent out and the replies to be received.

A written enquiry should be in the form of a letter setting out the following information:

- The project title, the location, and the name of the Principal
- An indication of the authority delegated by the Principal to the writer of the letter
- An outline of the work under the Contract
- The nature of the Contract (e.g. Lump Sum, Schedule of Rates)
- The planned dates for the issue of the Enquiry Documents, submission of tenders, award of Contract, and completion
- An indication of the numbers of tenderers being invited to bid
- Whether or not there is a charge for the Enquiry Documents and details of the charge
- An invitation to be included as a tenderer with a request for a written reply

If the enquiry is made by telephone, the contractor should be given the same information and and it should then be confirmed in writing.

From the replies received, a final list of tenderers can be prepared. Usually a minimum of four and a maximum of seven tenderers comprise the list.

Pre-qualification of Tenderers

The aim of this procedure is to prepare a list of suitably qualified tenderers whose capability and experience have been checked prior to the issue of the Enquiry Documents.

Pre-qualification is the recommended procedure for major projects where the proper and timely completion of the works is of prime importance. It ensures that tenders are sought only from contractors who have already been checked as having the required resources and capacity to perform satisfactorily the work under the Contract. It also gives added encouragement to contractors to respond to invitations to bid for those projects which they are best suited to undertake and it avoids unnecessary work by both the contractor and the Engineer in the preparation and evaluation of tenders.

Invitation to pre-qualify The decision to use this procedure must be taken very early in the documentation stage because it requires a substantial lead time to be effective. It involves publishing an advertisement inviting interested contractors to apply for pre-qualification documents upon which their applications are to be made. The applications are then analysed and a list of selected tenderers is prepared. The procedure should be initiated 10 to 12 weeks before the planned date for the issue of the Enquiry Documents.

Where time is limited, the procedure can be accelerated by expanding the invitation advertisement to include a schedule of information to be submitted with the application in lieu of issuing a questionnaire.

However, the preferred option is to use a prepared questionnaire. The use of a standard form on which the answers are to be made will help to maintain uniformity in the return of information sought and so make the replies quicker and cheaper to provide while making their analysis and comparison easier.

Where pre-qualification documents are to be issued, the Notice of Invitation to Pre-qualify should be brief and, where practicable, contain the following information:

- A heading – 'Pre-Qualification of Tenderers'
- The name and address of the Principal (or of the Consulting Engineer)
- The project title and location
- An outline of the project and the scope and scale of the work
- The planned dates for the issue of the Enquiry Documents, submission of tenders, award of the Contract, and completion
- Any other major requirements
- The name and address of the Principal or of the Consulting Engineer under

whose authority the advertisement is issued and from whom Pre-qualification Documents can be obtained

Pre-qualification documents The pre-qualification documents should be issued to all respondents to the Invitation to Pre-qualify. The documents should include the following:

- A statement relevant to the project
- Instructions relating to the submission of the application
- Information to be submitted with the application (the Questionnaire)

The statement relevant to the project should, as far as possible, repeat and enlarge upon the information contained in the published Invitation to Pre-qualify. In addition, it should include:

- The nature of the Contract (e.g. Lump Sum, Schedule of Rates)
- An outline of the authority delegated to the person or firm issuing the documents
- The scope of any work to be undertaken by Designated, Selected and Nominated Subcontractors
- An outline of the performance standards to be met
- Any other special requirements for the work under the Contract such as maintenance or commissioning
- Any unusual aspect of the work
- Whether or not there is a charge for the Enquiry Documents and details of the charge

Instructions relating to the submission of the application should include where practicable:

- The number of copies of the application documents required
- The name, address, and latest date for the submission of the application
- Details of any particular requirements
- Attitude of the Principal to joint ventures

The latest date for the submission of applications should allow from four to six weeks for the selection process.

The Questionnaire should be drawn up in a manner similar to that of the schedules prepared for the actual tender and should follow the format for the various schedules described in Sec. 9.4 – 'Forms, Schedules, and Statements, for Tendering'. The questions should cover the matters outlined in the following tender schedules:

- Tenderer's Management and Administration Structure
- General Financial Statement
- Schedule of Key Personnel Resources
- Schedule of Major Items of Constructional Plant
- Schedule of Proposed Subcontracted Work
- Details of Fabrication and Manufacturing Facilities
- Any additional information that the contractor considers to be relevant

Analysis of pre-qualification applications In analysing the applications, the first stage is to identify those firms considered to be clearly not suited to the project and who therefore do not qualify to be included in the list of tenderers.

The second stage is to rank the remaining applicants in order of suitability and to select the required number of tenderers by working down from the top of the list.

The evaluation of the suitability of each applicant should be made primarily on the basis of the answers to the questionnaire. This may be supplemented by knowledge of previous experience with the contractors (both by the Principal and the Engineer) and by confidential enquiries to previous clients and reference to trade associations, directories, or national company registers. Where appropriate or practicable, interviews with the applicants may be held.

At all times, the selection process should be conducted fairly and be fully documented.

Notification of tenderers When the list of tenderers has been prepared, a confidential report setting out the reasons for selecting those named and the reasons for rejecting the others should be prepared by the Engineer and the tenderers then approved by the Principal.

Following receipt of the Principal's approval, the selected contractors should be advised of their selection and requested to confirm in writing their intention to submit a valid tender in response to the issue of the tender enquiry documents. If any of the contractors wish to drop out at this stage, the next best placed on the selection list could be offered the same invitation.

When all the invited contractors have acknowledged their intention to tender, the rejected contractors should be advised that their applications have been unsuccessful and thanked for submitting their application.

4.4 PROCEDURES DURING THE TENDER PERIOD

Disclosing the Names of Tenderers

The question of whether or not to reveal the names of tenderers to other parties often arises during the tender period. A request to reveal the names of tenderers usually arises from one of two sources:

- From other tenderers
- From hopeful subcontractors or suppliers who want to submit quotes to tenderers

The Principal may have a definite policy on the matter. Some prefer to treat the names of tenderers as confidential and to refuse to disclose them to other parties. Others have a more relaxed attitude and see no reason why the names of tenderers should be confidential. If tenders are being sought from nominated or pre-qualified tenderers, there is no real reason why tenderers should not be told who are their competitors. They will usually find out in any case. The question then to be resolved is whether or not to advise all tenderers as a matter of course or just to answer specific requests.

With regard to enquiries from subcontractors or suppliers, most contractors have their own stable of such firms and if they want further quotes they do not hesitate to advertise in the press. Revealing the names of tenderers to subcontractors or suppliers could cause tenderers to be inundated with unwelcome enquiries.

If an enquiry from a subcontractor or supplier appears to be of particular interest, the enquirer could be asked to put the request in writing and a copy of this could then be circulated under cover of a Notice to Tenderers. However, in doing so, a disclaimer should be added to the covering Notice to Tenderers advising that the enquiry is circulated without prejudice and that the Principal takes no responsibility for the integrity or acceptance of the workmanship of or materials supplied by the subcontractor or supplier. The problem with this procedure is that circulating one enquiry inevitably leads to circulating all such enquiries.

One reason sometimes put forward against disclosing the names of tenderers is based on the premise that if tenderers find out who else is tendering, there is a possibility of collusion. The contractors' grapevine is usually very efficient, however, and any tenderer who wants to find out the names of other tenderers usually has no difficulty in getting the information. The same thing applies in reverse to subcontractors.

Visits to Site by Tenderers

When the Contract involves sitework, the Enquiry Documents should require tenderers to examine the Site and its surroundings and to become acquainted as far as practicable of all relevant physical conditions. Arrangements must therefore be made to enable each tenderer to inspect the Site and to obtain the relevant information.

Tenderers should be notified whether visits to the Site will be made individually or collectively. This decision will be dependent upon a number of factors such as the location and nature of the work. Where practicable, the Engineer or a representative of the Principal should be present during the inspection of the Site, but any discussion should be limited to the verification of facts. Should a site visit reveal pertinent information not included in the Enquiry Documents, all tenderers must be informed by a Notice to Tenderers.

Where the work involves alterations or extensions to an existing plant, it may be necessary to place restrictions on the number, time, and duration of the visits. Arrangements for visits to the Site should be made so that equal opportunities are available for all tenderers.

It should be made clear to all tenderers that they must make their own arrangements for and bear the costs of travel and accommodation. It is the responsibility of the Principal to make only those arrangements necessary for the actual inspection of the Site.

Dealing with Enquiries from Tenderers

Enquiries from tenderers regarding errors, omissions or matters requiring clarification in the Enquiry Documents must be handled promptly and fairly, keeping in mind the need to ensure impartiality in dealing with all tenderers.

Options for procedure The alternative methods for handling such enquiries during the tender period are:

• By correspondence
• By a tenderer's briefing

The correspondence method is the normally recommended procedure because it is simpler, cheaper to all concerned, and less time-consuming. If there are many amendments, some of which may be complicated, a meeting to brief all tenderers may be more suitable. The appropriate procedure to be followed should be clearly defined in the Enquiry Documents, preferably in the Instructions to Tenderers.

In either case, any tenderer requiring clarification of the Enquiry Documents should be required to submit the query to the Engineer in writing on or before a nominated date. The closing date for receipt of queries should be at least 14 days before the date for the submission of tenders. In no circumstance should verbal enquiries be accepted unless they are confirmed in writing. Queries received after the closing date for the receipt of queries should only be considered in exceptional circumstances.

Correspondence method In this procedure, written replies to a tenderer's query should be prepared and despatched without delay. Unless the query is of a confidential nature or relevant to a particular tenderer's expertise or proposed method of work, these replies, together with the text of the query (without identifying the source), should be issued to all tenderers, preferably as a Notice to Tenderers.

Should a late query involve an error or omission in the Enquiry Documents which could have a significant effect on tenders, a decision must be made whether to advise all tenderers immediately or to deal with the matter during negotiations prior to accepting a tender. If the first option is adopted, it may be advisable to consider extending the date for the submission of tenders.

Tenderers' briefing method In this procedure, all tenderers are invited to send representatives (preferably not more than three from each tenderer) to a meeting, at which queries previously received in writing will be answered. This tenderers' briefing should be held about mid-way through the tender period and after all tenderers have had an opportunity to visit the Site if sitework is involved.

The Engineer should promptly acknowledge receipt of all queries and confirm the time, date, and place for the meeting to all tenderers at least 10 days beforehand. At this meeting, the queries and the replies should be read out to all the tenderers present. At the conclusion of the reading, copies of the text of the queries and replies should be distributed. These should not identify the source of the queries and the material should be arranged by subject matter in the same order as in the Enquiry Documents.

It may then be advisable to adjourn the meeting for a brief period to enable the tenderers to review the replies and to submit in writing any supplementary queries arising therefrom.

On reconvening, the supplementary questions and replies should then be read out, the anonymity of the questioners still being maintained. In the event that a question cannot be answered immediately, the reason for the delay should be announced and the meeting advised that a written reply will be sent out to all tenderers as soon as practicable.

Within a reasonable time after the meeting, a full set of minutes of the meeting recording both the original and supplementary queries and replies should be sent to each tenderer, whether they were present at the meeting or not. The tenderers should be required to acknowledge receipt of the minutes. These minutes are deemed to form part of the Enquiry Documents.

The above procedure may seem somewhat elaborate and time-consuming, and it should therefore be only contemplated where circumstances justify it.

Submission and Receipt of Tenders

The procedure for lodging the tenders should be clearly defined in the Instructions to Tenderers. It is the responsibility of tenderers to ensure that their properly completed tenders are delivered to the place nominated by the due submission date and time.

Tenders may be delivered by hand or by mail to the place nominated on or before the time stated in the Enquiry Documents. Most tenderers prefer to hand-deliver their tenders because they are then more certain of delivery and because they tend to leave it to the last minute to submit their tenders.

When a tender is received, the time and date of receipt should be noted on the envelope or package together with the name or initials of the person receiving the tender. The Instructions to Tenderers should require that the envelope or package containing the tender be marked with the name of the tenderer and the name and number (if appropriate) of the Contract. The tenders should then be placed in a safe place until the time nominated for their opening.

Many organizations who deal frequently with tenders may have a locked Tender Box at the reception desk of their main office into which the tenders can be placed during normal business hours. It is usual for this Tender Box to be opened each day and tenders deposited in it to be removed to a safe place after being logged, although some organizations prefer to leave the box locked until the closing date.

It is suggested that the receipt of tenders be logged as they are received in a schedule containing the names of tenderers to whom Enquiry Documents have been issued. At least 24 hours before the nominated closing time the schedule should be checked to ascertain which tenders have not yet been received. Tenderers who have not at that time deposited their tenders should be contacted by telephone, telex, or fax to ascertain if they still intend submitting a tender and to remind them of the closing time and date. This will also alert the tenderer if the tender has been delayed or lost in transit and a duplicate submission can be prepared and submitted.

When this duplicate tender has been received it should be marked accordingly. This procedure is, of course, not possible where open tendering has been adopted.

Tenderers, especially on small projects, tend to run late and frequently telephone, telex, or fax their prices to be confirmed in due course. Whether or not these tenders are to be accepted is at the discretion of the Principal. Provided legal or other requirements are not infringed, the opening of all tenders could be deferred to ensure consideration of late ones.

FIVE

THE TENDER

5.1 THE TENDER DOCUMENTS

The Tender Documents comprise the tenderer's offer to the Principal and are submitted in response to the Invitation to Tender.

The principal document is the Tender Form, which is issued with the Enquiry Documents and is completed and signed by the tenderer. It is accompanied and supported by the various forms and schedules which are listed in the Content of Tender and are also to be completed by the tenderer. The tenderer may include such additional material which the tenderer deems necessary to support and explain the tender.

The Conditions of Contract, the Specification and the Drawings issued for tender purposes with the Enquiry Documents are, by reference, deemed to form part of the Tender Documents.

5.2 THE OPENING AND CHECKING OF TENDERS

Opening the Tenders

Tenders can be opened in private or in public at the option of the Principal.

The Instructions to Tenderers should indicate if tenders are to be opened in public or in the presence of representatives of tenderers who wish to witness the procedure. The tenders are usually opened by the Engineer in the presence of a witness or a representative of the Principal and the representatives of the tenderers. Before each tender package is opened it should be checked by the Engineer and displayed to the audience to show that it is intact. As each tender is opened, the Engineer should announce and record:

- The name of the tenderer
- The date and time of receipt of tender
- The Tender Sum – for a conforming tender
                        – for any alternative tender
- The construction period or completion date
- The other relevant details (if applicable)

The Engineer should then announce (and record) the names of tenderers who have been issued with Enquiry Documents and who are disqualified owing to late or non-receipt of tenders.

As soon as practicable after opening the tenders, a list should be posted for display showing the names of the tenderers and their respective Tender Sums, arranged in ascending order from the lowest to the highest amount. A copy of the list should be mailed or faxed to each tenderer.

If tenders are to be opened in private, they may be opened by the Engineer in the presence of an appropriate witness. The details should be recorded as for public opening.

The record of the information scheduled at the opening should be signed by the Engineer and by the witness. A copy of the signed record should then be handed to the Principal or, if the Principal was not represented at the opening, delivered to the Principal with a covering letter.

Late Tenders

Whether to accept tenders received after the nominated closing time is at the Principal's option. In the case of publicly opened tenders, it would be difficult to accept such tenders. In the case of privately opened tenders, the opening of the tenders could be delayed briefly if it was known that one was on its way. Occasionally, tenderers will telephone or fax the principle details of their tenders with written confirmation to follow. Again, the validity of such tenders is for the Principal to decide.

This provision should be made clear in the Instructions to Tenderers. If it is decided not to accept a late tender, it should be returned unopened to the tenderer immediately, under cover of a letter explaining why it has not been accepted.

Checking the Tenders

The purpose of this operation is to verify that the tenders conform with the requirements laid down in the Instructions to Tenderers and that all the information required has been provided.

Each tender should be carefully examined to identify any disclaimer of responsibility or qualifying conditions proposed by the tenderer and should be checked for arithmetical correctness, errors or omissions.

Tenders for the supply of materials and equipment are often qualified by the inclusion of standard pre-printed Conditions of Sale or by quoting terms frequently abbreviated in a single-letter format. As is pointed out in Sec. 9.3 – 'Outline of Clauses for Instructions to Tenderers' – the inclusion of such conditions and terms may result in the tender being judged 'non-conforming'. The Engineer should be aware of the possibility of ambiguity and obscurity arising from the use of such qualifying abbreviations. Some of these qualifying terms and their usual abbreviated forms are listed in Appendix C.

It is recommended that, before commencing the examination of the Tender Documents, a schedule be drawn up of all the documents listed in the Content of Tender and other matters to be checked. The following checklist, while not claimed to be completely exhaustive, is sufficiently detailed to be used as a basis for preparing the schedule.

Checklist of Items to Consider when Checking a Tender

- Have all the documents listed in the Content of Tender been completed correctly and returned with the tender?
- Has the Tender Form been properly completed and correctly signed?
- Has Stamp Duty, if applicable, been paid?
- Does the Tender Sum entered on the Form of Tender agree with total of prices in the Schedule of Prices for Tendering or the Schedule of Rates?
- Is the Period or Date for Practical Completion stated?
- Is the Period or date for 'milestone' dates or Separable Portions stated?
- Has the Schedule of Prices for Tendering or Schedule of Rates been properly completed with quantities and rates correctly extended and totalled?
- Has the correct number of Tender Documents been submitted where more than one copy is specified?
- Are Alternative Tenders correctly identified and signed?
- Has endorsement been given regarding the Notices to Tenderers received (by number and date)?
- Is any tenderer's disagreement with or qualification of any provision in the Enquiry Documents stated clearly and in specific terms which relate directly to that provision?

- Is there any inclusion of standard conditions of sale or other conditions proposed by the tenderer?

5.3 THE EVALUATION OF TENDERS

Purpose of Evaluation

Tenders are deemed to be under evaluation from the time they are opened until a Contractor has been appointed and the unsuccessful tenderers notified or until the Tender Validity Period has expired, whichever occurs first. The evaluation process comprises four phases:

- Preliminary Evaluation
- Post Tender Interview
- Final Evaluation
- Risk Analysis

Following completion of these four phases, the Engineer should compile an Evaluation Report and Recommendation.

Preliminary Evaluation

This is the first phase of the evaluation process. The aim is to identify conforming and acceptable Alternative Tenders and then to ascertain matters which may require further clarification.

Any qualifications made by a tenderer which are not in accordance with the Enquiry Documents and which are unacceptable should first be determined. The tenderer should be notified and given the opportunity of withdrawing such qualifications unreservedly in writing. The tenderer should only be allowed to do this provided there is no change in the Tender Sum and no other qualifications raised. Otherwise such tender should be rejected as non-conforming.

Alternative Tenders complying with the provisions laid down in the Instructions to Tenderers, should be appraised to ascertain those which appear to be viable.

The forms and schedules returned with tenders should have been prepared so that all the required information will be supplied with the tenders. Nevertheless, it is almost inevitable that some of the information provided will be incomplete or ambiguous and the Engineer will need to seek clarification. The next step is then to examine each tender and identify those matters requiring amplification. At this stage it is not necessary to determine the significance of the information supplied , only to assess if it is in sufficient detail to enable a final evaluation and comparison of tenders to be made.

Tenderer's management and administrative structure

- Have all the listed questions been clearly and adequately answered?
- If the tenderer is a corporation, have all the details of any parent and subsidiary companies (as applicable) been provided?
- Is it clear what person/firm/company holds a controlling interest in the tenderer and should that person/firm/company be required to guarantee in writing the tenderer's performance?
- If a consortium or joint venture is proposed, have details of the partners been made available, is it made clear how it is to function and what is the proposed management structure?

Financial statement

- Are the tenderer's proposals for funding the project clearly defined?
- Is a banker's statement required to verify the tenderer's capacity to undertake the work?
- Has the tenderer indicated how the requirements for Security and Retention will be met?
- Has the tenderer made any qualifications to the specified arrangements for payments? If so, are they clearly stated?
- If the tenderer has nominated a price fluctuation formula, are details of base dates, definition of indexes, numerical values of indexes at base dates, and numerical values and make-up of wages and allowances provided?
- Are there any other financial or commercial matters which should be raised?

Alternative Tender

- If an Alternative Tender has been submitted, have all deviations from the Enquiry Documents been clearly stated and have all other necessary details been provided to enable a proper assessment to be made?

Tenderer's background and experience

- Has the tenderer's background and experience been given in sufficient detail to confirm whether or not the tenderer is capable of undertaking the work?
- Is the tenderer's current work load given in detail?
- Has the tenderer's current workforce been given in adequate detail?

Tenderer's industrial relations record

- If there is the possibility of industrial relations problems arising, has the tenderer's past record in industrial relations been adequately stated?

Bill of Quantities

- If a Bill of Quantities is to be part of the Contract, have all the items been priced and correctly totalled?
- Has the tenderer made any alterations or qualifications to the Bill?

Schedule of Rates/Schedule of Prices for Tendering

- Has the tenderer completed the Schedule as issued with the Enquiry Documents or has an alternative schedule been submitted?
- If the latter, does the alternative Schedule adequately reflect the whole of the work under the Contract?

Schedule of Daywork Rates

- Does the Schedule cover all classifications including subcontractor's labour?
- Do the rates submitted include all penalty rates such as ordinary time, time-and-a-half and double time?
- Do the rates include tool expendables and handheld tools, including power tools?

Changes to prequalification documents

- If applicable, have all changes been noted and do they require amplification?

Statement on tenderer's plan of approach to the work

- Does the tenderer's proposed method of construction/fabrication include any unusual or novel techniques? Are these clearly explained?
- Is the nature and extent of 'temporary works' clearly defined?
- Does the tenderer appear to understand the requirements in respect of items of unusual or difficult nature?
- Have the tenderer's requirements for Site establishment been given? Has the tenderer defined what provision and allowance have been made for fencing, security, lighting, access, parking, and services?

- Has the tenderer stated what allowance has been made for handling Site administration in regard to managers, engineers, supervisors, and foremen?

Programme of work

- Is the tenderer's programme submitted in sufficient detail?
- Are Site start dates, manufacture start dates, completion dates, and key milestone dates shown?
- Are working days and hours stated?
- Has the tenderer stated what allowance has been made to allow for short-term interruptions to the work?

Schedule of key personnel

- Are CVs provided for key personnel?
- Has the tenderer named the person who would be actively and continually responsible for the whole of the Contract?
- Has the senior Site officer been named?
- Have the qualifications, experience and competence of each of the persons individually responsible for management, adminstration, financial reporting, cost accounting, and construction or fabrication been stated?

Schedule of subcontract work

- Has the tenderer expressed any reservations about the nominated, designated, or selected subcontractors named in the Enquiry Documents? If so, have these doubts been substantiated?
- Has the tenderer listed other parts of the work which would be subcontracted?
- Are the subcontractors for these parts named by the tenderer?
- Has the tenderer explained procedures for the supervision and coordination of subcontractors?

Schedule of major items of constructional plant and equipment

- Has the tenderer listed all the necessary items of major constructional plant and equipment – which are readily available or obtainable – required to undertake the work in a practical and efficient manner?

Schedule of imported items

- Are current exchange rates quoted for buying foreign currency for imported items?

- How are the item costs qualified? Are there any 'hidden' costs and charges, such as delivery costs, not included in the Tender Sum?
- If the quoted costs are subject to a Cost Adjustment formula, is the formula supplied, together with all data for its operation?

Schedule of tender drawings

- Have all the drawings listed in the Schedule been included in the tender?
- Are the drawings competently prepared and do they provide all the information required by the Enquiry Documents?

Schedule of transport and delivery

- Does the Schedule cover all critical items of equipment?
- Are there any potential delivery problems leading to delay in the work?

Schedule of insurance policies

- Are details of all the required policies provided?
- Are there any exclusions?
- Is the amount of Excess stated in each case?

Schedule of Design Data Schedules

- Have all Data Schedules been completed?
- Are there any doubtful matters?

Schedule of substitutions

- Are any substitutions proposed? Are they clearly defined?

The answers to these questions could be obtained by correspondence but that can be time-consuming and the Engineer may be tempted to speed up the process by a telephone call. This may be satisfactory for a simple query but the conversation should, nevertheless, be immediately confirmed in writing in a Memorandum of Telephone Discussion, detailing the matters discussed, the time and date of the call and the names of the persons involved.

However, a Post Tender Interview with one or more selected tenderers may be more effective. From the preliminary evaluation it should be possible to determine which, if any, of the tenders would be of interest to the Principal. A shortlist of from one to three tenders should be prepared and those tenderers invited to a Post Tender Interview.

Post Tender Interview

This is the second phase of the evaluation process. The prime function of the Post Tender Interview is to obtain further information from tenderers in clarification of their tenders; it is not the occasion for negotiating any alternative offers. It can also be used to ensure that the tenderers know about and understand all important and potentially troublesome matters and to reinforce the safeguarding of the Principal and the Engineer in the event of future disagreements with the Contractor. Where two or more tenderers are to be interviewed, each interview is conducted separately.

Before each interview is held, a list of questions arising from the Preliminary Evaluation should be prepared and printed under an appropriate heading. This list, prepared individually for each tenderer, should preferably be sent to the selected tenderers with the invitations to attend the interviews. The invitations should give the tenderers sufficient notice to permit them to consider their replies carefully. A written list of queries will also tend to minimize misunderstandings as to the meaning and intent of the questions.

The interview with each selected tenderer should be held at a time, date and place nominated by the Engineer. The Principal and the tenderer should each be represented by at least two persons; the Engineer and one other person could represent the Principal. The invitation should ask the tenderer to advise the Engineer of the name and authority (or responsibility) of each of the representatives attending the meeting.

Each meeting should be chaired by the Engineer and arrangements made to take notes from which formal minutes would be prepared. At the commencement of each meeting the Engineer should explain the purpose of the meeting and should point out that matters outlined in the minutes of the meeting should, when approved by both parties, be incorporated in the Contract. If copies of the list of questions have not been previously forwarded to the tenderer, they should now be handed over.

As far as is possible, the discussion should be restricted to the queries listed and the replies should be explored in sufficient depth to enable the Engineer to make an assessment of the point raised in relation to the final evaluation. As soon as is practicable after each Post Tender Interview, minutes of the meeting should be forwarded to the tenderer concerned under cover of a letter requesting that they reply immediately with their agreement or comments. These minutes should set out:

- Date and place of the meeting
- Names of those present (with their positions)
- Matters discussed
- Decisions made or replies given

Final Evaluation

This is the third phase of the evaluation. Following the Post Tender Interviews, it should be possible for the Engineer to make a final evaluation of the tenders leading to a recommendation for acceptance by the Principal.

The Final Evaluation takes into account the analysis and assessment of three components:

- General Contractual and Administrative Review
- Financial Appraisal
- Technical Evaluation

The appropriate basic factors and the method of appraisal should first be established so that an objective result can be obtained from the evaluation and comparison of tenders.

In assessing each of the three main components of the evaluation process, a number of factors need to be considered. These include:

General contractual and administrative review

- Conformity with Enquiry Documents and Notices to Tenderers
- Completeness and validity of tender
- Exclusions and qualifications
- Insurance arrangements
- Tenderer's administration proposals and expertise
- Tenderer's record in industrial relations
- Source of labour and working hours
- Mobilization and demobilization of labour

Financial appraisal

- Estimated capital cost
- Financial standing of the tenderer
- Financing arrangements by the tenderer
- Discounted cash flow and programme of payments
- Arrangements for security and retention
- Guarantees and bonds
- Adjustment for fluctuations in costs
- Currencies and exchange rates
- Rates for Daywork

Technical evaluation

(a) Applicable generally

• Technical capacity of tenderer
• Conformity with the Specification and Drawings
• Programme of the work and completion/delivery dates
• Extent of subcontracted work
• Supervision and quality control
• Location of off-Site facilities
• Quality of materials and fabrication

(b) Applicable to civil/structural work

• Method of construction or fabrication
• Extent of temporary works
• Construction plant and equipment (available or required)

(c) Applicable to mechanical/electrical work

• Efficiency of the design
• Estimated service life
• Ease of installation
• Ease of maintenance
• Availability of spare parts
• Level of operator training available/required

When tenders are to be analysed in detail, the data applicable to the various offers should be tabulated for comparison purposes. A typical blank analysis sheet is shown in Appendix A.

For civil and/or structural work, the comparison will largely be a subjective analysis of the financial assessment and the evaluation of technical matters, many of which are difficult to tabulate. The objective analysis would primarily be restricted to a comparison of the Tender Sums and Date(s) for Practical Completion. However, for Schedule of Rates contracts, it is sometimes useful to use an analysis sheet to test the sensitivity of the Tender Sum to significant variations in the estimated quantities used for tender purposes, particularly those items whose quantities are more uncertain.

In mechanical and/or electrical plant contracts, an analysis sheet can be very useful, particularly where comparisons are to be made between locally manufactured and imported items. Where there are a number of components, a separate sheet may be required for each unit, with a final summary sheet to encapsulate the results. The analysis for each component may be in two parts – a commercial comparison and a technical comparison.

The commercial comparison would be primarily concerned with cost and delivery or completion time. For example, for an imported unit of equipment, the items on the analysis sheet could be as follows:

- Item of equipment
- Country of origin
- Cost ex-works (country of origin currency)
- Fixed price or subject to adjustment
- Terms of payment
- Exchange rate
- Cost ex-works (local currency)
- Shipping costs (local currency)
- Total landed cost (local currency)
- Cost of transport to Site
- Insurance costs
- Cost of installation
- Total installed cost
- Shipment port – loading
              – unloading
- Delivery times – ex works
               – on Site

When making the commercial comparison, it is important to ensure that the tenderer's estimated costs are realistic. Sometimes tenderers deliberately quote underestimated costs (such as transport and shipping costs) hoping that they can claim reimbursement for an 'unforeseen' escalation in such costs. The technical comparison would, of course, depend upon what factors the Engineer considers significant.

Some large organizations have standard, pre-printed analysis sheets for various types of equipment, but in most cases the Engineer should be able to prepare a suitable form for the project in hand.

On a financial basis, the tender with the lowest overall estimated cost should be judged to be the most favourable. It would normally be accepted by the Principal, provided that the administrative and technical appraisals are satisfactory. If they are not, then a value judgement must be made as to whether or not to attempt to negotiate an acceptable contract.

In appraising qualifications or exclusions included in tenders, and the acceptability of any alternative tenders, consideration should be given to any resulting cost or benefit (direct or indirect) during the performance of the work under the Contract and during the estimated life of the completed Works.

Risk Analysis

The final stage of the appraisal is a Risk Analysis. Risks are inevitable in all projects and the identification and allocation of all foreseeable risks to either the Principal or to the Contractor should have been evaluated and defined in the Enquiry Documents. It is advisable that these risks be reviewed and a value judgement be made of their magnitude and possible consequences in the light of the tenderer's offer. This is particularly important for large and complex projects.

The possible consequences of the following risks should be appraised:

- Inadequate performance by the Contractor
- Poor supervision and quality control
- Inability to meet the Date for Practical Completion and other programme 'milestone' dates
- Failure of temporary works or elements of the Works
- Failure to meet performance requirements for mechanical and electrical plant and services
- Effect of delays due to industrial disputes, taking into account the tenderer's track record in industrial relations
- Effect of lack of collaboration with the Principal and other parties involved in the work

The lowest Tender Sum and the most satisfactory result from the Financial Appraisal may not be the best tender for the Principal to accept. All factors considered in the evaluation process, including the Risk Analysis, should be taken into account.

Evaluation Report and Recommendation

Following completion of the four phases of the evaluation process, the Engineer should be in a position to compile an Evaluation Report and Recommendation.

This Report should first identify the Contract and give a brief description of the scope of the work under the Contract. There should follow a description of the procedure adopted and the action taken in receiving, opening and evaluating the tenders.

The Report should then separately name all tenderers who:

- Were invited to tender
- Submitted tenders
- Declined to tender

The tenders received should then be identified as:

- Conforming tenders
- Non-conforming tenders
- Acceptable Alternative Tenders

The basis for consideration of Alternative Tenders and the reasons for the rejection of non-conforming tenders should be stated and the results of the comparative analysis of the conforming tenders and acceptable alternative tenders should be set out.

In civil and structural engineering contracts, provided that there are one or more conforming tenders within the price range previously established by the Principal and the Engineer, and the Contractor has the required expertise and experience, the Engineer should be able to make a firm recommendation on the basis of the Tender Sum. In the event that there are no conforming tenders but there is an acceptable Alternative Tender, the Engineer should again be able to make a recommendation to the Principal provided that the Alternative Tender complies with the provisions laid down in the Instructions to Tenderers for such tenders. If neither of these conditions is met and no acceptable tenders are received, the Engineer will need to consult with the Principal as to the next step to take.

For contracts involving the design, supply and installation of mechanical or electrical plant or equipment, the tenders may need to be analysed in greater detail. In addition to taking into account the Tender Sum and delivery/completion date(s), consideration must be given to a comparison of quality and efficiency, as well as the cost of installation, operation and maintenance.

Procedure if no Satisfactory Tenders are Received

It is when there are no acceptable tenders received, either conforming or alternative, or the Tender Sum is beyond the limit established by the Principal, that the Engineer will need to reassess the situation.

There are three options open to the Principal:

1. Abandon the project.
2. Negotiate an acceptable contract with one of the tenderers.
3. Invite new tenders.

Should the Principal choose the first option, the Engineer should notify all tenderers accordingly (stating the reasons why the Principal does not wish to proceed), arrange for the return of any tender deposits and request the tenderers to return all copies of the Enquiry Documents. Under such circumstances, consideration could be given to compensating tenderers for all or part of their tendering expenses.

The second option should be approached with caution. Any such negotiations must be conducted discreetly so as to ensure confidentiality and impartiality and so that neither the tenderer nor the Principal will have an unfair advantage. It should be appreciated that entering into negotiations with tenderers, particularly where an attempt is made to canvass the possibility of a lower Contract Sum, may place the Principal at a disadvantage. This course of action should only be attempted where there appears to be the possibility of a compromise over some qualification(s) by the tenderer.

If it is a case of the Tender Sum being too high, the only practical solution may be to reduce the scope of the work under the Contract. If this can be achieved by the deletion of some discrete part or section of the work, it may be practicable to ask one or more of the tenderers to submit a quotation for the deletion of that part or section. The question then arises as to which of the tenderers should be asked. This is a matter to be discussed between the Engineer and the Principal and the decision will depend largely upon the Engineer's evaluation of the tenders received. Whatever the decision made it should be based on the principle of maintaining the probity and integrity of the parties. Neither the Principal nor the Engineer should lay themselves open to charges of unfair practices.

In the event that a satisfactory revised tender is obtained, the other tenderers should be advised that a tender has been accepted, have tender deposits returned and be requested to return the copies of the Enquiry Documents.

If this procedure is not considered feasible or if the changes to the extent of the work are more widespread, or if it was felt that there was lack of interest in the work leading to insufficient competition among the tenderers, the third option is probably the most practical solution. All tenderers should be advised of the decision not to accept any of the tenders submitted and the reasons for it; all tender deposits should be returned whether or not the tenderers are to be invited to submit a new tender. Tenderers should be told of the intention to invite new tenders and a brief outline given of the proposed changes to the Enquiry Documents. They could be asked to signify if they would be interested in being included in the new list of tenderers. It would be pointless to invite new tenders on the basis of the original Enquiry Documents solely with the intention of obtaining a lower Tender Sum.

The Enquiry Documents should be amended to include the revised scope of the work and to incorporate any relevant matters covered by Notices to Tenderers issued during the first tender period. New tenders should be invited as if it was an entirely new project.

Extending the Tender Validity Period

All possible steps should be taken to avoid delay in the acceptance of a tender. Because of unforeseen or unavoidable circumstances, however, the acceptance of a tender may be delayed beyond the limit of the Tender Validity Period as nominated in the Instructions to Tenderers (Conditions of Tendering), in which case all tenderers should be advised in writing of the delay and asked if they would agree to a specified extension of the Validity Period. The letter should indicate that tenderers who do not agree will be deemed to have withdrawn their tenders. This could give rise to a fine legal point, which the Engineer should discuss with a legal professional.

When the Enquiry Documents do not provide for cost adjustment due to fluctuations in the cost of wages, services, and materials, consideration could be given to allowing tenderers to adjust their Tender Sums accordingly.

An extension of the Validity Period then raises the question of the Tender Deposits. If these are in the form of a Banker's Guarantee or a Security Bond, the Engineer should examine the documents and ascertain if there is any time limit to their validity. Rather than attempt to renegotiate these warranties, it might be easier to return all Tender Deposits. Since it could be argued that the Principal had breached the Conditions of Contract, it may be difficult to enforce any warranty.

THE CONTRACT

6.1 AWARDING THE CONTRACT

The Letter of Acceptance

As soon as practicable after the decision is made to accept a tender, a *Letter of Acceptance*, signed by the person authorized to do so by the Principal, should be sent to the successful tenderer.

As already pointed out in Sec. 2.2 – 'The Law of Contract', a legally binding contract is formed when an offer made by one party is accepted *unconditionally* by another party. If the original conforming tender or an alternative tender is accepted without qualification or amendment, the Letter of Acceptance need only accept the nominated tender as submitted in order to form a legally binding Contract.

If an original offer has been amended or qualified in subsequent negotiations, the agreed changes must be documented and then proposed or acknowledged by the tenderer as a revised offer. The Letter of Acceptance can then unequivocally accept the amended tender to form a valid Contract.

In addition to accepting the tender, the Letter of Acceptance should:

- Nominate those Enquiry Documents and any documentation of amendments, minutes of meetings and qualifications which will be incorporated in the Contract Documents.

- Confirm that an Instrument of Agreement will be prepared by the Engineer and, together with the updated Contract Documents, forwarded to the tenderer (now the Contractor) for signature.
- Name the Superintendent or nominate the Consulting Engineer or other agent who will appoint the Superintendent.
- State that all directions concerning the Contract will henceforth be issued by the Superintendent and all further correspondence in connection with the Contract should be addressed to the Superintendent.
- Draw attention to the provision in the Conditions of Contract for the lodging of Security.
- Point out that the Specification and Drawings issued with the Enquiry Documents are provisional and must not be used for construction purposes unless or until otherwise approved or amended.
- Nominate that the date of the Letter of Acceptance is the Date of Acceptance of Tender or the Date for Commencement of Work, as appropriate.
- In the case of Lump Sum contracts, confirm the Lump Sum.

Until the Agreement is signed, the Letter of Acceptance and the referenced documents will form the Contract.

Letter of Intent

If for some reason it is not possible to issue a Letter of Acceptance immediately after a decision is made to accept a tender, a *Letter of Intent* may be sent to the successful tenderer as a precursor to the Letter of Acceptance. The purpose of a Letter of Intent, by advising the tenderer that the Principal intends to accept the tender, is to avoid unnecessary delays to the work under the Contract by authorizing the successful tenderer to commence preliminary planning and mobilization.

It must be emphasized that a Letter of Intent is not an acceptance. Unless the Letter of Intent makes specific provision, the successful tenderer would be unable to recoup the cost of such preliminary work in the event that the Principal decided not to proceed.

The Letter of Intent should, therefore:

- Advise the tenderer that it is the Principal's intention to accept the nominated/amended tender within a stated period or by a certain date.
- Authorize the tenderer to proceed with certain nominated preliminary work up to a specified cost limit.
- Confirm that in the event that the Letter of Intent is withdrawn and the tender not accepted, the Principal will pay to the tenderer the cost of such

of the authorized work undertaken on a basis to be set out in the Letter of Intent.

- State that when the Letter of Acceptance is eventually issued, the provisions therein will supersede those in the Letter of Intent and
- Request the tenderer to acknowledge receipt of the Letter of Intent and confirm acceptance of the conditions therein.

Notifying Tenderers

On the issue of the Letter of Acceptance or the Letter of Intent, all other tenderers should be individually notified that a tender has been accepted; no public announcement should be made until all tenderers have been notified. All Tender Deposits should be returned and, where requested, the unsuccessful tenderers requested to return their copies of the Enquiry Documents. The Tender Deposit of the successful tenderer should be retained until any Security Deposit required under the Contract is lodged.

A question often raised is whether or not it is advisable to tell other tenderers the amount of the successsful Tender Sum. Where tenders have been opened publicly or in the presence of the tenderers, the point does not arise. In other situations, it is a matter in which the Principal may seek the advice of the Engineer before making a decision.

Some authorities suggest that it would be of assistance to tenderers generally to know where they stood in relation to their competition. Their suggestion is to include a list of tenderers arranged alphabetically in the letter to each tenderer, together with a separate list of Tender Sums arranged in order of cost. Each tenderer could then see how their tender stood in relation to those of the other tenderers without disclosing any tenderer's own price. However, the Principal could be placed in a quandary if there have been some post-tender negotiations with the successful tenderer, resulting in an amended Tender Sum.

The value of making this information available is debatable. The contractors' 'grapevine' can be very efficient and some of the more cynical members of the engineering profession believe that in many cases most tenderers are well aware of the tender sums submitted by their competitors even before the tenders are opened by the Engineer. This viewpoint has been reinforced by the evidence given at the Royal Commission on Building in New South Wales, which seems to indicate that there is a remarkable amount of 'cooperation' between major, and otherwise respectable, contractors when tendering for large building and engineering projects.

6.2 PREPARING A FORMAL CONTRACT FOR SIGNATURE

The Requirements for a Formal Contract

Provided that the Letter of Acceptance identifies all the documents and encompasses all the provisions which comprise the agreement between the parties, a simple contract is formed by the issue of the Letter. While in law, this may be sufficient to evidence the Contract, the parties may, either as required by the terms of the Contract or else through subsequent agreement, merge the simple Contract into a formal one by signing an Instrument of Agreement (the Agreement). Since both the Principal and the Contractor will, in all probability, be limited-liability corporations, their Articles of Association may require this procedure to be followed. The Engineer should have determined the Principal's requirements in this regard when preparing the Conditions of Tendering in the Instructions to Tenderers.

Assuming that a formal Agreement is required, the final stage of the tendering process is, therefore, for the Engineer to assemble the Contract Documents and arrange for the parties to the Contract to sign the Agreement.

The Contract Documents

The Contract Documents comprise all the documents required to evidence the Contract as negotiated by the parties. They include, but are not necessarily limited to, the following:

- Agreement
- Tender Documents
- Letter of Acceptance
- Conditions of Contract
- Specification
- Drawings

Since the Specification and the Drawings, and, to a lesser extent, the Conditions of Contract, will be referred to by many people during the performance of the Contract, it is first advisable to *engross* the Contract by incorporating all the changes and amendments to the conditions and scope of the work which have arisen during the Tender Period.

Amending the Documents

Most engineering offices today are well equipped with modern copying, printing, and binding facilities, backed up by efficient word-processing and desk-top publishing programs.

These make easier the task of physically incorporating the amendments and printing the revised documents, but great care must be taken to ensure that all the changes and revisions are correctly and accurately made.

The first step is to embrace all the amendments to the Conditions of Contract and the Specification included in the Notices to Tenderers. Any amendments to the Drawings would be made by issuing amended drawings with the relevant Notice to Tenderers. There may also be some typographical errors picked up during the Tender Period and these can also be corrected.

The second step is to incorporate data provided by the Contractor in response to the Enquiry Documents. This would include:

- Inserting details nominated by tenderers in their tenders for inclusion in the Annexure to the General Conditions
- Replacing the *pro-forma* Data Schedules in the Specification with copies of the completed schedules included in the Tender Documents
- Any other relevant data supplied in response to requests in the Enquiry Documents or submitted by the Contractor amplifying the tender

The third and most difficult step is to incorporate all changes to the Conditions of Contract and the Specification negotiated before the award of the Contract and set out in the documents accompanying the Letter of Acceptence. It is essential that these amendments are incorporated in exactly the same words as used in the Letter of Acceptance documents.

The Engineer should carefully list *every* amendment to the documents and advise the Contractor accordingly when the Contract is submitted for signature.

The Agreement

The Agreement itself need only be a short document incorporating the respective promises of the parties, identifying the work under the Contract and specifying the consideration. This is best accomplished by marking each of the documents annexed to and forming part of the Agreement 'A', 'B', 'C', and so on, and listing them in the Agreement with their identifying marks.

Most General Conditions provide a *pro-forma* Form of Agreement, ranging from the elaborately worded form in the ICE Conditions of Contract to the relatively simple statement in the SAA General Conditions. The Engineer's choice of the form of the Agreement will depend upon local legal requirements; in any case, the Principal's legal advisers may wish to draw up the Agreement.

Date of the Agreement

Most Forms of Agreement commence with the words 'This Agreement made [date inserted] ...'. The significance of the date inserted is primarily for convenience in referring to or identifying the document. However, unless the Date of Acceptance of Tender or the Date for Commencement of Work (as applicable) is clearly stated in the Letter of Acceptance or elsewhere in the Contract, the date on the Agreement will be construed as that date.

Assembling the Documents for Signature

It is usual to prepare three copies of the Contract Documents for signature marked 'Original', 'Duplicate' and 'Triplicate' respectively. The Original is for the Principal, the Duplicate is for the Contractor and the Triplicate is for the Superintendent.

Where practicable, all the documents, apart from the Drawings and the Priced Bill of Quantities (if applicable), should preferably be bound in a single volume in such a manner that removal and replacement of individual documents or pages would be difficult. Where the total thickness of the documents makes it possible, they can be bound together with three or more staples along the left-hand edge. Thermoplastic comb binding, while possibly suitable for job copies of the Specification, should not be used for the Contract Documents.

The covers, on which appropriate identification details have been printed, can be a good-quality cover board, plastic-laminated after printing. Where the thickness renders stapling impracticable, the documents could be bound as two or more separate volumes. Alternatively, consideration should be given to having the documents professionally casebound (in hard covers). The Priced Bill of Quantities will have been separately bound by the Quantity Surveyor.

Where only a few drawings are involved, they can be folded and bound behind the Specification. Otherwise they can stapled together with a cover sheet on which is printed, in addition to the usual identification details, a list of the drawings enclosed. The binding edge and staples can be covered with bookbinder's tape.

6.3 SIGNING THE AGREEMENT

Where practicable, the three sets of the Contract Documents should be signed by the authorized representatives of the Principal and the Contractor in the presence of the Engineer. Several days before the date set for the signing, the Duplicate copy should be sent to the Contractor and the Original

```
┌──────────────────────────────────────────────────────┐
│                                                        │
│  This is document ...... comprising ....... sheets referred to in the │
│  Agreement dated . . . . . . . . . . . . . . . . . . . │
│  Principal . . . . . . . . . . . . . . . . . . . . . . │
│  Contractor . . . . . . . . . . . . . . . . . . . . .  │
│                                                        │
└──────────────────────────────────────────────────────┘
```

```
┌──────────────────────────────────────────────────┐
│                                                    │
│  This is the set of ....... drawing referred to in the │
│  Agreement dated . . . . . . . . . . . . . . . .   │
│  Principal . . . . . . . . . . . . . . . . . . .   │
│  Contractor  . . . . . . . . . . . . . . . . . .   │
│                                                    │
└────────────────────────────────────────────────────┘
```

```
┌──────────────────────────────────────────────────┐
│                                                    │
│  This is one of the drawings referred to in the    │
│  Agreement dated . . . . . . . . . . . . . . . .   │
│  Principal  . . . . . . . . . . . . . . . . . .    │
│  Contractor  . . . . . . . . . . . . . . . . . .   │
│                                                    │
└────────────────────────────────────────────────────┘
```

Figure 6.1 Contract document identification.

to the Principal for examination and approval, with the request that they each bring the copy to the place nominated for the signing on the date and at the time advised. The three copies (including the Triplicate retained by the Engineer) can then be signed and witnessed. If it is required under local regulations, the Contract should be registered and the appropriate Stamp Duty paid. This is usually undertaken by the Engineer, after which they can be distributed as indicated.

Where it is not practicable to have the signatories formally meet for the signing, the Engineer can send the Original and the Triplicate to the Contractor and the Duplicate to the Principal for examination and approval, with the request that they be returned to the Engineer after signature and witnessing. When the signed copies have been received by the Engineer, the Duplicate (with the Principal's signature) can be sent to the Contractor and the Original (with the Contractor's signature) sent to the Principal for signature. They can then each sign and return their copies to the Engineer for registering if this is required under local regulations. The Triplicate (signed by only the Contractor) remains in the possession of the Engineer.

Strictly speaking, every page of both the Original and Duplicate copies should be signed or at least initialled by the persons signing on behalf of both the Principal and the Contractor. In an engineering contract where several hundred pages could be involved this can be time consuming and tedious. One possible solution is to have a suitable note printed on the cover sheet of each document along the lines of those shown in Fig. 6.1. A rubber stamp could be made for this purpose. Nevertheless, where the Agreement comprises more than one page, all pages of the actual Agreement should be signed by both parties. All costs associated with preparing and registering the Contract Documents are usually borne by the Principal.

Before arranging the signing procedure, the Engineer would be well advised to consult and seek the approval of the Principal's legal advisor.

PART
THREE

PREPARATION OF THE DOCUMENTS

SEVEN

ORGANIZATION OF THE WORK

7.1 PROGRAMMING AND BUDGETING

The Need for a Programme

The meticulous preparation of the designs and documents for an engineering project is both time-consuming and costly. Having made the decision to proceed with a project, an Owner will be understandably anxious to 'see something happening', and, unless made fully aware from the outset of the time required to carry out this stage of the project in a competent and thorough manner, may pressure the Engineer into making unrealistic promises for the completion of this stage.

Owners and Principals who have had little or no previous involvement in engineering contracts often find it difficult to appreciate the amounts of time and money expended during the design and documentation phase when there is little to show for it. It is then the task of the Engineer to explain the procedure and to assure the Owner or Principal of the need for the expenditure.

At the earliest possible opportunity, the Engineer should prepare, in a suitable form, a detailed programme for the preparation of the documents required for the tender stage of the project, together with achievable cost and time budgets. This programme should then be presented to the Principal/ Owner for approval.

The function of the programme is to enable the Engineer to allocate and manage effectively the available resources during the design and documentation of the project. Unless this aspect of the work is closely controlled and monitored, time can be wasted and unnecessary expense incurred. A properly coordinated and realistic programme will enable the Engineer to complete this phase of the work on time and within budget.

Preparing the Programme

In preparing this programme, the Engineer should first review carefully the Project Plan, so as to make clear both the nature and extent of the task to be undertaken and the Engineer's responsibilities. There are three identifiable stages in the documentation process:

1. Collation and Review of Design Criteria
2. Development of the Design
3. Final Design and Documentation

Collation and review The Engineer should review the data available and the design criteria arising from the Conceptual Design Study to determine what additional information is required before final design can be carried out. It is necessary for the Engineer to make an assessment of the reliability of the data used in the Conceptual Design Study, and if the Engineer is not completely satisfied with the integrity of the information or the dependability of its source, it may be advisable to obtain fresh data from known and more reliable sources. Such a decision can have significant effect on the time and cost budgets and would be a matter for the Principal to understand and approve.

In this review, the following matters should be considered in so far as they may affect the work:

- Cadastral and Topographical Survey data
- Details of existing structures, facilities and services affected by the work under the Contract
- Meteorological data
- Geotechnical information
- Environmental parameters and constraints
- Requirements for Environmental Impact Statements
- Requirements of all government and statutory authorities having jurisdiction over the project

The Engineer should then prepare a schedule of the additional information required and determine how and from where it is to be obtained.

Where the Engineer is able to research and obtain the required information without outside help, the sources from which the data is to be sought should be listed and the time required for its collection and collation estimated. Where external assistance is required, the Engineer should determine who is to do the work and then prepare time and cost estimates for obtaining the required data. In many cases, it will be necessary to obtain quotations from firms specializing in the type of work involved and this can take time.

Developing the design This is the principal analytical stage when the Engineer considers in detail the option (or options) identified in the Conceptual Design Study as being the most appropriate.

The task is then to:

- Confirm or revise the choice of the recommended option
- Select the final design approach
- Undertake the detailed analysis and development of the final design, and then to
- Prepare a draft outline of the requirements for the Enquiry Documents

On completion of this stage, the Engineer will have determined the appropriate design approach and provided the designer with firm directions on the procedures to be followed.

Final design and documentation In this final stage of the documentation process, the Engineer completes or supervises the completion of all the detailed calculations and sketches required for the preparation of the Drawings and the Specification. The Engineer's responsibility during this phase is then to:

- Supervise the preparation and checking of the Drawings
- Prepare the detailed Specification for the work
- Calculate quantities and prepare cost estimates
- Coordinate and prepare the Enquiry Documents

Time and Cost Budgets

In preparing the programme and estimating the cost of data collection by others, the Engineer will need to rely on the estimates or quotations submitted by the specialist firms appointed to do the work. This work will need to be cordinated by the Engineer, who may also be involved in data collection using in-house resources.

If there are a number of different organizations involved then the Engineer would be well advised to build in an adequate 'float' to provide for the possible failure of any of the organizations to perform as promised or unforeseen difficulties arising during the investigation.

Estimating the time required to do the actual design and documentation will largely depend upon the Engineer's knowledge and experience. Unfortunately, engineers are often too optimistic when it comes to estimating the time it takes to do this work, with the result that there is a strong temptation to take short cuts in the face of a difficult deadline.

There are a number of ways for the Engineer to estimate the time required to do the design itself. One of the most reliable is to prepare a schedule of all the drawings required, and from this to calculate the time required to complete the drafting. On a large project, the average time required to complete a drawing is about 40 hours. From this the total work-hours of drafting time can be calculated and from the number of drafters available, a drafting programme can be determined. Allowance should be made for a gradual build-up of the drafting team to full strength; it is rarely practicable for the full team to start operating effectively at the same time.

The work-hours of engineering design time usually amount to about 50 per cent of the drafting work-hours. To this must be added engineering time for coordinating and managing the design team and preparing the written documents. When the engineering time required for organizing, collating and reviewing data collection and receiving and evaluating tenders is included, the total engineering work-hours will be almost the same as the drafting work-hours. The engineering design will need to be commenced some time before the drafting can commence and, as with the drafting, there should be a gradual buildup of worker resources.

Each organization will have its own method for estimating costs but, working on an hourly rate of three times the actual wage or salary rate, the total cost of engineering and drafting should be between 4 and 6 per cent of the estimated project cost. Any significant difference from this range should prompt the Engineer to review the design programme.

The budget cost estimate for the project itself may be suspect, but there could be circumstances peculiar to the nature of the work which could account for this discrepancy. The above estimates are based on manual drafting; the use of a CAD system could require a different approach.

Monitoring the Programme

It is pointless to prepare a programme and then ignore it. At regular intervals during the design phase the Engineer should review the progress of the work both as regards time and cost. If the work appears to be falling behind schedule, the reason should be investigated and steps taken to rectify the situation. If the Engineer has underestimated the task, the solution may be to allocate additional resources, provided they are available. Alternatively, if time is not critical, the programme can be revised. Either course of action could increase the budget cost and the Engineer may have some explaining to do.

In evaluating progress, it would be self-defeating to express the situation as a percentage completion by calculating the ratio of the cost to date with budget cost. The most reliable way is to assess the amount of work remaining to be done and add the time required and the cost to the corresponding values for the work already completed. If these figures are above budget, the work would appear to be behind schedule.

The Engineer should carry out these reviews independently of any formal project management system instigated by the Principal.

7.2 KEEPING RECORDS

Keeping a Job Diary

The Engineer should recognize the importance of keeping adequate records. Not only should letters, invoices, receipts and other documents be filed for future reference, but written records of all verbal discussions arising from telephone conversations, meetings, and conferences should be made as soon as practicable after the event. For this purpose a Job Diary can be a useful means of recording such material.

Usually it is sufficient to record names, places, dates, times, and subjects of the discussion in a few words. If the matters discussed or decided are significant – such as receiving amended instructions or reaching a decision with which the Engineer does not wholeheartedly agree or which may be controversial – a more detailed account setting out the pertinent facts may be made and incorporated in a 'Memo to File'.

Above all, the Engineer should keep in mind that everything the Engineer says or writes may one day receive close scrutiny by a member of the legal profession. More than one engineer has been thankful that even the briefest note had been kept on a scrap of paper.

Recording the Design

Many engineers regard written calculations as an unnecessary evil. They are usually scrawled in a haphazard manner with inadequate identification, are frequently illegible, and often have quantum leaps from one point in the analysis to another several steps away. The intervening steps may be quite obvious to the designer who often overlooks the fact that the calculations are not for the designer's use alone. Apart from being a notepad to record the designer's thought processes during the design analysis, written calculations serve two main functions:

1. To provide a permanent record of the analysis and design process
2. To provide written instructions to the drafter for the preparation of the Drawings

Each page of calculations should be numbered and dated and should identify the project and the particular unit being designed. The name or initials of the designer should also be recorded.

Before commencing the actual calculations, the designer should clearly define the task, identify the design approach and list the constraints. All loads, forces and environmental factors affecting the design should be noted, with their source and code reference, where applicable. Any unusual loading conditions should be specifically identified.

If the designer intends to investigate a number of options, the option being studied should be clearly noted and when a conclusion is reached the solution should be conspicuously identified. It is not unknown for a drafter to incorporate on a drawing one of the options that has already been tried and rejected because the designer has not made clear the final decision. If such an error is not picked up in the checking process or on the job before construction or fabrication, a costly and possibly dangerous situation could arise. Many an engineer's professional reputation has been damaged as a result.

On completion of the project, the calculations will be filed, possibly on microfilm, and retained for many years. At some future time, another engineer may need to refer to the calculations in order to modify the unit for another purpose. Unless the original designer's intentions are quite clear, the second engineer may spend many frustrating hours trying to interpret the design.

EIGHT

GENERAL REQUIREMENTS FOR DOCUMENTS

8.1 LOCATION OF SUBJECT MATTER

The documents evidencing an engineering contract are made up of a large number of individual statements comprising instructions, requirements and provisions. Together these define what has to be done, how it is to be paid for and what are the responsibilities of the parties to the contract.

It is most important that this material is assembled and presented in such a way that a particular item can be readily located and interpreted. There are widely varying, and sometimes inconsistent, approaches to the question of where in the Enquiry Documents or the Contract Documents a particular matter is to be covered. The lack of a standardized approach has sometimes led to difficulties including omissions, duplications, and redundancies.

Omission of an important provision or direction is all too frequently a source of dispute between the parties to an engineering contract. Duplication – or the repetition of the same subject matter in more than one location – can cause uncertainty. It may also have unforeseen legal consequences if, as is frequently the case, exactly the same wording is not used in each repetition. Redundancy – the inclusion of unecessary material – can be confusing and can lead to the Contractor developing an indifferent attitude to the documents.

These problems can best be avoided by taking great care in the drafting and review of the various documents. The Engineer can reduce the possibility of difficulties arising by developing a logical and consistent approach to locating subject matter in the most appropriate place in the documents.

The guiding principle to be followed right through the preparation of contract documents, a principle which cannot be emphasized too much, is that information and directions should be grouped in a logical and consistent order in an appropriate document.

The first step is to separate tendering provisions from contractual provisions. It is important to remember that the Requirements for Tendering pertain to relationships between the parties before the Contract is signed and not to the performance of the work. Arising out of this, there are two important points to consider when selecting material for the Requirements for Tendering:

1. When the Principal has decided which, if any, tender is to be accepted, the documents comprising the Requirements for Tendering cease to have any further relevance and therefore they *will not* form part of the Contract.

   The Invitation to Tender and the Instructions to Tenderers must not contain any information relating to the performance of the Contract.

2. Once an agreement has been reached, the successful tenderer becomes the *Contractor* and the tender, incorporating any negotiated amendments, *will* form part of the Contract.

   The words *tender*, *tenderer* and *tendering* must therefore appear only in the Invitation to Tender and the Instructions for Tendering and they must not be used in any other document issued to tenderers and/or incorporated in the Contract.

Failure to observe these two rules is a major cause of confusion and dispute during the contract administration stage of the project.

Having decided that a particular item is a tendering provision, whether to allocate it to the Invitation to Tender or to the Instructions for Tendering is largely a matter of personal preference. However, the Engineer is advised to consider the guidelines in Chapter 9 – 'The Requirements for Tendering'. The Engineer should have little difficulty in separating tendering provisions from contractual provisions.

It is at the next step that the Engineer may encounter difficulties. The Engineer is required to decide in which particular group of Contract Documents a particular contractual provision is to be placed – in the Con-

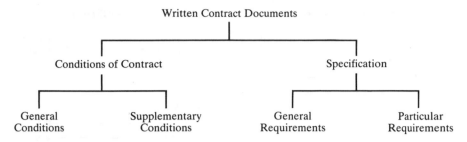

Figure 8.1 Written documents comprising a contract.

ditions of Contract or in the Specification. Each of these two groups of documents itself comprises several items, as Fig. 8.1 shows.

It should be understood that this separation of provisions into one or other document is for convenience only and has no legal significance. A provision is no less valid for appearing in one particular document when one would logically expect it to be found in another. All the documents comprising the Contract must be treated as the one instrument. The main reason for grouping the provisions together as suggested is to reduce the possibility of error or of one of them being overlooked or misunderstood.

The difficulty lies in determining whether a particular topic belongs in the Conditions of Contract or in the Specification. Engineers are not alone in this predicament; many standard General Conditions contain items which should logically belong in the Specification. The answer lies partly in whichever member of the Contractor's organization is most concerned with the particular item. The Contractor will have appointed a person to have overall responsibility for the Contract; how the Contractor designates them is immaterial, but for the purposes of this discussion the title 'Project Manager' is used.

The Project Manager will normally be located in the Contractor's head office and will have access to support staff located there such as accountants, bookkeepers, estimators, purchasing officers and so on. On the Site, which includes the workshops, there will be a person appointed to have the day-to-day responsibility for the work (the 'Works Supervisor') who will report to the Project Manager.

While the Project Manager and the head office staff will need to have access to all the Contract Documents, the Works Supervisor and Site personnel will be mainly concerned with the Specification. In some cases, where the Contractor may wish to restrict the ready availability of some sensitive contractual matters, the General Conditions and the Specification may be bound in separate volumes.

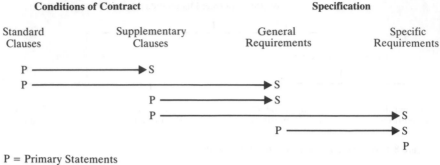

Figure 8.2 Relationship between primary and secondary statements.

Put in simple terms, the Conditions of Contract contains the 're-sponsibility-related' provisions, while the Specification contains the 'work-related' provisions. Unfortunately, this division can sometimes be difficult to analyse and in putting it into practice the Engineer is often compelled to resort to a rather arbitrary solution. A good rule to follow is:

> If the provision directly concerns what has to be done on Site and is the responsibility of the Site personnel then it is a Specification item. If the provision is an administrative matter and is unlikely to be the responsibility of the Site personnel then it is a General Conditions item.

There will, of course, be some 'grey areas' in applying this rule, such as the ordering of material or labour. This may be the function of the head office staff, in which case it will be a Conditions of Contract item, but the process may be initiated by the Site staff in which case it could be a Specification item.

One way to overcome the problem is to express the terms of a particular provision in two related statements – a primary and a secondary. The primary statement covers generally applicable basic principles. The secondary statement supplements or qualifies the primary statement by adding details, procedural requirements, or specific data, or adapts the principles enunciated in the primary statement to the particular requirements of the Contract. This arrangement is illustrated in Fig. 8.2.

A primary statement can appear in any one of the four documents indicated in Fig. 8.2 and its qualifying secondary statement in any one of the subsequent documents.

There may be occasions when it is necessary to have more than one secondary statement in different subsequent documents but this should be avoided if possible.

As will be pointed out, the General Conditions is usually a pre-printed, standard document suitable for most contracts and covering the rights and responsibilities of the parties. It follows, then, that the provisions dealt with in the General Conditions are all primary statements.

The provisions in the Supplementary Conditions are either secondary statements qualifying statements in the General Conditions or primary statements in their own right. Occasionally, secondary statements qualifying General Conditions statements may best be located in the Specification.

Primary statements in the Supplementary Conditions can be qualified by secondary statements in the Specification – either in the general requirements or in the particular requirements parts of the Specification.

8.2 ANNEXURES, APPENDIXES, SCHEDULES, AND FORMS

Annexures, Appendixes, Schedules, and Forms are widely used in contract documentation as practical methods of collecting and presenting information.

Unfortunately, the terms used for these supplementary documents are frequently used with little thought being given to their precise meaning. The meanings usually attributed to these terms, including those given in dictionaries, often differ and, unless precisely defined in the Contract, may not have the meaning intended by the Engineer. If one or more of these terms is used to refer to any part or parts of a contract document then it is important to make it clear what each such term is intended to mean and what is its function.

For example, if 'Appendix' or 'Schedule' is used to describe an attachment to one of the documents then the Contract must make clear its function and that it is intended to form an essential part of the Contract Documents. Otherwise it may be argued that it only has some contributory value and is not essential to the meaning of the terms of the Contract.

The following are definitions usually accepted for these supplementary documents and which are applicable to their use in contract documentation:

annexure A supplement annexed (i.e. attached) to a document.
appendix An addition subjoined to a document having some contributory value but not essential to its completeness.
addendum An alternative term for Appendix.
schedule In a strictly legal sense, an annexure to a legal instrument containing a statement of details. In a wider sense, any tabulated or classified

compilation of information or details. In the USA, a schedule can also be a timetable.

Form Dictionaries give many interpretations for this term (the *Macquarie Dictionary* gives 49 definitions). There are three meanings which are applicable to the use of this term in contract documentation:

- A set order of words as for use in a legal document.
- A typical document to be used as a guide in framing others for like uses.
- A document with blank spaces to be filled in with particulars before it is executed. Forms completed in this way become, in effect, schedules.

Appendix This is often employed to identify a supplement to Conditions of Contract or a Specification. In standard General Conditions, particulars which are expected to vary from contract to contract, and which are unsuitable for inclusion in the main printed document, are usually set out in an Appendix to the Conditions. Standards Australia more correctly identifies such an item as an 'Annexure'.

Elsewhere in the documents, appendixes should be used only where absolutely necessary. Supplementary documents such as geotechnical reports, meteorological information, and survey data may be included in the Enquiry Documents, normally as appendixes to the Specification. Where these documents have been prepared by consultants or other parties, it is necessary to obtain their approval before reproducing them or including them in the Enquiry Documents.

Schedules These can be used three ways in contract documentation:

1. Schedules prepared in the form of questionnaires issued with the Enquiry Documents and required to be completed by tenderers and submitted with their tenders, e.g. a Schedule of Rates.
2. Schedules prepared by tenderers and submitted with their tenders, e.g. a Schedule of Work to be Subcontracted.
3. Schedules completed in their entirety and issued as part of the Specification, e.g. Data Schedules.

All Schedules of these types, when completed, will be incorporated in the Contract Documents and form part of the Contract.

All schedules, including those required to be prepared entirely by the tenderer, should be identified by name and numbered. This will make easier the task of checking the contents of the tenders submitted.

Forms These are usually issued with the Enquiry Documents and can be used in three ways:

1. Forms to be completed by tenderers and submitted with their tenders, e.g. a Form of Tender.
2. Forms issued as an indication of the intended order of words, e.g. a Form of Instrument of Agreement.
3. Forms to be used by the Contractor and submitted during the course of the work under the Contract, e.g. a Payment Claim Form.

One copy of every form and schedule required to be completed and returned by tenderers should be bound with the Enquiry Documents. A second copy can be included loose with the Enquiry Documents for completion and return.

8.3 GUARANTEES AND BONDS

The Function of Contract Guarantees

At two stages in the tendering and contract procedure, tenderers, and later the Contractor, may be required to provide guarantees, backed by financial consideration, that they will fulfil their obligations as defined in the Enquiry Documents. The requirements for providing these guarantees should be outlined in the Enquiry Documents.

The first of these guarantees is the *Tender Deposit*, which may be required to be submitted by tenderers with their tenders as evidence of their good faith. It is a guarantee that if a tender is accepted, the successful tenderer will proceed to enter into a formal agreement with the Principal within the period specified in the Enquiry Documents. If the tenderer whose tender has been accepted fails to comply with this provision, the deposit will be forfeited to the Principal to contribute towards the difference in cost between the accepted tenderer's offered price and the price for which the Principal legally contracts with another party to undertake the work under the Contract.

The period of guarantee for a Tender Deposit is only the tender Validity Period. The Deposit is returned to *all* tenderers (including the tenderer whose tender has been accepted) when the Principal has accepted a tender or at the end of the Validity Period, whichever comes first. A Tender Deposit does not guarantee that the Contractor will perform the Contract.

The second of these guarantees is the *Security Deposit*, the basic function of which is to indemnify the Principal in the event of default on the part of the Contractor during the term of the Contract. The Security Deposit may be required to be lodged by the Contractor within a nominated period after acceptance of the tender. Although they have the same object, a Security Deposit should not be confused with *Retention* (or *Retainage*), which is the withholding of a percentage of moneys due to a Contractor when a *progress payment* is made.

In each case the Enquiry Documents usually provide that the financial consideration supporting the guarantee may be in any one of a number of forms. Cash (banker's cheque), government bonds or inscribed stock, an interest-bearing bank deposit, or an unconditional undertaking in the form of a banker's guarantee or a surety bond, may all be accepted forms of security.

Cash security can be a nuisance. The Principal, or the party acting on behalf of the Principal, will have to account for the funds and pay any interest accrued to the party depositing the funds when the deposit is returned. Principally for this reason, the tendency today is to provide the financial consideration in the form of a Bank Guarantee or a Surety Bond.

Bank Guarantee

A *Bank Guarantee* is an unconditional undertaking by a bank that it will pay on demand any sum or sums which may, at any time, be demanded by the Principal to the maximum aggregate of the amount specified in the undertaking. It is the responsibility of the Principal to ensure that such demands are not made without sufficient justification. Otherwise the Principal may be subject to a claim for damages, which could be quite substantial.

Surety Bonds

A *Surety Bond* is an Agreement between a tenderer or Contractor and a financial institution other than a bank (usually referred to as the *Surety*) whereby the Surety provides a financial guarantee to the Principal that the tenderer or Contractor will fulfil certain obligations as defined in the Bond. This guarantee is made provided that the Principal will also fulfil certain obligations in return. A Surety Bond is *not* an insurance policy. It is simply an undertaking by one party to indemnify a second party in the event of a default by a third party who has commissioned the Bond.

The obligations defined in the Bond can vary, from the payment of money to the Principal to an undertaking to seek competitive tenders from other contractors in order to complete the work abandoned by the Contractor.

Surety Bonds are a means of ensuring responsible contract performance and financial security without the tenderer or Contractor having to provide funds for a guarantee, or other security, which could tie up working capital. The upper limit of the amount the Surety is required to pay in the event of default is defined in the Bond. In the event of default, the Surety will endeavour to recover the cost from the defaulting party. There are three types of Surety Bond used in engineering contracts:

- Tender (or Bid) Bond
- Performance Bond
- Payment Bond

A *Tender Bond* is provided as a Tender Deposit. The amount of the Bond should be not less than the full amount of the required Tender Deposit as specified in the Enquiry Documents. A Tender Bond does not guarantee the performance of the Contract by the Contractor. It only undertakes to indemnify the Principal, up to the amount nominated in the Bond as the maximum liability of the Surety, in the event that the tenderer fails to enter into a formal contract with the Principal or as otherwise provided by the Bond.

A *Performance Bond* is provided as a Security Deposit. As with a Tender Bond, the amount of the Bond should be not less than the amount of the required Security Deposit as specified in the Contract. The purpose of the Security Deposit is to cover, wholly or in part, the additional cost to the Principal of completing the work under the Contract in the event of default by the Contractor. The liability of the Surety under these circumstances is limited to the amount specified in the Bond. A Performance Bond does not cover claims against the Contractor by suppliers and subcontractors for materials and labour. If the Principal and/or the Contractor requires indemnification against such claims, separate provision must be made.

A *Payment Bond* is a guarantee that all subcontractors and suppliers who have a *direct* contract with the Contractor will receive payment for the provision of materials and labour as defined in the Bond. The requirement in the Contract that such an indemnity be provided is not at present common, but with the increasing complexity of the law of liability many Principals are beginning to see the need for such protection.

Bond Format

There are many forms of Bonds. Some legal jurisdictions have specific laws and regulations covering not only the authorization of institutions dealing in bonds but also the actual wording of the bonds. For this reason it is not practicable to give specific examples of surety bonds. The Engineer is advised to consult experts in local practice when dealing with bonding matters. As a guide only, a Surety Bond should contain the following information:

1. The name of the party which is bonded (the Contractor)
2. The name of the party to whom the Bond is payable (the Principal)
3. The name of the party who issues the Bond and who guarantees the obligations under the Contract (the Surety)
4. The amount of the Bond
5. Clear identification of the Contract covered by the Bond
6. The conditions of the obligations under the Bond

The Bond should be signed under seal both by the party who is bonded and the party who issues the Bond.

If Bonds are required or permitted under the terms of the Contract, a draft of each Form of Bond, applicable to local conditions or regulations, should be included in the Tender Enquiry Documents. Most General Conditions of Contract provide recommended Forms of Bond suitable for the legal jurisdiction under which the General Conditions operates.

Claims Under Bonds

In the event of a default by a tenderer or a contractor, the procedure for initiating a claim under a Bond can be a complex legal matter. The Engineer is advised to consult legal experts before undertaking such a step.

Specific Warranties and Guarantees

In addition to the guarantees outlined above, engineers frequently require warranties in respect of specific materials and workmanship. These requirements are usually defined in the Specification and refer to items whose service life may be limited, such as metal roof and wall cladding, waterproof membranes, elastomeric sealants, and protective surface treatments. The manufacturers and suppliers of these often claim extended service lives for their products and the Engineer, seeking to indemnify the Principal in the event of a product failing to perform as claimed, may require a written guarantee.

There are two points to keep in mind when specifying such warranties. The first is that this type of warranty is rarely backed by a financial consideration, and the party being indemnified has to rely on the form and wording of the warranty and the goodwill of the guarantor for redress. The second point is that the guarantor is usually a subcontractor of the main Contractor, and therefore may not have a direct contractual responsibility to the Principal. When incorporating requirements for such warranties in the Specification, the Engineer should make sure that:

- The aims of the warranty are realistic and achievable.

- The guarantor is someone of substance and repute.
- The warranty specifically identifies the Principal by name as the party indemnified.
- The period of the warranty and the precise nature of the reparations guaranteed are clearly defined.
- The responsibility of the main Contractor in ensuring that the guarantor honours the obligations under the warranty is clearly specified.

The responsibility of the Engineer in regard to warranties is also referred to in Sec. 11.1 – 'Drafting the Specification'.

8.4 STANDARD DOCUMENTS

The Engineer can draw upon a wide range of standard texts to assist in the preparation of the Enquiry Documents. These can be classified into two separate groups:

- Documents published by various organizations and available to the public at large
- Documents prepared in-house by the firm or organization for whom the Engineer works

Such standard documents can be of immense help to the Engineer and should be used as much as practicable. However, the Engineer must read carefully any standard document intended for use and understand its intent and ramifications thoroughly before making use of it.

Most such texts comprise a collection of standard clauses drafted to cover, as far as practicable, generally used provisions for the particular type of document. Since engineering contracts cover such a wide range of activities and situations, it is simply not possible to draft a standard text to provide for every situation. In every case there will be irrelevant clauses to be removed as well as omissions to be rectified.

The use of such documents is discussed in subsequent chapters.

CHAPTER NINE

THE REQUIREMENTS FOR TENDERING

9.1 PREPARING THE INVITATION TO TENDER

When drafting the Invitation to Tender, the information outlined in Sec. 3.3 – 'Requirements for Tendering' – should be dealt with in the following manner:

Project identification The heading for the Invitation should identify the Contract by stating the name of the particular project and the assigned contract number, or other reference.

Formal invitation This is a simple statement inviting the submission of a tender in accordance with the Enquiry Documents as specified in the Instructions to Tenderers.

Outline of work This is a brief summary of the work under the Contract (not more than 100 words, if possible).

Location of the work If the Contract involves construction or installation, the location of the Site should be stated. If the Contract is for the supply only of plant or equipment, the point of delivery should be stated.

Who is involved The name and address of the Principal and of any other party (such as a Consulting Engineer) involved in the project should be given. The name, position, telephone, fax, and telex numbers and business address of the person to whom all enquiries regarding the Enquiry Documents should be directed, should be given in this statement.

Type of contract The type of contract envisaged as stated in the terms outlined in Sec. 2.3 – 'Types of Contracts'.

Programme for the work Attention should be drawn to the Instructions to Tenderers regarding the times for commencement and completion. Tenderers may be asked to nominate a completion date based on a provisional date for awarding the Contract, or details of the proposed programme for the work may be outlined in a programme schedule attached to the Enquiry Documents.

Closing time, date, and place The Invitation to Tender must advise tenderers the closing time, date and place for the lodgement of tenders.

Procedure for opening tenders Tenderers should be told if tenders are to be opened in public or in the presence of tenderers or their representatives. If tenders are to be opened in either manner, tenderers should be told the time, date and place for the opening.

Intention to tender Tenderers should be asked to confirm, as soon as practicable, whether or not they intend to submit a tender. Tenderers should be asked to notify the Principal in writing (by telex, fax, or letter) of the dispatch of their tenders, advising them of the method of delivery.

Changes to pre-qualification documents Where tenderers have been selected from a pre-qualification procedure as outlined in Sec. 4.3 – 'Procedures for Inviting Tenders' – they should be asked to provide in their tenders, on the statement sheet provided in the Enquiry Documents, details of any significant changes in the data supplied with their pre-qualification application.

9.2 INSTRUCTIONS TO TENDERERS

Tenders which have been prepared in accordance with clearly defined requirements are easier to evaluate and compare.

In addition to clearly prescribing the Principal's requirements regarding the preparation and submission of tenders it is also important that tenderers be made aware of the rules under which the Principal will evaluate and assess tenders. By laying down and then following well-defined and acceptable procedures for determining the most suitable offer, the Principal can avoid being accused of being biased or unfair, and thence possibly subject to legal action.

Since the early 1980s, Canadian courts have delivered a number of significant legal decisions which have overturned some traditional and widely held presumptions about the tendering process. Although these rulings have been made under Canadian law, they are considered relevant, and it is quite possible that similar decisions may eventually be made by courts in other jurisdictions.

The Canadian courts have held that once a tender has been submitted, a binding contract exists between the tenderer and the Principal which imposes obligations on both parties during the tender period. It is also pointed out that in the cases before the Canadian courts there was a 'valuable consideration', in the form of a tender deposit, which may have had some bearing on the situation. Nevertheless, anyone involved in the tendering process should proceed cautiously and act as if the concept of a bidding contract, as envisaged by the Canadian courts, would apply.

These judgements have highlighted several important principles which should be followed when preparing the Instructions to Tenderers, irrespective of which legal jurisdiction is applicable.

- Where tenders are to be submitted in accordance with clearly stated requirements, those requirements must be strictly complied with and both the party submitting the tender and the party receiving it will be bound by those requirements.
- Where the requirements for tendering specify the rules under which the Principal will determine which offer to accept, the Principal must follow those rules or be exposed to a claim for damages by any tenderer.
- Where the tendering requirements specify that the lowest, or any, tender may not necessarily be accepted there is, nevertheless, an obligation on the Principal not to award the contract to any tenderer whose tender does not comply with all the Enquiry Documents.
- Tenderers are obliged to comply only with the issued tendering requirements. If the Principal has any undisclosed conditions or preferences not made known to all tenderers, the Principal may be exposed to action for damages by unsuccessful tenderers.
- The requirements for tendering cannot be unilaterally altered after submission of tenders.

Many government and statutory authorities, as well as some private engineering organizations, have their own standard Instructions to Tenderers or Conditions of Tendering. The engineer working for one of these groups will have access to that document and most probably will be required to use it. The engineer who does not have access to such a document will have to prepare independently the necessary Instructions to Tenderers.

A checklist of items to be considered when preparing the individual clauses for the Instructions to Tenderers under the headings in Sec. 3.3 – 'Requirements for Tendering' – is given in Table 9.1.

To assist the Engineer in the task of preparing these clauses, each item listed in Table 9.1 is then discussed in turn. Since the requirements may differ markedly between individual contracts, it is not practicable to give a draft text for each clause. The Engineer should be able to prepare the required clauses based on the comments given. It is suggested that the clauses be included in the order given in the table, but this is a matter for individual preference.

9.3 OUTLINE OF CLAUSES FOR INSTRUCTIONS TO TENDERERS

Heading

The Instructions to Tenderers should be a complete and separate document with its own title page, heading and numbering system.The title page should identify the Project and the Contract by name and number and should include the name of the Principal. The document should be readily identified as the Instructions to Tenderers.

The Enquiry Documents

It is important to identify clearly the individual documents which comprise the Enquiry Documents and to set out the conditions under which they are supplied.

Schedule of Enquiry Documents This clause should list all the documents which comprise the Enquiry Documents as issued, including reference to annexures and appendixes and to the forms, schedules, and statements listed in the Content of Tender.

Tenderers should also be advised that all pages (and possibly drawings) in the documents have been consecutively numbered. They should be advised to check that they have been included and compiled in their correct place in the documents and that all annexures, appendixes, forms, schedules, and statements referred to have been included.

Table 9.1 Checklist of items to be considered in preparing the instructions to tenderers

The Enquiry Documents
  Schedule of Enquiry Documents
  Ownership of Enquiry Documents
  Charge for Enquiry Documents
  Notices to Tenderers
Requirements for the Preparation of Tenders
  Preparation of Tenders
  Non-Conforming Tenders
  Alternative Tenders
  Endorsement of Tenders
  Expenses of Tendering
Conditions of Tendering
  Lodgement of Tenders
  Qualifications of Tenderers
  Tender Deposit
  Acceptance or Rejection of Tenders
  Advertising and Publicity
  Confidential Information
  Formal Agreement
  Withdrawal and Amendment of Tenders
Commercial Requirements
  Contract Sum Adjustment
  Schedule of Rates
  Schedule of Prices for Tendering
  Schedule of Daywork Rates
  Bill of Quantities
  Time for Completion
  Subcontractors
  Sales Tax
  Import Duty
  Currency
  Stamp Duty
  Insurance
Site Data
  Examination of Documents and Site
  Visits to Site by Tenderers
  Site Information
Miscellaneous Information
  Language
  Units of Measurement

Ownership of Enquiry Documents Tenderers should be advised that all Enquiry Documents issued are and remain the property of the Principal. Some engineers require unsuccessful tenderers to return all Enquiry Documents to the point of issue within fourteen days of being notified that their tenders have been unsuccessful, with tenderers who decline to tender after receiving Enquiry Documents being required to return them immediately they disclose that they will not be submitting a tender. Whether or not this policy is adopted should be determined by the Principal.

When the documents have been prepared on behalf of the Principal by another party, such as a Consulting Engineer, the question of the ownership of the copyright of the documents is a separate issue and should be resolved independently by the Principal and the Consulting Engineer.

Charge for Enquiry Documents This clause should state whether or not there is to be any charge for the Enquiry Documents and whether or not the charge is refundable. Tenderers often require more than one set of documents for a variety of good reasons, and a decision should be made as to whether or not a charge should be made for supplying additional sets of documents and how much that charge should be. This point is discussed in more detail in Sec. 4.2 – 'Guidelines for Tendering'.

Notices to Tenderers This clause should point out that amendments to the Enquiry Documents contained in Notices to Tenderers issued during the Tender Period will form part of the Enquiry Documents and will supersede the appropriate references in the original Enquiry Documents. Tenderers should be instructed to endorse their tenders with the confirmation that the tender is submitted in accordance with each Notice received, identified by Notice Number and date of issue. The Tender Form may be drafted to include an appropriate statement.

Requirements for the Preparation of Tenders

Tenderers must be given clear instructions as to how their tenders are to be prepared and presented.

Preparation of Tender This clause must state that to ensure a Conforming Tender, tenderers must complete all the forms, schedules and statements listed in the Content of Tender and issued with the Enquiry Documents. Points to be considered when drafting this clause include:

● The name and address of the tenderer must be stated on the Tender Form in accordance with the following:

- if the tenderer is a person, the full given names, surname and address of the tenderer
- if the tenderer is a firm, the full given names and surname of each member of the firm
- if the tenderer is a corporation, the registered name and the address of the registered office of the corporation.

- Changing the Tender Form in any way may lead to the tender being deemed non-conforming and thereby rejected.
- All the Enquiry Documents as nominated in the relevant clause above are deemed to form part of the Tender Documents.
- The number of copies of the tender to be submitted should be stated (under normal circumstances, one copy should be sufficient). If more than one copy is required, one copy should be marked 'Original' and the other(s) 'Copy'.

Non-conforming tenders This clause should define the rules by which a tender may be judged to be non-conforming. A non-conforming tender is usually defined as one which has been improperly completed or which does not comply with the Enquiry Documents, and the clause should state that such a tender may not be accepted by the Principal. This leaves the Principal with the option of whether or not to consider such a tender. The Principal may also reserve the right to waive any minor irregularity in a tender although, as previously pointed out, this procedure should be approached with care.

Tenderers often submit their own standard Conditions of Sale with a tender. This usually applies to tenders for the supply of plant or equipment. Consideration should be given to perhaps pointing out that the inclusion of such terms in a tender may make it non-conforming and liable to be rejected at the Principal's discretion.

Alternative tenders This clause should define the conditions to be observed for an alternative tender to be considered. An *Alternative Tender* is usually defined as one specifically nominated as such by the tenderer and containing a provision or provisions which contradict or are inconsistent with one or more provisions of the Enquiry Documents.

A separate Tender Form, clearly marked 'Alternative Tender', should be completed for each Alternative Tender submitted. A Schedule of Deviations from the Enquiry Documents, detailing all deviations from the work as specified and/or shown, must be attached to each Alternative Tender Form, together with other relevant schedules and statements. Where more than one tender is submitted, only one copy of those schedules and statements applicable to all tenders need be provided.

Should Alternative Tenders not be acceptable, this clause should specifically state that such tenders will be excluded.

The Principal may choose to include a provision that consideration will be given to an Alternative Tender only if it is accompanied by a conforming tender.

Endorsement of tenders This clause should specify the manner in which the Tender Documents are to be endorsed.

- Tenderers should be told how to sign the Tender Form and have the signature witnessed. If the tenderer is a corporation, the common seal of the corporation must be affixed in the manner prescribed in the corporation's articles of association. If the tenderer is an individual or a firm, the tender must be signed by that individual or an authorized member of the firm.
- All documents accompanying the tender must be signed and dated by the tenderer or by an officer authorized to do so in the case of a corporation or firm tendering.

Expenses of tendering Tenderers should be advised that all costs and expenses incurred by tenderers in the course of the preparation and submission of their tenders shall be borne by the individual tenderers. These costs should include all expenses in connection with visiting and inspecting the Site, attending meetings called by the Engineer and the preparation of such preliminary designs and drawings required for tender purposes.

Conditions of Tendering

Lodgement of tenders This clause should set out clearly the procedure for lodging the tenders and the conditions under which tenders will be received. It is essential to ensure that the time, date and place for the receipt of tenders is made clear to tenderers.

A decision will need to be made as to where in the Enquiry Documents the closing time and date are nominated. It is possible to give this information in one of three places:

- In the first paragraph of this clause
- On the title sheet inside the front cover of the Enquiry Documents
- In the Invitation to Tender accompanying the Enquiry Documents (the preferred option).

Any one of these methods is satisfactory, but if the information is placed in more than one place, care must be taken if the closing time and/or date is amended during the tender period. Any Notice to Tenderers advising of such a change *must make reference to each and every place in the Enquiry Documents* where the original closing time and date was stated. For this reason, it is preferable to give the closing time and date in *only one place* in the Documents.

Tenderers should be directed to enclose each tender in a sealed envelope or package marked with the name of the tenderer and the name (and number if appropriate) of the particular contract for which the tender is submitted. Other points to be considered in drafting this clause include:

- It should be pointed out to tenderers that the closing time and date have been selected so as to provide adequate time for the preparation of tenders in accordance with generally accepted trade practice.
- Applications for extension of the tender period will be considered only in the most exceptional circumstances.
- Applications for extensions of time received less than seven days before the nominated date for the receipt of tenders will not be considered.
- Tenders received after the time and date nominated may be considered informal and liable to rejection. Acceptence or rejection of such tenders will be at the discretion of the Principal.

If tenders are to be opened in public or in the presence of representatives of any tenderers interested, the details of the procedure should be outlined in this clause.

Qualifications of Tenderers Where unrestricted tendering applies, the basis upon which tenderers' qualifications will be assessed should be clearly stated. Typical requirements include:

- Tenderers must be established contractors experienced in the type of work described.
- Tenderers must have access to adequate financial resources.
- Tenderers must have within their establishment sufficient experienced professional staff to direct and supervise the work.
- Tenderers must be able to satisfy the Principal that they fully understand the work and can perform the work in the time stated in the tender.
- Tenderers who propose to subcontract the whole or the major part of the work will not be considered.

This clause may also state the Principal's attitude to consortia, whether they are formed specifically for the work envisaged or exist already.

Tender deposit The Principal may require tenderers to provide a Tender Deposit with their tenders in the form of cash, bank guarantee, or surety bond. Its prime purpose is to discourage tenderers from withdrawing their tenders during the Tender Validity Period, since this could involve the Principal in unnecessary expense.

If bank guarantees or surety bonds are acceptable, it is advisable to include a form of Guarantee or Bond, as appropriate, with the Enquiry Documents.

Tender deposits are normally forfeited if a tenderer withdraws a bid during this period. Tender deposits are returned to all other tenderers, including the accepted tenderer, when the Principal has accepted a tender or at the end of the Tender Validity Period, whichever comes first.

Acceptance or rejection of tenders This clause defines the conditions for accepting a tender. The clause should state that the Principal is not bound to accept the lowest or any tender.

This can be important as it can deter, if not prevent, an unsuccessful tenderer from taking action against the Principal in the event that the lowest or any tender is not accepted. It is important to make sure that there is a full disclosure of the conditions attached to this procedure. There must be no 'hidden' conditions – conditions not made available to all tenderers – such as preference for local contractors. The existence of such 'hidden' conditions may leave the Principal open to a claim for damages from an unsuccessful tenderer.

Advertising and publicity The Instructions to Tenderers should point out that the Principal reserves the sole right to all publicity and advertising in connection with the Works in any verbal, printed or visual medium. Tenderers and their subcontractors should be permitted to take photographs or video records at the Site for tendering purposes only and such material shall not be used for publicity.

Confidential information The Instructions to Tenderers should point out that all the Enquiry Documents and Tender Documents should be treated as confidential by the Principal and by all tenderers. No information or document should be given or shown to any other party not involved in the tender procedure.

Formal agreement This clause should advise tenderers if the successful tenderer is to be required to sign a formal Agreement and that it is to be signed as a Deed. A copy of the draft Agreement should be included in the Enquiry Documents.

Withdrawal or amendment of tenders Tenderers must not be permitted to amend their tenders after the closing time and date. Since tenderers nearly always leave the lodging of tenders until the last minute, it is unlikely that a request would be received to amend a previously lodged tender before the closing time.

However, the Engineer may consider that a provision should be included to cover such a possibility.

It is usual for Enquiry Documents to require tenderers to hold their tenders valid for a fixed period after the submission of their tenders, usually 60 days. This period is usually referred to as the *Validity Period.*

The question as to how binding on the Contractor is a lodged tender will depend upon the legal jurisdiction under which the documents have been prepared and issued. It would, of course, be imprudent to force a tenderer to sign a contract which he is unable or unwilling to perform.

The main problem occurs when there is a Tender Deposit involved. In some jurisdictions (e.g. the Canadian and Scottish) the established situation is that the Contractor forfeits any such deposit.

Commercial Requirements

Contract Sum adjustment This clause should indicate if the Contract Sum or Schedule Rates are to be subject to adjustment due to fluctuations in the cost of labour and/or materials. The appropriate formula should be included in the Conditions of Contract and tenderers requested to submit the requisite data for the operation of the formula by completing the appropriate schedule. Alternatively, tenderers should be asked to submit for consideration any formula which they would be prepared to accept.

Schedule of Rates It is important that the attention of tenderers be drawn to the clause(s) in the Conditions of Contract regarding the items, quantities, and rates in the Schedule of Rates. Tenderers should be instructed:

- That if they consider that the items described in the Schedule do not include the cost of the whole of the work under the Contract, they should amend the Schedule as necessary to include whatever additional items they consider necessary to form a correct estimate for the whole of the work.
- To provide a rate and/or price for each item in the Schedule extended by multiplying the rate by the estimated quantity.
- That the summation of the extension of the quantities and rates in the Schedule will be the *Tender Sum.*

The above instructions may be included either as a clause in the Instructions to Tenderers or as a Preface Note on the first page of the Schedule of Rates. If the instructions are included in a clause in the Instructions to Tenderers they will not form part of the Contract. However, if they are included in a Preface Note on the Schedule Form, they will form part of the Contract. The Engineer should consider the implications of each option before deciding where to place the instructions.

Schedule of Prices for Tendering This is a schedule sometimes included in the Enquiry Documents for Lump Sum contracts to cover items, quantities and provisional sums for the whole of the work under the Contract. *It is not a Schedule of Rates* and its function and operation are outlined in Sec. 10.4 – 'Co-ordinating the Supplementary Conditions and the Annexure'.

The clause in the Instructions to Tenderers covering a Schedule of Prices for Tendering should carry a disclaimer that, while the items and quantities are believed to be correct, no guarantee can be given as to their accuracy. Unfortunately, errors in such schedules do occur and can give rise to claims by the Contractor even with this disclaimer.

One way to overcome this problem is for this clause to require tenderers to prepare and submit their own version of the Schedule based on the Schedule issued with the Enquiry Documents. The clause should also point out that, if tenderers adopt the Schedule issued with the Enquiry Documents, they accept the items and quantities as being correct. This will place the responsibility of accuracy and completeness on the tenderers.

Schedule of Daywork Rates There are two ways in which this information can be provided by tenderers:

1. By nominating hourly rates for individual employee categories or
2. By nominating a percentage surcharge to be applied to actual wage rates.

In the first option, the tenderer nominates the actual hourly rates, inclusive of statutory and other overheads, administration costs and profit, for the various employee categories. Those categories can be either listed by the Engineer in the schedule or the tenderer can be required to nominate the categories employed on the work.

In the second option, the tenderer provides a percentage on-cost to be applied to actual wage rates to cover overheads, administration costs and profit. In both options, tenderers should be asked to provide percentage on-costs to be added to:

● current commercial casual rates for constructional plant and
● invoice costs for the supply of services and materials.

Bill of Quantities A description and explanation of a Bill of Quantities is given in Sec. 10.4 – 'Co-ordinating the Supplementary Conditions and the Annexure'. Where a Bill of Quantities is issued with the Enquiry Documents, the Conditions of Contract must state whether or not it will form part of the Contract. Tenderers must be advised that:

- When the Bill of Quantities forms part of the Contract, each item must be priced and extended by tenderers and the Priced Bill of Quantities submitted with their tenders.
- When a Bill of Quantities does not form part of the Contract, the Contractor must submit a Priced Bill of Quantities within the period after the award of the Contract, as specified in the Conditions of Contract.

The main point to be decided is whether or not the Bill will form part of the Contract. In the latter case, the Priced Bill will not be submitted until after the agreement has been reached, and it is unreasonable for the Principal to be committed to a document which has not previously been seen. Bills of Quantities are discussed in more detail in Sec. 10.4 – 'Coordinating the Supplementary Conditions and the Annexure'. Unless there are other considerations to be taken into account, the Priced Bill should *not* form part of the Contract.

Time for completion If the duration of the contract period or the completion date is to be nominated by the Principal, the relevant details should be stated in the Conditions of Contract. It may be advisable to draw attention to this requirement in the Invitation to Tender.

If the Principal specifies that tenderers are to nominate a contract period or completion date in their tenders, this requirement should be defined in this clause and attention drawn to the requirement in the Invitation to Tender. The Tender Form should make provision for this information to be included on the Form or in a Schedule attached to the Form.

Subcontractors Most General Conditions require the Contractor to obtain the approval of the Principal (or the Superintendent) before subcontracting any part of the work. Since subcontracting is today an almost universal element in engineering contract work, once the Contract has been awarded, the Engineer should expect the Contractor to request approval to subcontract parts of the work. The Engineer should consider the desirability of anticipating these requests and take steps at the tendering stage to reduce possible delays to the works programme while these requests are investigated and answered. There are a number of ways to deal with this:

1. Ignore the potential for possible delays and leave it to the Superintendent

to deal with such requests as they arise.

2. Require tenderers to nominate all subcontractors to whom they intend subcontracting parts of the work.
3. Require tenderers to submit with their tenders a schedule of trades or work they propose to subcontract; within a nominated period after award of the Contract, the Contractor is required to submit the names of the subcontractors for approval, such approval not being unreasonably withheld.
4. Require tenderers to submit with their tenders the names of proposed subcontractors for certain nominated items of supply or work.
5. Specify items of supply or work to be carried out by selected, designated and/or nominated subcontractors.

The first option should be adopted only if there are other compelling reasons which make it a viable attitude.

As regards the second option, it is debatable whether it is practicable to require tenderers to name their intended subcontractors in their tenders. As a general rule, would-be contractors only like to commit themselves to subcontracts once they have the job, when they can usually negotiate a better subcontract price. In most cases, this does not really matter.

The third option is one way of approaching this problem. It is a practical way of dealing with those minor trades such as are traditionally subcontracted in the building industry. An alternative is the procedure adopted by the SAA General Conditions, which provides for the Principal to list in the Annexure work which cannot be subcontracted without approval.

However, it may be that the Principal considers that particular parts of the work, plant or equipment are so important that it must be known which subcontractors are to be engaged for it before awarding a contract, in which case the tenderers will be required to name the relevant subcontractors in their tenders, or else accept the subcontractors the Principal nominates for these items options 4 and 5).

Which procedure is adopted will be a matter to be decided at an early stage of the documentation process. Since the Requirements for Tendering will not form part of the Contract, it will be necesary to cover the procedure elsewhere in the Contract, preferably in the Conditions of Contract.

Sales Tax It is important to clarify the matter of Sales Tax, variously described as Goods and Services Tax, Consumption Tax and Value Added Tax. Which materials and equipment will be subject to such taxes can vary from country to country and from time to time.

It is a very complex question and requires a knowledge of the relevant

Acts and Regulations generally outside the average engineer's expertise. The Engineer should seek the advice of an appropriate authority.

Import duty Where imported goods and materials are involved, the amount of duty applying to each item and used in the tender should be stated in the tender. An appropriate Schedule should be prepared for completion by tenderers.

Currency This clause should nominate which currency is to be used when stating the tender sum. Where that currency differs from that of the country of origin of the Enquiry Documents, tenderers should be required to nominate the exchange rate used, quoting the conversion factor adopted and the date applying to that conversion factor. The same requirement should apply to the cost of imported goods and materials. Note that the currency in which payment will be made to the Contractor is usually nominated in the Conditions of Contract.

Stamp duty In some jurisdictions there is a requirement that Stamp Duty is applicable to tenders. This clause should place the onus on the tenderers to ensure that their tenders are duly stamped.

Insurances Where the Principal elects to provide insurance for the Works and/or Public Liability, tenderers should be so advised. A copy of the proposed policy should be included in the Enquiry Documents but, where this is not practicable, a copy should be made available at the Principal's office for perusal. Tenderers would be unable to prepare their bids properly if they were not aware of the terms of the insurances. They may wish to take out supplementary insurance if they do not feel that the cover is adequate.

Where the Contractor is to provide the insurance cover, an appropriate Schedule requiring details of the amount of cover, excess and other matters should be prepared for completion by the Contractor. This clause should cover all these points.

Site Data

Examination of Documents and Site The Enquiry Documents should require tenderers to acquaint themselves with all conditions relating to the proposed contract as set out in the Enquiry Documents. Where the Contract includes construction or installation, tenderers should be required to examine the Site and its surroundings and to determine, as far as practicable, all relevant physical conditions. Tenderers should be directed to make written requests to the Principal to clarify any point in the documents about which they are in doubt. Any such clarification will only be valid if issued by the Principal in writing. Tenderers should be advised that any clarification given for the purposes of this provision may also be made available to all other prospective tenderers.

Alternatively, tenderers may include in their tenders a statement of the interpretation upon which they have relied when preparing their tender.

The intention of this clause is to make it clear that it is the responsibility of tenderers to obtain clarification of any point in the Enquiry Documents about which they are in doubt.

Visits to Site by tenderers Where site visits are required, arrangements must be made to enable each tenderer to inspect the Site. Tenderers should be notified whether visits to the Site will be made individually or collectively. This decision will depend upon a number of factors such as the location and nature of the work. Where practicable, the Engineer or a representative of the Principal (or Owner) should be present during any inspection of the Site, but any discussion at the time should be limited to the verification of facts.

Tenderers must be told that, should a site visit reveal pertinent information not included in the Enquiry Documents, that information will be circulated to all tenderers by a Notice to Tenderers.

Where the work involves alterations or extensions to an existing plant, it may be necessary to place restrictions on the number, time, and duration of the visits. Arrangements for site visits should be made so that equal opportunities are available for all tenderers.

It should be made clear to all tenderers that they should make their own arrangements and bear the costs of travel and accommodation. It is the responsibility of the Principal to make only those arrangements necessary for the actual inspection of the Site.

Site information It is essential that all site information in the possession of the Principal be made available to tenderers. This information should, where applicable, include the results of all subsurface investigations, information obtained from topographic, cadastral, and geological surveys and details of known existing utilities, adjacent structures, and installations. Tenderers are entitled to assume that all such information provided by the Principal is accurate and correct.

Where practicable, this information should be copied and issued with the Enquiry Documents. If this is not possible or practicable, the information must be made available for inspection by tenderers at some specified time and place. This clause should clarify this point.

Where tenderers request copies of such information, a charge can be made to cover the cost of copying and collating the data. Where the information is in reports prepared by consultants or others, their approval must be obtained before copying and issuing the information.

Miscellaneous Information

Language The Instructions to Tenderers should nominate the language to be used in all correspondence with tenderers and in all documents submitted by tenderers. The Conditions of Contract usually have a clause specifying the language to be used during the work of the Contract.

Units of Measurement The Conditions of Contract usually nominate the units of measurement to be used in specifying physical quantities in the Contract. However, it is advisable to specify the units of measurement to be used in the Tender Documents.

9.4 FORMS, SCHEDULES, AND STATEMENTS FOR TENDERING

General Requirements

So as to ensure that all relevant data is provided by tenderers, wherever practicable, the Engineer should prepare schedules in the form of questionnaires to be completed and returned by tenderers with their tenders. Where questionnaires are not feasible, such as where tenderers are to supply details in their own format, a blank statement sheet for supporting statements should be provided. These forms, schedules, and statement sheets should be listed in the Content of Tender and, when completed, will comprise the tender.

It is emphasized that not all the information listed below for each schedule is required in every instance. The Engineer should evaluate each situation and use discretion in selecting the questions to be asked. Only information necessary to enable the tenders for the particular project to be evaluated should be sought. Asking unnecessary questions only complicates the issue and could irritate the tenderers.

All schedules, whether questionnaires or statement sheets, should have an appropriate heading which should include:

- Contract identification (see Sec. 3.2 – 'Contract Identification')
- Schedule title and number
- A statement that the Schedule forms part of the tender dated [date to be inserted by tenderer]

- Space for the name of the tenderer to be inserted
- Place for signature

The schedules should be consecutively numbered to make easier the task of checking the contents of the tenders submitted. Questionnaires and forms should be self-explanatory but statement sheets should have a Preface Note outlining the information required.

The forms, schedules and statements which may be required to be included in the Enquiry Documents are listed in Table 9.2. The following notes are to assist the Engineer in their selection and preparation.

Tender Form

The *Tender Form* is the key document in the Tender. It is the document signed by the tenderer as a legally binding offer to undertake the work under the Contract. Most standard General Conditions of Contract include a recommended Form of Tender, or the Form of Tender in Appendix A can be used. However, the Engineer may prefer to prepare a Tender Form specifically tailored to suit the particular contract. The Tender Form must be the same for all tenderers. A Tender Form should include the following:

- Contract Identification – Name of project
  – Assigned contract No.
- Name and address of tenderer
- Name and address of Principal
- Tender Sum: Lump Sum and/or Sum determined by measured quantities at the Schedule Rates
- Statement that the Prices and Rates are
  (a) Fixed or
  (b) Subject to Adjustment
- Statement that the tender complies with the Enquiry Documents or that the tender offered is an Alternative Tender as set out in the Schedule of Deviations
- Signature of Tenderer or Authorized Signatory
- Date

Tenderer's Management and Administrative Structure

This schedule should preferably be in the form of a questionnaire to elicit details of the tenderer's management structure. Where tenders are being invited from a list of nominated tenderers prepared by the Engineer, this information may already be at hand and the form may not be required.

Table 9.2 Checklist of forms and schedules for content of tender

Where tenderers are to be selected from a pre-qualification procedure, those forms and schedules marked * may form part of the Pre-qualification Documents

---

Tender Form
*Tenderer's Management and Administration Structure
*Financial Statements – General
                   – Specific
Alternative Tender – Schedule of Deviations from the Enquiry Documents
*Tenderer's Background and Experience
*Tenderer's Industrial Relations Record
Bill of Quantities
Schedule of Rates
Schedule of Prices for Tendering
Schedule of Daywork Rates
Changes to Pre-Qualification Documents
Statement on Tenderer's Approach to the Work
Programme of Work
*Schedule of Key Personnel
Schedule of Subcontract Work
*Schedule of Major Constructional Plant and Equipment
Schedule of Imported Items
Schedule of Tender Drawings
Schedule of Transport and Delivery
Schedule of Insurance Policies
Equipment Design Data Schedules
Schedule of Substitutions
Schedule of Recommended Spare Parts and Price List

Similarly, where tenderers have been pre-qualified, this form may have been used as one of the Pre-qualification Documents.

The questionnaire should require the following information to be supplied by tenderers:

1. Name of tenderer
2. Form of incorporation
3. Business address
4. Registered office address
5. Telephone, telex, and fax numbers
6. Outline of Contractor's experience (number of years in business, engineering fields covered, geographical spheres of activity)
7. Names and addresses of associated companies (including parent and subsidiary companies) to be involved in the work under the Contract
8. If the tenderer is a subsidiary company, details of the parent company and its involvement in the work under the Contract

If a joint venture is proposed then similar information should be requested in respect of all firms comprising the joint venture, with a clear explanation of how the joint venture is to function.

Tenderers should be asked to attach an organization chart to the Schedule, showing the company structure and indicating the names and positions of key management and administrative personnel.

Financial Statements

The information required in the Financial Statement may be divided into two parts – a General Statement and a Specific Statement relative to the Contract. The two parts should each be in the form of questionnaires to be completed by the tenderers. The following information should be requested:

General Financial Statement (The information requested in this part of the statement may have been obtained in a pre-qualification procedure, in which case it would not be necessary to ask for it again.)

1. Details of Authorized and Issued Capital
2. Annual value of work undertaken in each of the past three or five years
3. Approximate value of work currently in hand
4. Name and address of the bank or financial institution to whom reference can be made.

Specific Financial Statement
5. Financing arrangements for the Contract
6. Discounted cash flow and programme of payments
7. Arrangements for Security and Retention
8. Details of insurance policies to be provided
9. Provision for Contract Sum adjustment including alternative formulas (if applicable)
10. Details of payments which would be made to workers and which are outside the relevant award or industrial agreement

Consideration may also be given to asking tenderers to attach copies of audited Capital Accounts and Profit and Loss Accounts for the past three/ five years.

Alternative Tender – Schedule of Deviations from Enquiry Documents

Where the Instructions to Tenderers permits alternative tenders to be submitted, tenderers should be required to provide full details of all deviations from the work specified and/or shown in the Enquiry Documents. Tenderers should give specific references to those matters which do not comply with the provisions in the Conditions of Contract, the Specification and the Drawings.

This Schedule should be provided as a statement sheet with the appropriate heading to be completed and attached to the Tender Form for the Alternative Tender.

Tenderer's Background and Experience

This Schedule can be provided either as a questionnaire or in the form of a statement sheet for information to be supplied by tenderers in their own format. Its purpose is to find out if the tenderer has the necessary experience and resources to undertake the work under the Contract. It may only be required for unrestricted tendering, as the information may already be to hand where restricted tendering is being adopted. In the latter situation, the Schedule may be used as one of the Pre-qualification Documents.

Tenderers should be asked to provide the following information as considered appropriate:

- Details of contracts of a similar nature or magnitude previously undertaken by the Contractor.
- What is the tenderer's work commitment on other projects during the currency of the proposed Contract?
- What is the tenderer's present total labour force (own employees: numbers and classifications)?
- How many of these would be available for work on the Contract?

Tenderer's Industrial Relations Record

The Engineer will need to assess the importance of asking tenderers details of their industrial relations record. It will depend upon the nature of the work, the current industrial climate and the possibility of industrial relations becoming a major issue during the Contract. This could be particularly relevant when work is being carried out within the Owner's or Principal's existing premises. As with the previous Schedule, the information can be provided either as a questionnaire or in the form of a statement sheet for information to be supplied by tenderers in their own format. Alternatively, the relevant questions can be incorporated in the previous Schedule (Tenderer's Background and Experience). Questions which could be asked include:

- Has the tenderer a good history of industrial relations?

- How does the tenderer achieve good industrial relations?
- Who in the tenderer's organization would directly handle industrial relations?
- Who would be the person on the Site who would be responsible for industrial relations?
- What are the unions whose members would be employed on the Site?
- What industrial awards or agreements would apply to labour on the Site?

Bill of Quantities

The format and function of a Bill of Quantities is outlined in Sec. 10.4 – 'Coordinating the Supplementary Conditions and the Annexure'. Since it is a substantial document comprising a large number of pages, unless it forms part of the Contract it is not normally attached to the Tender Form but is a separately bound item included in the Enquiry Documents. This situation applies only where the Bill of Quantities forms part of the Contract.

Schedule of Rates

The format for a Schedule of Rates is almost identical to that used in a Bill of Quantities, the difference between the two documents being set out in Sec. 10.4 – 'Coordinating the Supplementary Conditions and the Annexure'.

The attention of tenderers should be drawn to the clause in the Supplementary Conditions detailing the conditions relating to the Schedule of Rates and the clause in the Instructions to Tenderers setting out the requirements for the completion of the Schedule. The first page of the Schedule is the alternative location for these requirements as a Preface Note. A typical *pro forma* for a Schedule of Rates is included in Appendix A.

Schedule of Prices for Tendering

This Schedule is similar in form and layout to a Schedule of Rates. An explanation of its function is given in Sec. 10.4. A typical *pro forma* for a Schedule of Prices for Tendering is included in Appendix A.

Schedule of Daywork Rates

Depending upon which option is adopted as outlined in Sec. 9.3 – 'Outline of Clauses for Instructions to Tenderers', (subsection 'Commercial Requirements', this Schedule may be in the form of either a questionnaire or a statement sheet.

Changes to Pre-qualification Documents

This Schedule should be provided in the form of a statement sheet for information to be provided by tenderers in their own format. It is only applicable where tenders have been invited as the result of a pre-qualification procedure.

Statement on Tenderer's Plan of Approach to the Work

Tenderers should be asked to provide a brief outline of their proposed approach to the work under the Contract. This Schedule may be in the form of a statement sheet itemizing the required information with particular reference to:

- Proposed method of construction and/or fabrication.
- Nature and extent of temporary works, including supports for plant, bracing of structures, diversion of roads and services, dewatering and the diversion of surface water, and protective covers for plant installed before permanent protection is built.
- Site area requirements for temporary buildings and storage of materials and construction camp (if applicable).
- Proposed arrangements for acquiring the labour force, including sources and mobilization and demobilization procedures and provisions for acquiring additional labour for short-term peak requirements.
- Provisions for supervision of the work and quality control.
- How and where the work will be engineered (if applicable).
- Provisions for the procurement of services.
- Arrangements for project control including planning, scheduling and cost control.
- Proposals for commissioning and training operations personnel (if applicable).

Where tenderers are required to nominate the Date(s) for Practical Completion, they can be stated in this Schedule.

Programme of Work

Tenderers should be asked to attach a programme for the work supporting their contention that they can meet the specified or tendered Date(s) for Practical Completion. This programme can be in a bar chart or other suitable form and should indicate proposed working hours and working days. The programme should indicate Site start date(s), manufacture start date(s) and any 'milestone' dates.

Schedule of Key Personnel

Notwithstanding the tenderer's previous experience and track record, it is the quality of the key personnel who will be engaged on the project which will have a significant influence on the Engineer's evaluation. It is this information which will play an important part in assessing the tenderer's offer.

Tenderers should be asked to prepare a schedule of key personnel for the work, together with details of their positions and responsibilities. This schedule should preferably be in the form of a statement sheet and should be supported by a brief CV for each person named. Without specific guidance, CVs submitted by tenderers tend to contain superfluous information. Sporting and recreation interests, hobbies, club memberships and the like are quite irrelevant; what really matters are details of technical skills, qualifications, and experience. Age, marital status, and family responsibilities would be relevant only if the project involved the employee being away from home or overseas. Similarly, the ability to speak and write other languages would be of value only if work overseas was involved. These points should be made clear in a Preface Note on the Schedule.

Schedule of Subcontract Work

The first section of this Schedule should be completed by the Engineer and may comprise three parts:

1. The Engineer should first list the work to be undertaken by nominated subcontractor(s), together with the names of the nominated subcontractors if known. If not known, the names should be noted as 'to be advised'.
2. The Engineer should then list the work to be carried out by designated subcontractors together with the subcontractors' names.
3. The Engineer finally lists the work specified to be undertaken by selected contractors together with a listing of the approved subcontractors. Tenderers should be asked to nominate which subcontractors they have selected for the work.

The second section of this Schedule is where the tenderers are asked to list the other items of work they propose to subcontract and, if possible, nominate the subcontractors as outlined in Sec. 9.3 – 'Outline of Clauses for Instructions to Tenderers', subsection 'Commercial Requirements'.

Schedule of Major Constructional Plant and Equipment

Tenderers should be asked to list all the major items of constructional plant which they propose to use on the work. *Constructional plant* comprises all items of plant and equipment used in the execution of the work under the Contract but not forming part of the Works. The Schedule should be in the form of a statement sheet in which tenderers should be asked to itemize separately:

- Items of plant and equipment already owned by the tenderer and available for use on the Contract
- Items of plant and equipment the tenderer proposes to acquire for the work, indicating their sources and whether they will be wholly owned or obtained under a hire-purchase agreement
- Items of plant and equipment which the tenderer proposes to hire or lease, indicating the reliability of source and availability

Schedule of Imported Items

It is important to obtain full details of all items of plant or equipment to be incorporated in the Works and which are to be imported. Tenderers should be asked to complete a schedule comprising a questionnaire for the following details:

Common to all Items:

Basis of Cost	Fixed or subject to adjustment Contract Sum Adjustment formula if applicable
Currency	Adopted for quote and exchange rate used and date applicable
Import Duty	If paid and the By-Law and Part applicable

For each individual Item:

Item Cost	Ex Works; FOB; FAS; CIF as applicable (see Appendix C)
Delivery Cost	If separate quotes required

Schedule of Tender Drawings

Where the Contract provides for all or some of the design to be the responsibility of the Contractor, tenderers may be asked to provide certain drawings with their tenders. The details of the requirement should be clearly stated in the Instructions to Tenderers and tenderers should be asked to list the drawings in this Schedule.

The prime purpose of the Schedule is to ensure that all copies of the drawings have been included in the tender. Tenderers should be asked to include in the Schedule drawing numbers, title, date of issue and number of copies supplied for each drawing.

This Schedule is distinct from those annexed to the Specification, which list drawings issued by the Principal with the Enquiry Documents and detail the requirements for submission of working drawings by the Contractor.

Schedule of Transport and Delivery

Transport and delivery of both locally manufactured and imported items is often overlooked or inadequately considered during the tender stage. It is important to know exactly how tenderers propose to handle this aspect of the work, and they should be asked to complete a schedule along the following lines:

Common to all items:
- Mode of Transport – Air, Sea, Road, Rail
- Point of Delivery, to be nominated – By Contractor
      – By Principal
- Handling – Offloading by Contractor
      – Offloading by others (nominate)
- Insurance – Overland
      – Marine
      – Insured value
      – Amount of excess
      – Insurance company
- Delivery Time – Weeks ex-Works
      – Weeks on-Site
- Shipment Details – Total mass of Shipment
      – Size and mass of largest item
      – Number of Items in Shipment

For Imported Items:
- Anticipated Date of Shipment
- Port of Shipment
- Port of Delivery
- Name of Ship, Shipping Company or Airline

Schedule of Insurance Policies

Where insurance is to be the responsibility of the Contractor, tenderers should be asked to provide details of insurance policies which they already hold or intend to effect in order to cover their obligations under the Contract. This should preferably be in the form of a questionnaire, with separate entries required for policies in respect of the Works, Workers' Compensation and Public Liability. The information to be provided should include:

- Nature of policy and risk covered
- Status of policy (existing/proposed)
- Name of insurer
- Amount of cover
- Amount of any excess

Equipment Design Data Schedules

The function of Equipment Design Data Schedules to supplement Job Specifications is outlined in Sec. 11.3 – 'The Specification Format'. Data Schedules which are to be completed and returned with tenders should be listed in the Content of Tender and copies included with the other Forms and Schedules for Tendering.

Schedule of Substitutions

Tenderers should be required to provide a statement sheet with details of any substitutions of specified make or manufacture of goods, materials, or catalogue items which the tenderer proposes to submit for approval.

Schedule of Recommended Spare Parts and Price List

Where the Contractor is to be responsible for the design of plant and equipment, the Principal may require tenderers to nominate in this Schedule a list of recommended spare parts with prices. Alternatively, where the Principal is responsible for the design, tenderers may be asked to price spare parts listed by the Principal in the Schedule. The requirements should be set out in a Supplementary Condition.

THE CONDITIONS OF CONTRACT

10.1 UNDERSTANDING THE CONDITIONS OF CONTRACT

The Role of the Conditions of Contract

Before commencing the preparation of any of the documents required for a Contract, it is important that the Engineer fully understands the role and function of the Conditions of Contract.

As pointed out in Sec. 3.4 – 'Contract Documents for Tendering', the Conditions of Contract contain all the clauses relating to the respective rights and obligations of the parties to the Contract. These are mostly administrative provisions as distinct from technical requirements. Technical matters should be confined to the Specification and the Drawings which, preferably, should not contain any administrative requirements. It is important to keep separate these two groups of requirements because misplacement of clauses is a frequent cause of their being overlooked and can possibly lead to a dispute.

Suggested guidelines for determining in which document a particular provision should be located are given in Sec. 8.1 – 'Location of Subject Matter'.

Responsibility for Preparing the Conditions of Contract

The dangers and possible adverse legal consequences arising from engineers attempting to work outside their areas of competence have already been pointed out. Preparing the Conditions of Contract is one of those situations where the Engineer must exercise particular care and discretion in this regard.

Most standard General Conditions have either been prepared by or have received close scrutiny and been approved by legally trained persons. The Engineer is therefore advised to have the Conditions of Contract which are to be included in the Enquiry Documents either prepared or reviewed by a member of the legal profession. Inevitably, the Engineer will be tempted to forgo this procedure on the grounds of cost or time, but should be aware of the potential for unforeseen legal consequences arising from such a decision.

This is one of the reasons why many large corporations which are continually involved in inviting tenders (such as government, statutory, industrial and commercial bodies), have teams of specialists, often including legally trained professionals, one of whose prime functions is to deal with legal aspects of Enquiry Documents. Frequently these teams are incorporated in a purchasing department within the organization.

In such cases, the Engineer prepares the Specification and the Drawings and the specialist team prepares the Conditions of Contract (and, frequently, the Requirements for Tendering) under instructions prepared by the Engineer. This specialist team may also invite and receive tenders and be involved in the evaluation process.

It will devolve to the Engineer who does not have access to such an in-house arrangement to draft the Conditions of Contract. Arrangements should then be made for the document to be reviewed by a legal professional experienced in contract matters.

Under either situation, the Engineer must retain ultimate responsibility for all the Enquiry Documents and should closely examine the documents drafted by the specialist team or amended by the legal adviser, to ensure that all the requirements have been met. While the documents as drafted or amended may be legally correct, they may not achieve the result desired by the Engineer. Lawyers can sometimes get things wrong, particularly if they have not been adequately briefed.

The Documents Comprising the Conditions of Contract

The General Conditions forms the basis for the Conditions of Contract. Unless the Principal has a firm policy regarding the use of a particular document, the Engineer must first select a General Conditions which comes closest to satisfying the requirements of the Contract. The Engineer will then need to qualify, amend or supplement those provisions which do not fully meet the requirements of the Contract.

This is achieved in two ways – by completion of an Annexure attached to the General Conditions or the Tender Form and by the preparation of the Supplementary Conditions which amends and complements the General Conditions. The Conditions of Contract thus comprises two parts:

- Part I   General Conditions (with Annexure)
- Part II Supplementary Conditions

10.2 THE GENERAL CONDITIONS AND ANNEXURE

Selecting the Appropriate General Conditions

Where the selection of the General Conditions is the responsibility of the Engineer, meeting the needs of a particular contract requires a complete understanding, not only of the nature and extent of the work under the Contract, but also of the terms and conditions of the various General Conditions available.

Where the Engineer is experienced in contract documentation, the choice of which General Conditions to use will be made on the Engineer's assessment of the requirements of the Contract, based on that experience. However, if the Engineer is inexperienced in the matter then advice and guidance should be sought from colleagues with the necessary knowledge. If such assistance is not readily available then the Engineer should approach the national standards authority, professional association or other organization which publishes standard General Conditions and obtain copies of their respective documents together with any commentaries available.

The various General Conditions have more or less a common structure. Although the order in which the provisions are dealt with may vary, they cover much the same ground. Indeed, it is not unusual to find clauses with almost identical wording in different General Conditions – even those from different countries. Table 10.1 lists (in alphabetical order) the headings under which the various provisions are usually covered.

In the United Kingdom, General Conditions have traditionally been, and still are, prepared and published by the various professional societies and associations such as the Institution of Civil Engineers and the Institution of Electrical Engineers. The Joint Contracts Tribunal, members of which include the Royal Institute of British Architects, the National Federation of Building Trades Employers, the Royal Institution of Chartered Surveyors and the County Councils Association, have prepared a series of standard

Table 10.1 Typical subject headings encountered in the general conditions
The items marked * are discussed in Sec. 10.4.

*	Assignment and subcontracting
*	Bill of quantities
	Care of the works
*	Certificates and payments
	Cleaning up
	Clerk of works and inspectors
*	Commencement and completion
	Constructional plant
*	Contract documents
	Contractor's representative
	Control of employees
*	Cost adjustment procedure
	Damage to persons and property
	Daywork
	Default or insolvency
*	Defects liability
	Definitions and interpretations
	Delay costs
	Disputes
	Evidence of contract
	Examination and testing
*	Insurance
	Labour
	Latent conditions
*	Liquidated damages
	Materials and workmanship
	Measurement and valuation
	Nature of the contract
	Patents and copyright
	Payment of workers and subcontractors
	Property in plant and materials
	Programming and progress
*	Provisional and prime cost sums
	Safety and security of works
	Security and retention moneys
*	Separable portions
	Service of notices
	Setting out the works
	Site, inspection and access
	Statutory requirements
*	Superintendent
	Sureties
	Suspension of the work
	Termination by frustration
	Taxation
	Urgent protection
	Variations
	Working hours

conditions principally for use in the building industry. On the industrial side, organizations such as the British Coal Corporation, the UK Atomic Energy Authority and large commercial and industrial corporations have also prepared Conditions of Contract for their own use.

For international use by consulting engineers, the Fédération International nationale des Ingénieurs-Conseils (FIDIC) has published a 'Conditions of Contract for Civil Engineering Work' (known as the 'Red Book'), and a 'Conditions of Contract for Electrical and Mechanical Work' (known as the 'Yellow Book'). These appear to have been modelled largely on the ICE and IEE Conditions of Contract and they are both published in English, French and Japanese language versions.

In Australia, the Standards Association has published a standard Conditions of Contract for general use with three other standard conditions covering mechanical and electrical equipment and subcontract work.

Each of these documents reflects the particular requirements of the individual bodies preparing them; there is no one generally accepted Conditions of Contract.

It is not practicable to give here a detailed summary and review of all the standard General Conditions available. The commentaries referred to above are the best source of information and the Engineer is advised to consult these.

However, reference will be made in the discussion in the following chapters to four standard General Conditions to illustrate differing approaches to the subject. These are:

United Kingdom
- *Conditions of Contract and Forms of Tender, Agreement and Bond for use in connection with Works of Civil Engineering Construction*, 6th edition, 1991, published by Thomas Telford Publications for the Institution of Civil Engineers, London (referred to herein as the 'ICE Conditions of Contract').
- *Model Form of General Conditions of Contract* (MF/1 – 1988), published by Mechanical Engineering Publications Limited for the Institution of Electrical Engineers, London (referred to herein as the 'MF/1 General Conditions').

International
- *Conditions of Contract (International) for Works of Civil Engineering Construction*, 4th edition, published by the Fédération Internationale des Ingénieurs-Conseils (FIDIC) (referred to herein as the 'FIDIC Conditions of Contract').

Australia
- *Australian Standard General Conditions of Contract* (AS 2124–1986), published by the Standards Association of Australia (Standards Australia) (referred to herein as the 'SAA General Conditions).

Since these General Conditions have a narrow field of application, they may not be suitable for contracts for multi-discipline projects covering more than one field of engineering. If the Engineer is required to prepare Conditions of Contract for such a contract, substantial amendments to the selected General Conditions may be required.

The Current Editions

The standard General Conditions of Contract referred to above have all been revised and amended a number of times since they were first issued, which has resulted in excessively prolix documents.

During the 1980s it became apparent that, in spite of the many revisions and amendments, these General Conditions had failed to keep pace with significant changes in community attitudes and current legal and industrial practice. As a result, each of the four organizations referred to above undertook major reviews of their Conditions of Contract, and in the latter half of the decade new editions were published. The major areas of concern included:

1. The layout and format of the documents left much to be desired. Many of the sentences were very long and while they may have been intelligible to a legal professional, engineers often found them difficult to follow and they were therefore open to misinterpretation.
2. The General Conditions were believed by many, particularly contractors, to be biased in favour of the Principal. If General Conditions are to be seen as fair and even-handed documents, it was necessary to remove any suggestion of bias in favour of either party.
3. The role and responsibilities of the Superintendent (Engineer) were either inadequately defined or gave the Superintendent unreasonable authority.
4. Gender specific personal pronouns (he, him, his) were widely used to refer to individuals who, in today's society, could be female. This practice in published documents is becoming increasingly unacceptable. (See the subsection 'Non-discriminatory Language' in Sec. 13.2.)

The manner in which each of the above four organizations dealt with these problems is briefly outlined as follows:

1. Presentation In each case the layout and presentation has been improved and the documents are easier to follow. The language is simpler and more in keeping with modern legislative drafting practice. However, some Conditions of Contract still have sentences with over 100 words.

2. Equitability The accusation of bias is difficult to assess. The Conditions of Contract should not necessarily be equitable to both parties – only fair and reasonable. After all, it is the purpose of the party offering the Contract (the Principal) which is to be served, not the security of the other party (the Contractor). Nevertheless, most of the more obvious grounds for discontent on this subject have been addressed and contractors now have little reason to claim the documents are biased.

3. The Superintendent There are usually only two parties to an engineering contract – the Principal and the Contractor; the Superintendent is not a party to the Contract. Under the principle of privity of contract (see Sec. 2.2 – 'The Law of Contract') the parties to a contract cannot make a third party, who is not a party to the contract, liable under the contract.

Conditions of Contract usually require the Superintendent to act fairly and impartially and allocate particular duties and responsibilities to the Superintendent. However, they rarely make it clear how the Superintendent can be made to act fairly and honestly in the discharge of those duties and responsibilities. They tend to be equivocal when defining to whom the Superintendent is responsible and what is the procedure to be followed in the event that one or both the parties is dissatisfied with a ruling or direction given by the Superintendent.

The ICE Conditions of Contract and the FIDIC Conditions of Contract have both tried to avoid the issue by requiring the Contract to specify those matters which the Superintendent must refer to the Principal for decision; but they do not lay down the procedure to be followed in the event of dissatisfaction with a ruling by the Superintendent. The MF/1 General Conditions follows a similar course but does allow either party to refer to arbitration a disputed ruling by the Superintendent.

Only the SAA General Conditions has grasped the nettle firmly and clearly states that it is the responsibility of the Principal to ensure that the Superintendent acts fairly and impartially. This point is discussed in more detail under 'The Superintendent' in Sec. 10.4 – 'Coordinating the Supplementary Conditions and the Annexure'.

4. Non-discriminatory language It is to be regretted that only in the SAA General Conditions has gender-specific language been deliberately avoided. In contrast, the Forms of Tender in the ICE Conditions of Contract, the MF/1 General Conditions and the FIDIC Conditions of Contract still address the Principal as 'Gentlemen'! Such so-called 'dignified' wording is archaic and no longer appropriate. It is not difficult to use non-discriminatory language without being specious, as has been done in this book.

The Engineer should read carefully the General Conditions and commentaries offered, paying particular attention not only to what *is* covered but also to what is *not*.

Where the General Conditions contain an Annexure there are usually cross-references to the Annexure in the text of each clause involved. In reading the General Conditions, the Engineer should note:

- The terminology used
- Any condition which requires the insertion of data in an Annexure
- Any condition with unsatisfactory provisions which require amendment or deletion
- Any condition which requires further amplification
- Any condition which may be required but which is not covered

Many standard General Conditions have been written on the premise that the Principal will supply the design, either directly or through the services of a Consulting Engineer, and that the work under the Contract will include installation or construction on a site provided by the Principal. If this is not the case, the Engineer will need to examine the General Conditions closely and determine to what extent amendments are required or whether another and more appropriate General Conditions should be used.

Terminology

It is at this point that the Engineer must determine the terminology to be used throughout the documents. This particularly applies to those terms used to refer to the parties to the Contract and their representatives. The terminology used in the selected General Conditions may not be consistent with that adopted in this book or that preferred by the Engineer.

Since the selected General Conditions will most probably be a standard pre-printed document, it is unlikely to be practicable to amend the General Conditions to conform with the Engineer's preference. In this case the Engineer will find it pragmatic to adopt the terminology of the General Conditions for all the documents. Consistency is most important.

Some of the provisions listed under the headings in Table 10.1 require data to be inserted in the Annexure; others may require amending or supplementing. In Sec. 10.4 – 'Coordinating the Supplementary Conditions and the Annexure' a number of these subjects are briefly discussed and attention is drawn to some of the problems which the Engineer may encounter in preparing the Conditions of Contract.

There is another group of terms about which engineers are sometimes confused; those which refer to the amount of consideration paid to the Contractor. In the various General Conditions this amount is described differently at each stage in the contract process. These are:

1. The amount stated in the Contractor's tender
2. The amount stated in the Contract
3. The amount to be paid to the Contractor

To illustrate this confusion, none of the referenced General Conditions uses a specific term for the amount stated in the Contractor's tender. Where this amount is stated in the respective Tender Forms, it is referred to therein as a 'sum'; in the ICE Conditions of Contract it is referred to as the 'sum [that] may be ascertained in accordance with the said Conditions of Contract'.

The amount stated in the Contract as the amount to be paid to the Contractor is variously described as the 'Tender Total' (ICE Conditions of Contract), the 'Contract Price' (MF/1 General Conditions) and the 'Contract Sum' (SAA General Conditions). Although in most cases the amount stated in the Contract will be the same as the amount stated in the tender, it may not always be so. In the negotiations with the preferred tenderer prior to reaching agreement this amount may be changed.

The amount to be paid to the Contractor is time-related; that is, it may change from time to time during the performance of the work as adjustments are made due to variations in the extent of the work and fluctuations in the cost of labour, materials and services as provided for in the Contract.

The term *variation* is used to refer to an adjustment in the cost of the work arising from an increase, decrease, omission, change in character or quality, change in position or dimension or demolition of any part of the work under the Contract.

A *fluctuation* refers to the increase or decrease in the value of the work under the Contract due to changes in the cost of labour, materials, or services during the performance of the work.

The amount paid to the Contractor is variously described as the 'Contract Price' (ICE Conditions of Contract) and the 'Contract Value' (MF/1 General Conditions). Neither the FIDIC Conditions of Contract nor the SAA General Conditions have a specific term, referring respectively to the 'value of the work done' and 'the amount due to the Contractor'. These two descriptions do not necessarily refer to the same thing; the 'amount due to the Contractor' could be the 'value of the work done' less any retention money.

Neither would include the cost of variations approved but not yet under-taken.

It can be seen that there is considerable confusion in the terms used to identify these amounts. It is suggested that the following terms only be used:

tender sum: the amount stated in the Contractor's tender
contract sum: the amount stated in the Contract

The Engineer should be careful when using specific terms to identify payments paid or due to be paid to the Contractor. If it is necessary to refer to such amounts, the Engineer should make it quite clear exactly what is meant.

Completing the Annexure

As pointed out in Section 3.4 – 'Contract Documents for Tendering' – General Conditions usually provide an Annexure as a form to be completed by the Engineer and issued as a Schedule with the Enquiry Documents. The purpose of an Annexure is to avoid the necessity to fill in blank spaces in the General Conditions for each new contract with data which may vary from one contract to another. These Annexures can vary from a simple form covering a limited number of items of data to be inserted to a more detailed format with a large number of items to be included.

The ICE Conditions of Contract and the SAA General Conditions both have places in the Annexure for inserting the name and address of the Principal and the Superintendent. The MF/1 General Conditions indicates that the name of the Superintendent and the addresses of the Principal, the Superintendent and the Contractor should be stated in the 'Special Con-ditions'. Other General Conditions also have space for the name and address of the Contractor to be inserted in the Annexure. It is difficult to see how the name or address of the Contractor can be given at the Tender Stage, because the identity of the Contractor will not be known until the Contract is awarded.

The FIDIC Conditions of Contract suggests that the name of the Prin-cipal and the Superintendent be included in the 'Conditions of Particular Application' and no reference is made to the Contractor in this regard.

Putting the name and address of the Principal, the Contractor or the Superintendent in the Annexure or in the Supplementary Conditions is really unnecessary. The Principal should be identified in the Invitation to Tender, which should also name the Engineer as being the person to whom all enquiries are to be directed during the Tender Period (see Sec. 9.1 – 'Prepar-ing the Invitation to Tender'). When the Contract is prepared the Principal and the Contractor will be named in the Agreement.

It is not necessary for the Superintendent to be identified by name in the Enquiry Documents or in the Contract. Most General Conditions define the Superintendent in terms such as 'the person approved by the Principal and named in the Annexure or Supplementary Conditions, or other person approved by the Principal from time to time'.

It is then the responsibility of the Principal to notify the Contractor of the identity of the Superintendent, or of the Consulting Engineer designated to appoint the Superintendent, as soon as practicable after the Contract is awarded. In the latter case, it will then be the responsibility of the Consulting Engineer to notify the name of the Superintendent to the Contractor. The notification should include the address and telephone, telex, and fax numbers through which communication with the Superintendent are to be passed.

The identity of the Superintendent may possibly, but not necessarily, be known at the time of calling tenders, particularly if the Engineer and the Superintendent are to be the same person; but this information is not essential for tender purposes. If the Superintendent is not named in the Contract, the Conditions of Contract should state that the Principal will, at all times, ensure that there will be a Superintendent nominated.

The Engineer will have to decide how best to insert information in the Annexure. Since the Annexure form is usually bound with the General Conditions or, in the case of the ICE Conditions of Contract, on the back of the Form of Tender, the information can only be handwritten in the form. This can be a tedious procedure and there is the ever-present danger that an error will be made on one of the copies or that some handwritten word or figure will be misread. There are several ways to overcome this problem, two of which are:

- Remove the Annexure (or Form of Tender) from each copy of the General Conditions, type the data on one of the forms and reproduce the required number of copies for reinsertion in the Enquiry Documents.
- Retype the whole Annexure with the required information using the form from the General Conditions as a model, but in the Engineer's own words.

The difficulty with the first option is that it could involve the Engineer in a breach of copyright. Some of the bodies publishing General Conditions appreciate this problem and appear to tacitly accept the situation; the SAA, in fact, publishes pads of blank forms of their Annexures for this purpose. However, the Engineer is advised to obtain the approval of the owner of the copyright before adopting this course of action.

The second option would appear to overcome the difficulty, but the question of copyright may still be present. Everyone has, at some time, encountered a form with inadequate space for data insertion or with items which are not strictly applicable to the circumstances. The Annexures are no different. The second option allows the Engineer to redesign the layout of the Annexure and so overcome this difficulty.

Where the information to be inserted is more than a single statement or figure, the best solution is to provide a separate clause in the Supplementary Conditions dealing with the matter and make a simple cross-reference in the Annexure such as 'See Supplementary Conditions'. When completing the Annexure, it is important to ensure that the data or information inserted is clear and unambiguous.

Amending General Conditions

Inevitably, the selected General Conditions will have some provisions which are not relevant to the Contract. Unless these are directly at variance with what is required, there is little point in deleting such requirements. Everyone realizes that such situations can occur when a standard document is used, and in most cases no harm is done if those requirements remain.

However, it may be that one or more of the conditions are unacceptable and the Engineer may decide that certain clauses require amendment. It must be reiterated that amending individual clauses in a standard General Conditions should be approached with caution.

Most standard General Conditions have been in use for a number of years and have been refined and amended so as to meet the requirements of most users. The clauses have been fully integrated with each other and most discrepancies and inconsistencies eliminated. Great care must be taken when making amendments to the wording of individual clauses.

The safest way to amend a clause in a General Conditions is to delete the clause entirely and substitute an amended or reworded clause; but beware the 'bumping truck' syndrome. Amending a clause in a General Conditions may affect one or more other clauses, which, in turn, may have repercussions to clauses 'further down the line'. Some of these effects may not be immediately apparent and if not picked up and corrected, may have unforeseen legal consequences. Thus, an amendment such as 'Clause X, paragraph Y, line Z, delete the words ".   .   ." and substitute ".   .   ."' is all too frequently seen, and it is regrettable that FIDIC suggests this method of amendment in their 'Guidelines for the Preparation of Part II Clauses'. Not only is such an amendment clumsy but it is also open to misinterpretation. Such an amendment is often unnecessary and is frequently the result of the Engineer not really understanding the full legal implications of the clause. If the Engineer is completely satisfied that the provisions of the clause are unsatisfactory, the clause should be deleted entirely and, if necessary, replaced by a completely new clause.

Where a clause is to be completely deleted or deleted and replaced by an amended clause in the Supplementary Conditions, a note to this effect should be placed in the margin. It is suggested that a rubber stamp, worded along the following lines, be made for this purpose:

Clause ————

Amended/deleted
See Supplementary
Conditions

or

Amended. See
Supplementary
Conditions

10.3 THE SUPPLEMENTARY CONDITIONS OF CONTRACT

The Supplementary Conditions of Contract serves five purposes:

1. To delete any inappropriate clauses in the General Conditions
2. To substitute an alternative clause in place of one deleted from the General Conditions
3. To add a new clause which supplements a clause in the General Conditions
4. To provide information normally included in the Annexure where the form and layout of the Annexure is inadequate
5. To add a new clause to cover matters not dealt with in the General Conditions

Since the Supplementary Conditions is unique to each individual contract, so as to take account of the particular circumstances and location, the provisions must necessarily vary, and it is not practicable to produce a standard document or even standard clauses. The Engineer must therefore draft the document to meet the requirements of the particular contract. However, both FIDIC and the IEE produce guidelines for the preparation of Supplementary Conditions appropriate to their respective General Conditions.

Having read the General Conditions carefully, the Engineer will have to decide what supplementary conditions are required. The individual clauses dealing with the above listed matters must be carefully drafted to ensure that there is no discrepancy or ambiguity in relation to the Annexure or the corresponding clauses in the General Conditions.

The Supplementary Conditions should preferably be a separate document with the clauses arranged in an order compatible with the General Conditions. However, the ICE General Conditions refers to supplementary conditions as 'Special Conditions' and requires them to be added to and numbered consecutively with the General Conditions. If this document is being used, the Engineer should adopt that procedure.

1. Deleted clauses Notwithstanding the use of marginal notes in the General Conditions, the Supplementary Conditions should contain a separate statement listing the clauses which have been deleted from the General Conditions. The Annexure (Part B) to the SAA General Conditions provides space for listing deleted clauses.

2. Alternative clauses Clauses substituted for clauses deleted from the General Conditions should be identified by using the same heading as for the clause deleted. The text should make it clear that the new clause is a substitute for a specific deleted clause. The Annexure (Part B) to the SAA General Conditions provides space for listing amended clauses.

3. Supplementary clauses Clauses which provide information or instructions which supplement an existing General Conditions clause should be clearly cross-referenced to that clause.

4. Annexure clauses Where instructions or data normally included in the Annexure require a clause in the Supplementary Conditions, the entry in the Annexure should read 'See Supplementary Conditions'.

5. New clauses New clauses covering matters not dealt with in the General Conditions may be placed at the end of the Supplementary Conditions. The Annexure (Part B) to the SAA General Conditions provides space for listing new clauses.

10.4 COORDINATING THE SUPPLEMENTARY CONDITIONS AND THE ANNEXURE

It is not practicable in this book to discuss comprehensively all the subjects covered under the headings listed in Table 10.1. For such a review, the Engineer should refer to one of the commentaries which have been published for most of the General Conditions produced by nationally based organizations.

However, some of the provisions require data to be inserted in the Annexure while others may require amendment or further amplification. To guide the Engineer in this task, some of these matters (marked with an asterisk in Table 10.1) are now briefly discussed.

Assignment and Subcontracting

Most General Conditions do not permit the Contractor (or, in some cases, either party to the Contract) to assign or subcontract the whole or any part of the Contract without the (written) consent of the Principal (or of the other party).

The various options open to the Engineer who wishes to anticipate requests to subcontract parts of the work have already been outlined in Sec. 9.3 – see 'Outline of Clauses for Instructions to Tenderers'.

Depending upon the provisions of the particular General Conditions adopted, it may be necessary to define, preferably as a secondary statement in the Supplementary Conditions, the terms and conditions under which subcontracting will be permitted.

Where Designated, Selected and/or Nominated subcontractors (as defined in Sec. 2.3 – 'Types of Contracts') are to be specified, the requirements should also be laid down in the Supplementary Conditions. These items of work and the names of the subcontractors should be included in the draft schedules to be returned with the Tender Documents (see Sec. 9.4 – 'Forms, Schedules, and Statements for Tendering', subsection 'Schedule of Subcontract Work').

Bill of Quantities

A *Bill of Quantities* is a detailed schedule of work under the Contract giving a full description of every item of work to be performed or equipment to be supplied together with a measured quantity for each item. The Bill is usually prepared by a Quantity Surveyor, whose function is to measure the work, calculate the quantities and make up the Bill in accordance with a standard or code prepared by an appropriate authority.

There is normally a separate bill for each trade or speciality involved and for preliminary items applicable to all trades and to the Contract generally. Each Bill is divided into a number of columns.

The columns containing the description of each item and the corresponding estimated quantities are prepared by the Quantity Surveyor; the columns for the price or rate for each item measured and for the total for each item, determined by engrossing the quantity multiplied by the rate or price quoted, are completed by the tenderer or by the Contractor. Bills of Quantities serve a number of functions:

- They indicate to a tenderer the extent and nature of the work to be priced.
- They can shorten the tender period and speed up the tender evaluation process by enabling all tenders to be compared on a common basis.
- They form a basis for calculating variations in Lump Sum Contracts.
- They determine the final contract price in contracts where the Bill of Quantities forms part of the Contract.

Bills of Quantities prepared by a Quantity Surveyor are not normally used in Lump Sum engineering contracts, only the exceptions being those cases of civil engineering work which incorporate a significant amount of building work.

The method of measurement used to prepare the Bill of Quantities is usually stated in the Preamble to the Bill. If not, details should be included in the Supplementary Conditions.

The principal advantage in using Bills of Quantities in large building works is that, owing to the complexity of the work, the time required and the cost incurred by tenderers in preparing their quotations can be substantial and find reflection in their tender prices. However, in smaller building projects, the use of a Bill of Quantities can have an opposite effect and may even result in increased prices.

When completed and extended by a tenderer or by the Contractor, the Bill is known as a *Priced Bill of Quantities*. The manner in which a Priced Bill of Quantities is dealt with will depend upon the type of contract and the Contract must specify its intended purpose and how and when it is to be submitted.

When a Bill of Quantities is included in the Enquiry Documents, the Conditions of Contract must state whether or not it will form part of the Contract. If it is to form part of the Contract, the Priced Bill of Quantities will have to be submitted by tenderers as part of their tenders. The Contract then becomes, in effect, a Schedule of Rates Contract and the work subject to remeasurement on completion and the Contract Sum adjusted accordingly. The Engineer must carefully check the wording in respect of each item in the Bill.

It is advisable to include a statement in the Supplementary Conditions to the effect that in the event of a conflict of wording between the Bill and the Specification, the Specification wording would take precedence.

Where a Bill of Quantities does not form part of the Contract, such as in a Lump Sum Contract, the Priced Bill of Quantities need only be submitted by the Contractor after the Contract has been awarded and within a time nominated in the Contract. In this situation, the rates in the Priced Bill of Quantities are used to assess valuations for progress payments and, as far as they are applicable, will constitute schedule rates for extra payments and variations authorized under the Contract.

The Priced Bill of Quantities should be checked by the Engineer as to its technical and mathematical accuracy. In the event that the check reveals any error, discrepancy or unreasonable apportionment of prices, the matter should be drawn to the attention of the tenderer or the Contractor. How the matter should be rectified will depend upon the circumstances. The Engineer must carefully check the relevant clause(s) in the General Conditions and amend or amplify the provisions in the Supplementary Conditions as required.

It should be noted that the ICE Conditions of Contract infers that the Priced Bill of Quantities forms part of the Contract and therefore any contract written under these conditions is, in effect, a Schedule of Rates Contract.

Certificates and Payments

The provisions regarding the issue of certificates and the authorization of payments are complex matters and are handled with varying degrees of success in different ways by the various General Conditions. The certificates required to be issued by the Superintendent fall into two categories:

- Payment Certificates
- Completion Certificates

Payment certificates The Contractor is normally required to submit to the Superintendent at certain nominated periods or times (usually after the end of each calendar month and at specified progress stages) a statement of claim setting out the Contractor's estimate of the amount owing at that time in respect of goods and services provided under the Contract. The Superintendent is required to check the claim and, after deducting payments previously made, together with any agreed retention sum, issues a Payment Certificate in respect of the amount to which the Superintendent considers the Contractor to be entitled. The Payment Certificate should indicate whether it is an Interim or a Final Payment Certificate.

This raises an important point regarding the authority of the Superintendent under the Contract. There is a significant body of legal opinion which believes that, while the Superintendent must fairly value all claims for payment, the Superintendent is not required to do more than form an opinion on the Contractor's entitlement. If the Superintendent's opinion is that the Contractor has an entitlement, the Superintendent is obliged to include in the Payment Certificate a reasonable amount in respect thereof. While the Principal must take the Superintendent's opinion into account, if the Principal considers the Superintendent's assessment to be wrong, the Principal is bound to pay the correct entitlement. It is the Principal's final responsibility to make the correct payment. Many engineers believe that the Principal is obliged to pay only the amount certified in the Payment Certificate; this point of view is debatable and has led to many disputes. In the latest review of its General Conditions, the SAA has adopted the approach that, as the Principal warrants the acts of the Superintendent, it is the Principal's responsibility to ensure that the correct payment is made.

For this reason, many engineering firms providing Superintendent services are today avoiding the use of the term 'Certificate' when referring to these documents and prefer to identify them in other ways such as 'Valuation Assessments'.

The Engineer should read carefully the provisions in the General Conditions regarding claims for payment and insert the appropriate data in the Annexure. A draft Payment Certificate is included in Appendix A.

Some legal jurisdictions require the Contractor's claim to include a statement that all employees' wages and claims by subcontractors outstanding at the date of the claim have been paid. However, the question of payment to Nominated Subcontractors can cause difficulties.

Some General Conditions allow the Principal to make payments directly to a Nominated Subcontractor in the event that the Contractor fails to make a payment. Exercising this option involves the Principal in interfering in the contractual relationship between the Contractor and the Nominated Subcontractor; this can lead to unfortunate legal consequences. The Contractor cannot exercise control of a subcontractor if the Contractor's right to withhold payment is undermined. The SAA General Conditions does not have this provision but it does have an optional clause providing for all payments to be made by the Principal. However, the Principal is required to withhold payment when requested by the Contractor.

The simplest way to deal with this is to include a requirement in the Nominated Subcontract that the Nominated Subcontractor is to submit claims on a monthly basis for the period ending on the fifteenth day of the month.

The Nominated Subcontractor's claim should be submitted to the Contractor with a copy to the Superintendent not later than the twenty-first day of the month. The Superintendent then certifies to the Contractor the valuation of the amount due to the Nominated Subcontractor not later than the last day of the month; the Contractor can then include in the monthly claim the amount certified as due to the Nominated Subcontractor.

It is also advisable to include an Application for Payment Form in the Enquiry Documents and to require the Contractor to submit all claims on a facsimile of that form. Examples of typical Payment and Valuation Certificates and Application for Payment Form are included in Appendix A.

Before submitting the monthly claim, the Contractor should agree with the Superintendent's representative on the Site or in the workshop the *amount of work* completed on which the claim is based. The Superintendent's representative on the Site is not normally in a position to place a monetary value on the claim.

Some General Conditions (notably the ICE Conditions of Contract) do not make it clear that on the issue of the Certificate of Practical Completion (or in the case of mechanical or electrical equipment, the Certificate of Acceptance) the Contractor is to hand over the Works to the Principal.

All the above points should be set out in a secondary statement in the Supplementary Conditions.

Completion certificates When the work under the Contract has reached the stage of Practical (or Substantial) Completion, the Superintendent is required to issue a Certificate of Practical Completion. In the case of contracts for the supply of mechanical or electrical equipment, this is usually referred to as a Certificate of Acceptance or Taking-Over Certificate. In this certificate, the Superintendent nominates:

1. The date on which the work under the Contract has reached Practical Completion
2. Those items of work which, at the Date of Practical Completion, remain to be completed or rectified
3. A period after the Date of Practical Completion within which these unfinished items of work are to be completed.

The Certificate should include a statement to the effect that if the unfinished items of work are not completed within the nominated period, the commencement of the Defects Liability Period is deferred until they are completed. A separate Completion Certificate should be issued for each Separable Portion of the work.

Although the ICE Conditions of Contract requires the issue of a Defects Correction Certificate, it is not necessary to issue a final completion certificate at the end of the Defects Liability Period and when all the remedial work has been completed. The issue of the final Payment Certificate can be evidence of the determination of the Contract.

Commencement and Completion

The Contract must state the dates by which the work under the Contract is to be commenced and is to be completed. Where the Contract is for the supply only of mechanical or electrical equipment, the term 'accepted' is often used instead of 'completed'.

Unfortunately, many General Conditions do not precisely define the meaning of 'completed'. Strictly speaking, the work under the Contract is not 'complete' until after the expiry of the Defects Liability (or Correction) Period and all remedial work has been completed. This may be up to twelve months (or even more) after the Works are handed over to the Principal.

For this reason, many General Conditions qualify the meaning of 'completed' by using the term *Practical (or Substantial) Completion*. This is usually defined as the stage when the Works are completed except for the following classes of minor omissions and minor defects:

• Those the Superintendent determines the Contractor has reasonable grounds for not immediately rectifying
• Those which do not prevent the Works from being reasonably capable of being used for their intended purpose or
• Those whose rectification will not prejudice their use

In other words, it is the stage when the Works can be handed over to and used by the Principal.

There are two dates which arise from this definition. The *Date for Practical Completion* (or *Acceptance*) is the date nominated in the Contract by which the Contractor is to execute the work under the Contract; the *Date of Practical Completion* (or *Acceptance*) is the date certified by the Superintendent as the date when the Contractor has actually handed the Works over to the Principal.

The Date for Practical Completion will depend on when the Contract is awarded and when the Contractor can or does start on work under the Contract.

The dates for commencement and completion can be specified in a number of ways. Tenderers can be told to do one of the following:

• Nominate in their tenders a period or time for (Practical) Completion after either the award of the Contract or being given possession of the Site as appropriate.
• Nominate in their tenders a Date for (Practical) Completion based on the Contract being awarded on or before a specified date.
• Confirm in their tenders that they can reach (Practical) Completion by the date or within the period specified in the Enquiry Documents, based on the Contract being awarded on or before the date therein nominated.

Where the Engineer wishes to nominate a date or period for Practical Completion, a provisional date for the award of the Contract or possession of the Site must be included either in the Annexure or in a Supplementary Condition, together with details of the nominated date or period.

Where the Engineer requires tenderers to nominate, in their tenders, times or dates for Practical Completion, similar details must be included in the Instructions to Tenderers and tenderers must be required to complete appropriate schedules setting out their offers.

Whichever option is chosen, the Date for Practical Completion must be stated in one of the Contract Documents. It is important to remember that the Instructions to Tenderers will not be a Contract Document.

Where sitework is involved, most General Conditions specify periods after the award of the Contract within which the Contractor:

- Is given possession of the Site
- Must also start the work under the Contract

The significance of the Date of Practical Completion is that it is the date of commencement of the Defects Liability Period and the date for the termination of the period to which any liquidated damages may apply.

Claims by the Contractor for extensions of time for Practical Completion are a frequent source of disagreement. This is largely due to most General Conditions being somewhat vague, not so much as to what constitutes grounds for an extension of time, but rather how the claim is to be assessed.

There is rarely any serious problem over extensions of time for delays such as (but not necessarily limited to) industrial disputes, acts of the Principal, latent conditions, or repudiation by Designated or Nominated Subcontractors; these can usually be agreed upon readily. A very common source of dispute is claims due to inclement weather conditions. The ICE Conditions of Contract refers to 'exceptional adverse weather conditions' without defining the meaning of 'exceptional'. Other General Conditions are equally imprecise.

The most practical way to deal with this problem is to place upon the Principal the entire risk for delays due to inclement weather. It would be the Contractor's responsibility to establish to the satisfaction of the Superintendent, preferably at the time, that continuation of work under the circumstances would be unduly difficult or dangerous. The SAA General Conditions takes this approach, and furthermore makes it clear that the fact that the Contractor can still reach Practical Completion without an extension of time being granted shall not be taken into consideration when determining an entitlement to an extension. This acknowledges the fact that the Contractor's own allowance for 'float' in the programme should not be used to make up time due to delays arising from inclement weather. The risk is entirely the Principal's.

An example of a typical Certificate of Practical Completion is given in Appendix A.

Contract Documents

Most General Conditions state that the several documents forming the Contract are to be taken as mutually explanatory and that in the event of any ambiguity or discrepancy being discovered the Contractor shall advise the Superintendent accordingly. The Superintendent is then required to direct the Contractor as to the interpretation to be followed.

Some General Conditions (such as FIDIC Conditions of Contract) include a clause listing an order of priority of documents for the interpretation of ambiguous or discrepant provisions. This can be dangerous because the 'correct' interpretation may be in a lower order of document. The Contractor could use the 'incorrect' interpretation in a document of greater priority without referring the matter to the Superintendent, particularly if it better suits the Contractor's purpose.

The procedure to be followed in the event of such a discrepancy being discovered during the tender period has already been discussed in Sec. 9.3 – 'Instructions to Tenderers', ' Examination of Documents and Site'. However, if a discrepancy is discovered during the performance of the work under the Contract, then the Contractor could claim that the Superintendent's direction involved additional costs not envisaged at the time of tendering. In most case, this can easily be resolved and the additional work costed as a Variation. However, a problem could arise if the Superintendent disputes the Contractor's claim. One way to anticipate this is to require the Contractor's interpretation of the discrepancy to be stated when attention is drawn to the matter. Even this procedure may not eliminate the difficulty.

The SAA General Conditions requires the number of copies of documents to be supplied by the Principal to the Contractor and by the Contractor to the Principal to be stated in the Annexure, or, if no such number is stated, five copies to be provided in each case. The ICE Conditions of Contract specifically requires the Superintendent (Engineer) to supply two copies of all documents required to the Contractor but makes no reference to the supply of documents by the Contractor to the Superintendent (Engineer). This appears to ignore the situation where the Contractor is responsible for all or part of the design. The Engineer should consider whether the selected General Conditions adequately covers the situation and, if necessary, draft an appropriate Supplementary Condition.

Contract Sum Adjustment Procedure

As pointed out in Sec. 2.3 – 'Types of Contracts', the Contract Sum can be either 'fixed' or 'subject to cost adjustment'. *Contract Sum Adjustment* is a procedure whereby the risk that the value of the work done will increase or decrease, owing to fluctuations in the cost of labour, materials and transport during the performance of the work, is borne by the Principal. Cost Adjustment can be applied to both Lump Sums and to Schedule Rates.

Most General Conditions today do not include a clause in relation to cost adjustment, leaving it to the Engineer to decide whether or not to make an appropriate provision in the Supplementary Conditions. The ICE provides drafts of two types of cost adjustment clauses as looseleaf inserts in the ICE Conditions of Contract which the Engineer may include in the Supplementary Conditions if required. The 'Guidelines for Preparation of Part II Clauses' accompanying the FIDIC Conditions of Contract also has a sample clause to cover cost adjustment.

Within each legal jurisdiction there are usually a number of formulas available for the calculation of the cost adjustment amount. These formulas are derived from a number of sources such as professional engineering societies, contractors' associations, and government sponsored national building industry councils. Each is normally designed for a particular type of work and the Engineer should obtain copies of the available formulas and become familiar with their purpose and operation.

The formulas are applied by multiplying a factor (the 'Price Fluctuation Factor') by a defined portion of the Value of Work Done (the 'Variable Amount' or 'Effective Value'). Most of the differences between the various formulas lie in the way in which the Price Fluctuation Factor is determined. This factor is usually derived from Index Figures published regularly by an appropriate government authority (such as the Department of the Environment in the UK or the Bureau of Statistics in Australia). The Variable Amount (or Effective Value) is the actual valuation of the work under the Contract carried out during the period since the previous valuation, less the following costs:

● Prime Cost and Provisional Sums
● Work and material supplied on a Day Labour basis
● Mark-up on Nominated Subcontractors work
● Imported materials and equipment
● Customs Duty if quoted separately
● Firm fixed price Variations
● Amounts for Cost Adjustment made previously

Some formulas provide for a further percentage reduction to allow for risk sharing between the Principal and the Contractor. This is sometimes done in the expectation that it will encourage the Contractor to resist more firmly unreasonable demands for site allowances. If the Engineer elects to include provision for Cost Adjustment in the Contract there are two ways to deal with the provision:

● To nominate in the Conditions of Contract the formula to be used and details of the relevant indexes to be used

- To require tenderers to nominate in their tenders details of the formula or formulas they wish to adopt

Either option is practicable and the choice will depend upon the Engineer's assessment of the current tendering situation. Whichever procedure is chosen, an appropriate provision should be included in the Supplementary Conditions.

Many engineers prefer to issue separate payment certificates for entitlements under a cost adjustment provision.

Defects Liability

Most engineering contracts require the Contractor to rectify any omission or defect in the work which may be revealed within a specified period after Practical Completion.

This period is usually referred to as the *Defects Liability* or *Defects Correction Period*, although some General Conditions still use the term Maintenance Period. This can be confusing, because Maintenance is, strictly speaking, a more widespread activity and encompasses servicing the Works and replacing consumables and parts subject to normal wear and tear in operation, as well as making good defects. Consequently, it usually applies to mechanical and/or electrical equipment.

Most General Conditions provide for the Defects Liability Period to be nominated in the Annexure. There are two points to consider when determining the Defects Liability Period.

The first is that Defects Liability, while time-related, does not necessarily have to be defined as an actual period of time. In mechanical installations, it can be defined as a throughput quantity. For example, in a bulk materials handling facility, the Period may terminate when a certain volume or mass of product has passed through the facility. In an installation which requires 'working up' to a nominated rate of handling or production, it can be for a set time after the facility reaches the specified capacity. Most General Conditions assume that the Defects Liability will be for a specific time period, and in these other situations the provision will require amendment by means of a Supplementary Condition.

The second is to ensure that where Separable Portions are specified in the Contract, the Defects Liability Period for each Portion must be separately defined.

The most common Defects Liability period for infrastructure, buildings, and structures is 6 months. In some cases, such as earthworks, this can be reduced. On the other hand, environmental control facilities, such as in building services, may need to be 12 months to ensure that the facility has operated through a full annual cycle. The Engineer must ensure that any Defects Liability must be clearly stated and realistically practicable.

Insurance

It is usual for engineering contracts to require the Contractor to make good any damage, accidental or otherwise, to the Works and to indemnify the Principal against all claims from third parties for damage to persons or property arising from work under the Contract; the obligation remains in force until all work under the Contract is complete.

In order to protect the rights and interests of the parties to the Contract, it is therefore usual to require the Contractor to insure against such events and claims. It is important to appreciate that insurance does not reduce the incidence of risk – it merely transfers it to another party. There are three main areas to be covered by such insurance, usually in separate policies. They are:

- Death or injury to employees
- Damage to the Works
- Claims by third parties

However, it is becoming increasingly common for the Principal to effect the insurance of the Works and against claims by third parties. Many large organizations have blanket policies to cover all their activities and may prefer to insure these contractual risks under such policies, particularly where the work is to be undertaken within their own existing plants or establishments. In a major project involving a number of separate contracts, the Principal or the Owner may elect to negotiate a single policy to cover the risks under all contracts.

If the Principal elects to provide insurance cover, a copy of the policy or policies must be included as an annexure to the Conditions of Contract with an explanation as a Supplementary Condition. The Contractor may then wish to provide additional cover as seen fit.

Insurance of employees (Workers' Compensation) is mandatory by law in most countries. Nevertheless, the Engineer should ensure that the Contractor has insurance cover against liability, whether by statute or by common law, for death or injury of employees of the Contractor and all subcontractors in the course of the work under the Contract. The insurance cover should be unlimited in amount and maintained until all work, including all remedial work, has been completed.

Insurance of the Works should cover loss or damage resulting from any cause whatsoever to the Works and all items of material, plant and equipment for which the Contractor has assumed responsibility, whether on or off the Site, in storage or in transit. The policy should be maintained until the Contractor ceases to be responsible for the care of the work under the Contract. Normally this would occur on the Date of Practical Completion, when the responsibility for the insurance of the Works passes to the Principal.

This also applies to Separable Portions. However, any work outstanding at that date, and damage caused by the Contractor in carrying out any testing required under the Contract and making good defects during the Defects Liability Period, should continue to be covered by the Contractor's policy.

The amount of the cover should not be less than the Contract Sum plus an appropriate allowance for the cost of demolition and removal of debris, consultant's fees and cost escalation. The policy should be effected in the joint names of the Principal and the Contractor and should cover the respective rights and interests of all subcontractors.

The question of to whom the money in settlement of a claim against the policy is to be paid is not always made clear in General Conditions. Since the payment is jointly the property of the Principal and the Contractor, the safest course of action is to require the money to be deposited in a bank account in the joint names of the Principal and the Contractor and to provide for the cost of reinstatement to be paid from this account on certificates issued by the Superintendent.

Insurance against claims by third parties should be by a Public Liability Policy in the joint names of the Principal and the Contractor. This policy should also cover the Superintendent, particularly if the Superintendent is not an employee of the Principal. The reason for this is that in the event of a claim for damages arising out of the work under the Contract it is becoming increasingly common for the claim to be made against all parties, however remote their connection with the event. If the Superintendent is an employee of an agent of the Principal, such as a firm of consulting engineers, then, unless the agent is named in the Public Liability Policy, the Superintendent's employer will have to defend the action, probably under direction of the firm's Professional Indemnity insurer. With two insurance companies involved in the defence of the claim, there is always the possibility of them having a different approach to the problem and a conflict of interest may arise.

It is therefore preferable to have all defendents represented by the one company. However, the Public Liability Policy will not necessarily indemnify a consulting engineer employing the Superintendent against claims based on allegations of professional negligence. The consulting engineer's own Professional Indemnity Policy will take precedence in such cases. The amount of cover to be provided must be realistic, taking into account damages being awarded by the Courts at the time for similar claims.

Many insurance policies do not pay the full value of a claim. The difference between the amount of the claim and the amount paid by the insurer is known as the *excess* and is specified in the policy. When evaluating tenders it is important to know the amount of excess in the policies proposed by tenderers, and they should be asked to provide this information with their tenders. If the excess is very large, the ability of the tenderer to bear the loss is relevant.

The question of insurance generally is a complex issue and is one which the Engineer should approach with caution. This is one of those areas where the Engineer may be tempted to venture outside the Engineer's sphere of competence. The Engineer should seek expert advice but a further word of caution is necessary. Expert advisers in the field of insurance are often closely associated with a particular insurance company or group of companies and their advice may not be unbiased, being influenced by the customary practices of their associated insurers. Where possible, the Principal's or Owner's insurance advisers should be consulted.

There are many problems to be resolved when dealing with insurance matters, but there are two in particular the Engineer should be aware of.

The first is the procedure in the event of the Contractor or insurer cancelling or failing to renew a policy. The Principal may be unaware of the situation and could be left without any insurance cover. It is therefore advisable to ensure that each policy contains a provision requiring the insurer to advise both the Principal and the Contractor in the event of the issue of any notice regarding the policy.

The second situation is if the insurer rejects a claim made under the policy alleging that the Contractor failed to disclose some relevant fact when completing the proposal form. The Superintendent and the Principal would have no means of checking this at the time the policy was effected, but would still be left without insurance cover through no fault of their own. There is no simple answer to this problem, except for the Principal to effect the insurance. In this event, the Contractor could be at risk if the Principal failed to disclose.

It may be necessary to amplify in the Supplementary Conditions the provisions for insurance set out in the General Conditions.

Liquidated Damages

Most, but not all, engineering contracts provide for the payment of *Liquidated Damages* by the Contractor in the event of failure to complete the work under the Contract by the agreed date. However, MF/1 General Conditions does not make any reference to Liquidated Damages. In this context, the term 'liquidated' means 'determined or apportioned by agreement'. The intention of the provision is to ensure the due performance of the contractual obligations undertaken by the Contractor and to agree in advance the amount of any damages in the event of a breach of the Contract, rather than leaving it to a court or arbitrator to make the assessment.

The assessment and imposition of Liquidated Damages is one of the most contentious issues encountered in the determination of a contract. Most disagreements can be attributed to the failure of either or both parties to understand the full implications of the provision. It is therefore important for the Engineer to have a clear understanding of the intent and operation of Liquidated Damages.

The Engineer must first appreciate the difference between a 'Penalty' and 'Liquidated Damages'. The basis for Liquidated Damages must be a genuine, agreed pre-estimate of damages; the essence of a Penalty is an amount paid '*in terrorem*' (as a threat) to the defaulting party.

It is of little importance which term is used, because in the event of a dispute a court or arbitrator will determine whether the payment is a Penalty or Liquidated Damages. It would be held to be a Penalty if the amount nominated is extravagant or unreasonable in comparison with the greatest loss that could be proved. Provided that it can be established that the amount of damages stipulated in the Contract is based on a genuine pre-estimate of damages made at the time the Contract was formed, it would most probably be held that it was in the nature of Liquidated Damages rather than a Penalty.

Most General Conditions require the Liquidated Damages to be nominated in the Annexure as a monetary amount for every day (or other nominated period) for the interval between the Date for Practical Completion and the Date of Practical Completion after due allowance has been made for authorized extensions of time.

If the Principal does not wish to nominate an amount for Liquidated Damages, but wishes to retain the right to general damages without a limit being imposed on those general damages, the clause(s) relating to Liquidated Damages should be deleted. It would be unwise to insert the word 'nil' for Liquidated Damages in the Annexure as by doing so the Principal may remove the right to recover damages at large.

In determining the amount of Liquidated Damages, the Engineer must make a realistic estimate and not arbitrarily guess a figure. The damages must be a fair estimate of the amount by which the Principal would be out of pocket as a result of the breach. Any assessment of damages could include, but not necessarily be limited to, the following costs:

- Interest payments on funds borrowed to finance the project
- Rental of premises by the Principal for storage or operations due to the unavailability of the Works

- Consequential damages or costs incurred by the Principal as a result of being unable to honour commitments due to the late completion of the Works
- Cost of hiring labour in anticipation of the Works being available at the due time

Some costs may be difficult to justify, and should not be taken into consideration, unless the Principal feels that a strong case for their inclusion can be made. These include:

- Loss of interest on the Principal's own funds
- Loss of profit or goodwill arising from the late completion of the Works

One way to establish the validity of an amount nominated for Liquidated Damages is for the Principal, before the Contract is signed, to disclose to and obtain the acknowledgement of the Contractor of the basis for the calculation of the damages. This would have two benefits:

- It would emphasize to the Contractor that the Principal intends to take a serious view of any delay in completion.
- In the event of a dispute over damages, while the quantum of the damages could be challenged, the basis for their assessment has been agreed.

Where Separable Portions of the Works have been specified, separate Liquidated Damages for each portion must be nominated.

The case for the imposition of Liquidated Damages can be substantially strengthened if the Contract provides for the payment of a Bonus where the Date of Practical Completion is earlier than the Date for Practical Completion. Whether or not to make this provision will depend upon the value the Principal places on early completion of the Works. The amount of Bonus should be calculated in a manner similar to that suggested for the Liquidated Damages, but it is not necessary for the two amounts to be the same.

In either case, it may be advisable to place an upper limit on the amount of Liquidated Damages or Bonus. The amount frequently adopted is 10 per cent of the Contract Sum.

Provisional and Prime Cost Sums

It is not surprising that engineers can have difficulty in appreciating the difference between Provisional Sums and Prime Cost (PC) Sums; the terms appear to have so far defied legal definition. Although the terms are widely used in contracts in the construction industry, legal cases concerning their use in connection with subcontracts have been unable to produce comprehensive and authentic definitions of their meaning.

However, it is generally accepted that *Provisional Sums* are monetary allowances for work, the nature of which can be defined but the extent of which is indeterminate; *Prime Cost Sums*, on the other hand, are monetary allowances for the purchase of items whose nature is determinable but whose precise form and price are uncertain. It is the dividing line between these two definitions which has proved difficult to determine.

Any clear difference which may have existed has now become indistinct. Although many General Conditions still use both terms (without defining their meaning), both the FIDIC Conditions of Contract and the SAA General Conditions now make no reference to Prime Cost Sums and adopt the single term 'Provisional Sums' to include all monetary sums, contingency allowances and prime cost sums. There are several points to watch when specifying these amounts; they mainly concern the manner in which they are administered.

The first point is that they are amounts included in the Contract Sum which are nominated by the Principal and not determined by the Contractor, and which are expended in whole or in part only as directed by the Principal (or the Superintendent). They are usually, but not necessarily, amounts to be paid to nominated or designated subcontractors for goods and services selected by the Principal.

The second point is that when these goods and services are provided by nominated or designated subcontractors, the Contractor is entitled to be reimbursed for any costs and charges associated with the expenditure of the sums. This is usually achieved by requiring tenderers to nominate in their tenders a percentage to be applied to the actual amount expended to cover the Contractor's profit and attendance.

The third point concerns determining the cost of the Contractor's labour associated with the work of nominated or designated subcontractors in relation to Provisional or Prime Cost Sums. For example, the Provisional (or Prime Cost) Sum may be for the supply of a particular item of equipment, the installation of which is to be undertaken by the Contractor under the Contract. When a Bill of Quantities is provided, the details of this work would be itemized by the Quantity Surveyor in the Bill and priced by the Contractor.

However, in a Lump Sum Contract, it will be necessary for the cost of this work to be included in the Lump Sum; it should be itemized and quoted either in a Schedule of Prices for Tendering or in a Schedule of Provisional Sums.

Finally, there is the question of Contingency Sums. A *Contingency Sum* is usually a Provisional Sum in the Contract, provided as a device to allow the Superintendent to authorize payment for minor variations arising from unforeseen items not covered in the Bill of Quantities, so that the Superintendent need not continually refer to the Principal for approval.

The provision of this Sum and the amount is usually determined by mutual agreement between the Principal and the Engineer at the time of preparing the Enquiry Documents. The question the Engineer will have to decide is whether to provide for a percentage for the Contractor's profit and attendance or to leave it to the Superintendent to obtain a firm quotation for the variation at the time. In most cases, the second option is usually preferred.

Schedule of Rates

A *Schedule of Rates* is any schedule showing a rate of payment for sections or items of work to be carried out under the Contract. The Schedule includes estimated quantities for each item or section and may also include provisional and lump sums. When the Contract is completed, the work carried out is measured and the Contractor receives payment for that amount of work at the appropriate schedule rate or price.

Where a Bill of Quantities forms part of the Contract, it is effectively a Schedule of Rates. However, there are two basic differences between a Bill of Quantities and a Schedule of Rates. The first is in the degree of detail used to describe the items of work and the second is in the manner of interpretation and application.

A Bill of Quantities is usually prepared by a professional Quantity Surveyor and describes almost every individual item of work. A Schedule of Rates is more often prepared by the Engineer or the designer and describes the work in more comprehensive packages. For example, in a Schedule of Rates, structural steelwork may be listed as a single item and the rate per tonne is required to cover supply, fabrication, delivery to site and erection. Alternatively, the work can be subdivided into items such as beams and columns, trusses and bracing and purlins and girts with separate rates required, one for supply, fabrication and delivery and the other for erection; or it can be broken down into smaller packages. The degree of detail is at the discretion of the Engineer. A Bill of Quantities, on the other hand, usually itemizes the steelwork in much greater detail.

The other difference is that in a Schedule of Rates it is the Contractor's responsibility to ensure that the rates quoted cover all the specified work under the Contract. In a Bill of Quantities, the Contractor can make a claim if there is an error or omission in the description in the Bill (but not for an error or omission in the rates inserted by the Contractor).

If a list of items and quantities is given in a schedule and the items are to cover the whole of the work under the Contract with no claims for omissions or errors allowed, then the document should be described as a Schedule of Rates. If claims for omitted items (as distinct from incorrect quantities) are permitted then the document should be described as a Bill of Quantities.

If the Contract includes a Schedule of Rates, it is important to define precisely how the quantities are to be measured. As this may differ from one of the standard methods used by quantity surveyors, it is necessary to prepare a Supplementary Condition describing how the quantities are to be measured.

It is advisable to state the limits of accuracy applicable to the quantities. This will determine whether or not either party may request a reassessment of the rates when final measured quantities are outside these limits. It is important that the clause makes it clear that:

- The items listed in the Schedule as submitted by the Contractor are deemed to cover the cost of the whole of the work under the Contract, including the services necessary for the execution of the work and the performance of all the Contractor's obligations under the Contract and no claims for alleged omitted items will be entertained.
- The omission of a price or rate for any item in the Schedule will be an acceptance by the Contractor that all costs applicable to that item are included elsewhere in the Schedule.
- The unit rates and prices quoted in the Schedule are deemed to include due allowance for variable overheads and profit.
- Any item for 'Preliminaries' is a fixed sum and is deemed to cover all fixed or non-variable costs and charges.

'Preliminaries' can be subdivided into two parts – 'Mobilization' and 'Demobilization' – the former covering costs associated with setting up the work and the latter with cleaning up and other costs at the end of the Contract.

Alternatively, the Contract can specify a percentage of 'Preliminaries' (say 60 per cent) to be included in the first progress payment and the balance in the final payment.

Schedule of Prices for Tendering

In Lump Sum Contracts it is sometimes useful to include a Schedule of Prices for Tendering among the forms to be completed and returned by tenderers. In form and layout it is similar to a Schedule of Rates, the principle difference being that the quantities are not remeasured and the rates are not used to determine the final amount due to the Contractor at the end of the work. Its prime function is to provide a basis for evaluating progress payments; it can also be of value when assessing and comparing tenders.

A useful device in contracts where a Bill of Quantities is issued with the Enquiry Documents, and is not to form part of the Contract, is to prepare and issue a Schedule of Prices for Tendering consisting of a schedule of lump sum amounts for each section or trade in the Bill – the total of such amounts being the Tender Sum. Tenderers should then be required to complete and submit with their tenders, without alteration, the Schedule of Prices for Tendering issued with the Enquiry Documents. The amount for each section or trade will then have to agree with the corresponding amount in the Priced Bill when it is submitted.

If a Schedule of Prices for Tendering is included in the Enquiry Documents, a clause in the Supplementary Conditions should state that the Schedule will form part of the Contract only to the extent necessary to evaluate progress payments and that the Contractor accepts that the Schedule submitted with the Contractor's tender covers the whole of the work under the Contract.

Separable Portions

The General Conditions usually makes provision for the situation where the Works are to be handed over to the Principal a stage at a time as each is completed in accordance with an agreed time schedule. During the course of the work, the Principal and the Contractor may agree on other portions of the Works to be treated similarly. Neither the Contractor nor the Principal (or the Superintendent) can unilaterally hand or take over any portion of the Works without the consent of the other party. To attempt to do so may result in a claim for additional costs or damages.

These stages are referred to as *Sections* (ICE Conditions of Contract and MF/1 General Conditions) or as *Separable Portions* (SAA General Conditions). The Annexure usually makes provision for the times for completion and Liquidated Damages applicable to each portion to be specified. The SAA General Conditions provides for separate Defects Liability Periods for each Separable Portion, although the ICE Conditions of Contract does not make any such provision. MF/1 General Conditions makes no specific reference to Separable Portions (Sections) in the Annexure or in the *Aide Mémoire* for the 'Special' Conditions.

Whichever General Conditions are adopted, the Engineer should check that if Separable Portions are to be included in the work then their extents must be clearly defined and the times for completion, Defects Liability Periods and Liquidated Damages for each portion be clearly specified either in the Annexure or in the Supplementary Condition.

Superintendent

Both the Principal and the Contractor will most probably be incorporated bodies. This means that they must each appoint a representative with the necessary authority to deal with day-to-day matters arising out of the Contract. Otherwise, each communication would need to be approved in a formally minuted Board decision. This is clearly impractical.

Matters of major importance will, of course, be dealt with by the governing body of each organization. The dividing line will have to be established by each organization when giving the authority to their respective representatives.

The Principal's representative is usually termed the 'Engineer' or the 'Superintendent'. For the reasons outlined in 'Terminology', at the beginning of this book, the term 'Superintendent' is used in this text.

The Superintendent is not a party to the Contract and can only act as the Principal's agent, whose main task is to ensure that the work under the Contract is being performed in accordance with the terms and conditions laid down in the Contract. As neither party to a contract can unilaterally change the terms and conditions of the contract, the Superintendent, as the Principal's representative, cannot change the terms and conditions of the Contract.

Although the Superintendent is not a party to the Contract, reference is made to the Superintendent in almost every clause in many General Conditions. At the same time, the accountability and obligations of the Superintendent are rarely adequately defined. Nevertheless, the duties and responsibilities of the Superintendent must be clearly and unambiguously stated in the Contract.

By tradition and by interpretation of the duties of the Superintendent as specified in many General Conditions, the Superintendent is expected to play a dual role:

● To administer the Contract as the agent of the Principal
● To act as a fair and impartial arbitrator in the event of a dispute between the Contractor and the Principal

In the first role, the Superintendent should act as an advocate for the Principal and protect the Principal's interests at all times. Nevertheless, the Superintendent should also protect the Contractor from unreasonable demands by the Principal.

In the second role, the position of the Superintendent may be invidious. A dispute between the Contractor and the Principal usually arises from a difference of opinion between the Contractor and the Superintendent. The Superintendent is then required to adjudicate on a dispute in which the

Superintendent has a vested interest. These two roles can be seen, particularly by the Contractor, to be mutually incompatible, whether the Superintendent is an employee of the Principal or of an independent Consulting Engineer. This conflict of interest may arise despite the personal integrity of the Superintendent.

Many General Conditions give the Superintendent wide powers to have a direction or instruction enforced, leaving the Contractor to substantiate claims for extra costs, extensions of time, or damages arising from complying with those directions or instructions. The anomaly was recognized by the SAA when redrafting their General Conditions (AS 2124–1986), which now quite clearly indicates that the Superintendent is primarily an agent of the Principal. Under these General Conditions it is the responsibility of the Principal to ensure that at all times there is a Superintendent appointed and that the Superintendent:

- Acts honestly and fairly
- Acts within the times prescribed in the Contract
- Arrives at a reasonable measure or value of work, quantities, and time

In other words, it is the responsibility of the Principal to ensure that the duties of the Superintendent are carried out competently. This means that in the event of a dispute over a direction or ruling by the Superintendent, unless it can be shown that the Superintendent has acted in tort or with criminal intent, any legal action by the Contractor must be directed at the Principal and not at the Superintendent. This has important implications for a consulting engineering firm appointed by the Principal to provide the Superintendent. In such a situation, however, the Principal may have grounds for a case for negligence against the Consulting Engineer under the terms of any agreement or arrangement between the Principal and the Consulting Engineer.

This arrangement clearly defines the responsibilities of the Superintendent and overcomes what many contractors see as an unsatisfactory situation. It is a more positive approach than the ambivalent procedure adopted by the ICE Conditions of Contract and the MF/1 General Conditions, which require that those duties for which the Superintendent (Engineer) is required to obtain the approval of the Principal before performing them should be listed in the Contract.

For practical reasons, the Superintendent must be named as an individual, not as an incorporated body. This has particular implications where the Superintendent is an employee of another organization, such as a consulting engineering firm. The Conditions of Contract usually require the Superintendent to perform a number of duties – give directions, issue certificates, authorize variations, evaluate entitlements to payment and the like – duties which for practical reasons must be performed by an individual.

To avoid the necessity for every decision by the Superintendent to be a minuted resolution by the Partnership or the Board, the Superintendent must be formally authorized by the firm to act on its behalf. For this reason, the Superintendent is normally a partner, director, or senior executive of the consulting engineering firm. Furthermore, the ICE General Conditions (Sixth Edition) requires the Superintendent (Engineer) to be a Chartered Engineer. While this may be desirable in most cases, there may be situations where a Superintendent with other qualifications may be equally suitable.

When the Superintendent is an employee of the Principal, the Superintendent can be identified by name or by title, such as 'The Chief Engineer of [the Principal]'. Alternatively, the Superintendent can be 'The person named from time to time by [the Principal]'. It will then be the responsibility of the Principal to advise the Contractor who is to be the Superintendent at the appropriate time.

Many consulting engineering firms are incorporated, either as registered partnerships or as proprietary companies. The Superintendent can then be identified as 'The person named from time to time by [the consulting engineering firm]'. It will then be the responsibility of the consulting engineering firm to advise the Contractor of the name of the Superintendent; where the Consulting Engineer is a sole practitioner, the problem does not arise.

The existence of a *Contractor's Representative* is rarely acknowledged in General Conditions. Nevertheless, the Contract should require the Contractor to have a representative at all times on the Site or where work under the Contract is being carried out. Any direction given by the Superintendent to the Contractor's Representative should be deemed to have been a direction given to the Contractor under the terms of the Contract.

Paradoxically, many General Conditions specifically define the responsibilities of the *Superintendent's Representative*. This person is usually one appointed to carry out specific duties on behalf of the Superintendent and is intended to refer to individuals such as Resident Engineers, Clerks of Works and Inspectors.

When considering the Conditions of Contract, the Engineer should be aware of the points outlined above and ensure that where the General Conditions do not adequately cover the requirements of the Contract in regard to the duties and responsibilities of the respective representatives of the Principal and the Contractor, an appropriate Supplementary Condition should be drafted.

ELEVEN

THE SPECIFICATION AND THE DRAWINGS

11.1 DRAFTING THE SPECIFICATION

The Specification Writer

The person assigned to write the Specification should be one who has a complete understanding of the work to be carried out under the Contract. It is assumed that the specification writer will be a professionally qualified engineer with the ability to write clearly and to express the requirements in a competent manner so that they can easily be understood by those whose job it is to carry out the work.

In many cases the Engineer will be the one to write the Specification, but in a large project, particularly one involving diverse disciplines, all or part of the Specification may need to be written by specialists in particular fields or disciplines. Nevertheless, the overall responsibility for the Specification must remain with one person – the Engineer.

Writing the Specification cannot start too early. Where the Principal is responsible for the design, the specification writer should form part of the design team at the earliest possible time. An early start to writing the Specification will allow better coordination and will ensure that the Drawings and the Specification are both completed on time.

It is important for the design engineer and the specification writer to decide at an early stage what is to be shown on the Drawings and what is to be described in the Specification. An alert specification writer can be of great help to the design engineer by preventing unnecessary information being added to a drawing which only has to be removed later. It has been estimated that the work hours involved in drafting a design are from 10 to 20 times the time required for writing the corresponding Specification. This indicates that there is a definite potential for saving considerable time and therefore cost by careful coordination of the Drawings and the Specification.

Presentation and Style

As a general rule, the end result should be specified rather than the method of achieving it. Unless what is required is outside the normal Contractor's experience and expertise, the Specification should not direct how the job should be done. That is the Contractor's responsibility and the Engineer should not try to tell the Contractor 'how to do it'.

There is also danger in specifying both the means and the end result. If the specified means are found to be inappropriate, the Contractor would have grounds for claiming extra payment for having to try other methods to achieve the required end result.

'Bad experience' clauses are the obverse of 'how to do it' clauses and can be even more objectionable. They are clauses the specification writer has included in an effort to overcome difficulties experienced in an earlier project. Frequently these difficulties arose from personality clashes and their inclusion will detract from the Specification. Before considering the use of such a clause, the Engineer should ascertain the background to the proposed provision and make sure that it is a genuine improvement. Unless it is really needed, its incorporation should be avoided.

As far as possible, workmanship should be specified objectively in terms of the required result such as dimensions, tolerances, fit, finish, colour and the like.

Materials, on the other hand, should be specified by reference to national or corporate standards wherever possible. A standard should never be specified before being examined by the Engineer to determine if it is relevant. Some standards give alternatives or a range of options and these must be qualified if the reference is to be valid. There are three methods of specifying products, manufactured items and assemblies. They are:

- By direct specification
- By prescriptive specification
- By performance specification

Direct specification, in which a brand name together with the catalogue number and the name of the manufacturer or supplier is specified, is the simplest and the most effective method where the required item can be clearly identified. If a particular unique product is required, the direct specification method is the only practicable way.

Prescriptive specification requires the critical characteristics of the item to be set out as objectively as possible (e.g. materials, dimensions, mass, strength, finish, colour, and other physical requirements). This method is appropriate when there is a range of generically similar items available, any one of which would be acceptable.

In the above two methods, the Engineer, by implication, has accepted responsibility for the satisfactory performance of the specified product. The responsibility of the Contractor is only to ensure that the product supplied is in accordance with the specified requirements and is properly installed.

The remaining option is to use the performance specification method wherein are specified the critical characteristics which the item will be required to exhibit when delivered or installed, whichever the case may be. It is the Contractor's responsibility to achieve the performance specified by whatever means the Contractor considers appropriate. This method is only suitable where the performance can be defined objectively, and it can be measured and tested. It is important to remember that laboratory testing may not relate to performance on the job and the cost of testing, particularly on-site testing, can be quite high. It should also be realized that the Contractor's method of achieving the required performance, while contractually watertight, may not be quite what the Engineer wanted. This method is best suited to where safety standards and the like are laid down in regulations and codes which allow the designer to use any one of a number of design solutions to meet the required standard.

The Specification text comprises direct instructions to the Contractor. There are two forms which can be used to express these instructions. The form usually adopted in engineering specifications is a direct instruction in the third person singular: 'The Contractor shall do so and so. . .'. Others, particularly architects, on the other hand, seem to prefer to adopt the imperative ('you' understood), since the Specification is addressed to the Contractor: '[You] Do so and so . . .'.

However, if the Specification refers to actions to be performed by persons other than the Contractor, (e.g. by the Principal or the Engineer), then it must say so and the first person singular form must be used for that particular direction. Although the imperative form saves words and space and is claimed to convey the meaning more forcefully, the need to use the third person singular form when referring to persons other than the Contractor can lead to a confusing mixture of styles. Note that most standard General Conditions use the third person singular form.

Common Faults in Specifications

Accuracy and clarity are most important in writing the Specification since faulty specifications are a frequent source of dispute. Because lawyers are more familiar with words, it is the Specification rather than the Drawings which will receive their closest attention. Common faults found in specifications include:

- Inadequate coordination with other documents
- Redundancy
- Misplaced insertions
- Duplication
- Ignored options in referenced standards
- Ambiguity
- Out-of-date, misquoted, contradictions to or ignored referenced standards
- Failure to keep abreast of technical changes
- Inadequate definition of responsibilties
- Omissions
- Gratuitous instructions to the Contractor
- Itemizing
- Impractical guarantees

Most pitfalls which specification writers fall into are either 'hardy perennials' or arise from unfamiliarity with the system. With regard to the 'hardy perennials', the following comments may help the specification writer to recognize them:

Inadequate coordination can be overcome only by a complete familiarity with all the Enquiry Documents.

Redundancy can come in many forms. This usually arises when the specification writer is using a Master Specification or when copying from a previous specification. Leaving in unwanted references to national or other standards, or clauses describing non-existent items, although not serious, can be puzzling and unfair to the Contractor. The Contractor may develop an indifferent attitude to the Specification if too many such situations arise.

Misplaced insertions, usually afterthoughts, put all together at the end of the section are not only irritating to the reader but makes duplication more likely. The material should be sorted so that like topics are dealt with together. This should not present a problem with modern word-processing facilities.

Duplication by an insertion covering ground already dealt with elsewhere can be serious, particularly as the new insert will invariably have significant differences in wording.

Options, particularly those arising from the use of national or corporate standards, must be carefully selected and unwanted items deleted.

Ambiguity can only be dealt with by careful use of the English language, relying on clear, concise and simple expressions.

References to national or corporate Standards which are out of date, misquoted, contradicted or ignored can have serious consequences. The legal attitude in cases of alleged professional negligence is to ask whether a normally proficient professional person would have done the same under similar conditions. The Engineer would have a case to answer if it could be shown that technical information available to peers was ignored.

Work 'by others' frequently ends up as 'by nobody'. It is imperative to define clearly the extent and limits of the work to be done by the Contractor. Only work already undertaken can be safely stated to be 'by others'.

Omissions can be avoided by a complete familiarity of the work under the Contract and a careful review of the Specification and Drawings before going to print.

Gratuitous instructions to the Contractor should be avoided at all costs. As already pointed out, it is the Contractor's right and function to carry out the work as the Contractor thinks fit. If the Specification trespasses on the 'Contractor's right and function', the Principal would also assume part of the responsibility which would normally belong solely to the Contractor.

Itemizing a list of things or acts that are required implies that other things and acts not mentioned in the list are not required. There is a time-honoured principle of law which states that '*Expressio unius est exclusio alterius*'. ('The express mention of one thing implies the exclusion of another'.) On the other hand, a general statement that is supposed to include everything may be too broad and cumbersome and may be subject to varying interpretation. The specification writer is called upon to use care and discretion in each particular case.

Guarantees which are impractically stringent are frequently called for and (not surprisingly) never received. Required guarantees must be realistic and, once asked for, must be obtained. If a problem arose with an item for which the Specification required a guarantee which the Superintendent failed to obtain then the Superintendent could be accused of professional negligence.

Some Important Considerations

Chapter 13 - 'Writing Effective English' – sets out recommendations for writing and editing technical documents generally. However, there are some points to be emphasized which have particular relevance to the Specification and these are briefly discussed in the following:

- Use normal everyday language but avoid colloquialisms. Be as precise as possible using no more words than are necessary to convey the meaning. Do not attempt to use 'legalese' language. Plain, direct language helps to avoid misunderstanding and disputes.
- Use only those technical terms which are current and well understood in the engineering industry. Whenever possible adopt the terminology used in the relevant national standards. Consistency is most important – the same term should be used for the same thing throughout. If there are two or more ways to identify an item or describe a procedure, the most appropriate one should be selected and consistently used. Abbreviations and acronyms should not be used unless they are universally accepted and used in the industry (e.g. BSI, PVC).
- Avoid using expressions such as 'take *special* care to . . .' or 'comply *strictly* with . . .'. The words in italic can be taken to mean that some specification requirements are more or less stringent than others. This can be dangerous.
- Avoid cross-references as much as possible and if they are unavoidable *never* cross-reference by clause or page numbers. Inevitable last-minute changes or insertions may involve renumbering clauses and pages and this can result in an incorrect cross-reference. The '*expressio unius est exclusio alterius*' principle, referred to earlier, may also be relevant here. A cross-reference 'as specified in Clause X' has been held by courts to mean that *only* Clause X has relevance. This may exclude vital information specified in another Part or Clause. The only safe way is either to cross-reference using 'as specified elsewhere herein' and leave the reader to find out where 'elsewhere herein' is to be found, or else, more helpfully to cross-refer to the title of the clause or part, with the added words 'and as specified elsewhere herein'.
- Government Acts and Regulations which apply to the Contract have precedence over whatever the Contract may say. This also applies to regulations promulgated under such Acts. Most standard General Conditions cover this point and it is unnecessary and undesirable to repeat the injunction in the Specification. It is the responsibility of the designer and the specification writer to ensure that the design, the Specification and the Drawings conform to the relevant Acts and Regulations.
- Wherever applicable, materials and workmanship should conform with relevant national and corporate standards. Not all such standards are necessarily relevant and a 'blanket' reference to the many potentially applicable standards is unsatisfactory and possibly dangerous. The criteria

for relevance to be applied to standards or codes are that they should be:
–Identifiable (published)
–Readily available
–Up to date
–Applicable to the circumstances
–Recognized, understood and used in the particular section of the industry.
Relevant national standards may include standards from other countries. Each listed standard should be closely checked for suitability. The text of a listed standard should not be repeated or paraphrased. The listed standard becomes part of the Specification by reference.

Checking the Specification

When each job specification has been written, it must be checked carefully to detect possible discrepancies, deficiencies and errors. In doing so, the Engineer should pay close attention to the following:

1. Does the Scope of the Work clearly define the extent and limits of the work described in the Specification?
2. Are the references to the relevant Drawings complete and accurate?
3. Are all the technical requirements clearly covered?
4. Do the requirements stated comply with all statutory rules and regulations?
5. Are all referenced standards correctly identified?
6. Is there any conflict or overlap with other job specifications, particularly those prepared for other disciplines?
7. Does the Specification comply with the overall criteria for the project?
8. If applicable, do the Schedule of Rates and Schedule of Prices for Tendering completely cover the work under the Contract?
9. Is the quality of presentation and the completeness and clarity of the text satisfactory?

11.2 REFERENCE AND SOURCE DOCUMENTS

The Engineer attempting to write a specification completely from first principles, without the assistance of reference or source documents, would be faced with a monumental task.

Fortunately, there is a wide range of reliable reference documents available which the Engineer can draw upon and which greatly simplify the task. These may be broadly classified into two groups:

• Standard Specifications
• Master Specifications

Standard Specifications

Standard Specifications themselves can be subdivided further into three types:

- National and International
- Corporate
- Manufacturer's

National and International Standard Specifications These are prepared and issued by nationally based and technically competent institutions, societies and associations. Some of these bodies exist solely for this purpose (e.g. the British Standards Institution) while others are industry-based and prepare and issue Standards as only part of their activities and only in the field of their particular industry (e.g. the American Concrete Institute).

The objective is to specify acceptable quality levels for goods and services, establish basic safety provisions and to standardize dimensions and tolerances so as to facilitate the interchangeability of components and encourage the reduction of unnecessary and uneconomical variety.

Following the Second World War and the formation of the United Nations, the need for internationally recognized standard specifications became apparent. For this purpose, a number of international bodies were established in the engineering field, the principal ones being the International Standards Organization (ISO) and the International Electrotechnical Commission (IEC). These two bodies are worldwide federations of some ninety national bodies and represent the consolidated views and interests of industry, government, labour and individual consumers. The scope of ISO covers standardization in all fields of engineering except electrical and electronic engineering, which have become the responsibility of IEC.

ISO coordinates the exchange of information on national and international standards, technical regulations and other standard-type documents through an information network linking most of the major national standards organizations. It is not uncommon for national standard organizations to adopt international standards either in identical forms with only minor editorial changes or as versions equivalent in technical content but with different presentation.

While national standards are naturally published in the language of the country concerned, ISO standards are usually published in separate English and French editions although certain standards, especially in the field of terminology, are published in bilingual or trilingual editions (English, French and Russian). On the other hand, IEC publications are usually bilingual with English and French texts on facing pages, with some standards published in English only.

Table 11.1 International Standards Organizations

International Standards Organization	ISO
International Electrotechnical Commission	IEC
International Special Committee on Radio Interference	CISPR
International Commission on Illumination	CIE
European Committee for Standardization Harmonization Document	CEN HD
European Committee for Electrotechnical Standardization Harmonization Document	CENELEC HD
International Commission on Rules for the Approval of Electrical Equipment	CEE
European Committee for Iron and Steel Standardization	EURONORM

As a general rule, Standard Specifications deal with specific materials and equipment, while Codes of Practice cover design, fabrication and installation or construction of elements incorporating materials and equipment specified in the relevant Standard Specifications.

Originally, Standard Specifications and Codes of Practice were independently identified as separate groups of documents. Inevitably, with the increasing complexity of modern manufacturing and construction techniques, overlaps occurred and the distinction became blurred. Today, most are identified generally as *National Standards* or *International Standards*.

These Standards are published documents freely available for purchase. They are periodically revised in accordance with latest thinking and new technologies.

Individual National, and some International, Standards may be legally recognized by government regulation and, where public interest and safety are involved, become mandatory.

The major organizations involved in the preparation of recognized Standards and Codes, with their respective abbreviations, are given in Tables 11.1, 11.2 and 11.3.

The use of International and National Standards When drafting the Project Specification, the Engineer should make as much use as possible of the many International and National Standards available. In most cases, the first choice is to use the National Standards applicable to the country where the work is to be undertaken. Where that country does not have a national standards organization, consideration should be given to referring to the appropriate International Standards.

These Standards should never be incorporated as complete and separate 'Parts' of a project specification. They are always specified in the text as

Table 11.2 National Standards Organizations

Australia	Standards Association of Australia	
	(Standards Australia)	SAA
Belgium	Institut belge de normalisation	IBN
Canada	Standards Council of Canada	SCC
Denmark	Dansk Standardiseringraad	DS
France	Association française de normalisation	AFNOR
Germany	Deutches Institut für Normung	DIN
Italy	Ente Nazionale Italiano di Unificazion	UNI
Japan	Japanese Industrial Standards Committee	JISC
New Zealand	Standards Association of New Zealand	SANZ
UK	British Standards Institution	BSI
USA	American National Standards Institution	ANSI

reference documents applying to a particular item or topic. Accordingly, it may not be necessary, or even advisable, to include a copy of an applicable Standard in the Specification.

When used with care and discretion, International and National Standards can play an important part in project specification and can simplify the task of the specification writer. However, there are a number of important points to observe:

1. Each Standard referenced must be clearly identified by its title, its reference number and the name of the issuing body. If alternative Standards are acceptable, then they must also be identified in the same manner.
2. The extent to which a particular item of material, equipment or work is to be covered by the referenced Standard must be clearly defined.

Table 11.3 Industry Standards Associations

American Chemical Society	ACS
American Concrete Institute	ACI
American Gas Association	AGA
American Institute of Steel Construction	AISC
American Petroleum Institute	API
American Society of Heating, Refrigeration	
and Air Conditioning Engineers	ASHRAE
American Society of Mechanical Engineers	ASME
American Water Works Assocation	AWWA
American Welding Society	AWS
Institute of Petroleum (UK)	IP
Society of Automotive Engineers	SAE
National Electrical Manufacturers Association	NEMA

3. The acceptability of the referenced Standard to any statutory authority having jurisdiction over the work must be verified. This is particularly important if the country of origin of the material or equipment differs from the country where it is to be finally used.
4. Many Standards provide for alternatives or options. The particular alternative or option required must be clearly specified.
5. If a Standard is to be used, the whole document must be referenced. Prescribing only part of a Standard as being applicable, or quoting extracts or paraphrasing sections, must not be attempted.
6. The Standards themselves must not be amended. If any part of a Standard is unsuitable, it should not be used at all and other more suitable references sought.
7. The Engineer should never prescribe a Standard without completely understanding its provisions.

Corporate Standard Specifications (referred to as *Corporate Standards*) These are specifications prepared for their own use by large engineering corporations – government, semi-government and private. They have the same objective as International and National Standards, except that they specifically define the minimum requirements acceptable to the individual organization rather than to the community or to industry generally.

For example, a Highway Department may have standard specifications for such items as road signs, crash barriers and line marking; an oil company may have standard specifications for pumps, pressure vessels and pipework. These standards directly relate to the activities and requirements of the particular organization.

Corporate Standards are readily available to engineers working within the organization, but for outside parties seeking to make use of them prior approval from the particular organization may need to be obtained.

In most cases, Corporate Standards are pre-printed documents intended for use without amendment. However, a Corporate Standard may be accompanied by a Data Schedule in which the Engineer inserts data appropriate to the particular item being specified.

Corporate Standards may not be as widely known as National Standards, although they may be familiar to engineers and contractors who have previously been involved with work for that corporation. For this reason it is usually advisable to include in the Specification a copy of each Corporate Standard referenced (see 'Master Specifications').

The use of Corporate Standards The points to be watched when using Corporate Standards are basically the same as those recommended for National Standards. However, particular organizations will usually have definite rules to be followed by the specification writer when using one of their specifications.

Manufacturer's Standard Specifications (referred to as *Manufacturer's Standards*) These are prepared by manufacturers or suppliers of materials, plant or equipment and relate specifically to their own products. In most cases they are in the form of printed sales brochures listing the basic features of each item and identified by trade name or reference number.

The use of Manufacturer's Standards Manufacturer's Standards are rarely used in direct project specification, except where the Engineer has determined that a specified item from a particular manufacturer is required or where the Engineer is not able to produce a satisfactory standard or job specification for the component. Their most common use is where they are incorporated in Tender Documents in answer to a request in the Enquiry Documents for information on a material or component offered. If they are referenced, then the Engineer must carefully consider the manner in which they are used and the possible ramifications.

Master Specifications

With the ready availability of electronic word-processing systems, many engineering organizations have prepared *Master Specifications* (sometimes referred to as *Guideline Specifications*) for their own use.

Master Specifications are source documents for standard specifications. They are normally confined to Corporate Standards, although commercial versions such as the Australian Building Industry Specifications (ABIS) and the Canadian National Master Specifications (CNMS) have recently come onto the market. These have become widely accepted by industry, but at the time of writing they appear to be confined mainly to architectural and engineering work for buildings.

Master Specifications usually comprise a collection of standard clauses, often with different options, from which the Engineer can select, copy and modify, if necessary, to compile the specification for a particular item or work. Master Specifications can cover a wide range of materials, components and work to meet the requirements of the particular organization, and most have been refined by experience over a number of years. The principal difference between pre-printed Corporate Standards and Master Specifications is that Master Specifications have been compiled and stored electronically on disk or tape, and kept up to date, so that they can be copied and modified to suit the requirements for the project in hand.

Master Specifications are never issued as they stand. They are always copied and the copy, when amended or completed as required, becomes part of the project specification.

In some cases Corporate Standards, particularly those requiring the insertion of data for their completion or to be accompanied by a Data Schedule, are retained electronically, (with the appropriate draft data schedule) as Master Specifications.

The use of Master Specifications When they are available, the Engineer should make full use of Master Specifications as base source documents. They will overcome many of the initial problems encountered by the specification writer. They will also provide much surer guidelines than will making use of a previously written specification for a similar project, which may contain matter which is irrelevant to or inconsistent with the current project. There are many other advantages in the use of Master Specifications:

- There is a major saving in time, because clauses do not have to be completely redrafted for each new job.
- The time required for checking and correcting typographical and other errors is substantially reduced.
- The requirements are presented in a concise and uniform manner.
- There is less likelihood of important points being overlooked, omitted or duplicated.

The procedure for using a Master Specification to compile a 'part' for an individual project specification will naturally depend upon the program and setup for the Master Specification. The organization providing the Master Specification will have specific instructions for its use.

It should be noted that once a Master Specification has been copied and amended it becomes a specification in its own right and is no longer a Master Specification.

11.3 THE SPECIFICATION FORMAT

Before commencing the task of actually writing the Specification, consideration must be given to the format. Format, in this context, means the arrangement of the provisions of the Specification.

Every specification is unique. It is written to define the requirements for the work for a particular project and is, in effect, a schedule of instructions to the Contractor.

No two Contracts are completely identical. Even if a Contract is for a repeat order for a single item of equipment, it will be different. The difference may be only a matter of a new identifying number or delivery date. But it will not be exactly the same. There may be other differences and if the Engineer is tempted to copy a specification written for a previous contract, it must be thoroughly checked to ensure that it does apply to the work in hand.

It is not practicable, or even possible, to lay down a standard format for every specification. Contracts can vary in size and complexity from the supply of a single piece of equipment to the design and construction of a major project, possibly comprising a number of individual facilities. The work under the Contract can comprise design only, construction to a design provided by the Principal or construction to a design provided by the Contractor. In a major project, it is quite possible for the work to comprise a combination of these services.

The Specification should be written as a head contract document. It should be addressed to the Contractor alone and never to the subcontractors. It is the Contractor's business and responsibility to decide how instructions are passed on to the subcontractors or suppliers. It is not the function of the Principal, by means of the Specification, to direct how the Contractor's business should be conducted, but this does not prevent the arrangement of the Specification being in a format designed to make the task of administration easier for both the Principal and the Contractor.

The Specification is a reference text for the work. The text should, therefore, be separated into 'Parts' or 'Sections' for easy reference. How this is done is entirely at the discretion of the Engineer, but it is recommended that the format should conform with the following outline:

Part A   Extent of the Work and General Description
Part B   General Requirements
Part C   Particular Requirements

Recommendations for the preparation of the individual Parts follow.

Part A – Extent of the Work and General Description

The requirement that the Contractor shall execute and complete the work under the Contract is usually covered in a clause in the Conditions of Contract. The documents deemed to form and be read and construed as part of the Contract are then listed or referred to in the Agreement.

So that there is no doubt as to what the Contractor has to do, there should be a clear and concise statement in the Specification under the above or a similar title describing in detail the extent of the work under the Contract. This statement should include particulars relating to the following:

- The type of contract classified by method of payment and the technical and administrative responsibilities of the Contractor
- A detailed description of the nature and extent of the work under the Contract
- For contracts involving installation, erection and construction, the location of the Works and a description of the Site
- A clear definition of any interfaces between the Contractor's work and any work which may be carried out by others
- Details of materials and/or services to be supplied by the Principal either directly or under another contract
- Any unusual features or requirements under the Contract

The classification of the type of Contract is outlined in Sec. 2.3 – 'Types of Contracts'.

Accepted meanings In defining the extent of the work, the use and accepted meanings of the following terms should be taken into consideration:

Design A description of the types of design likely to be encountered in an engineering contract is outlined in Sec. 1.2. – 'The Development of the Project Plan'.

Documentation The preparation of the documents required for tendering and contract purposes. As such, it is usually the responsibility of the Principal. The Contractor is, of course, responsible for ensuring that subcontracts are properly documented.

Fabrication The manufacture of plant, equipment and elements or components required for later use in the work. Frequently this work is undertaken off-site in a workshop or factory, frequently by a subcontractor, as part of a larger project.

Handling and delivery The delivery to the Site, or to a place nominated in the Contract, of work manufactured or fabricated elsewhere. The need to specify this activity correctly is often either overlooked or inadequately covered. This is particularly important where work is carried out elsewhere under another contract. It is essential to nominate clearly who is to be responsible for the method of handling, the means of transport, the point of delivery and, most importantly, at what point the deliverer's responsibility ends. The responsibility for unloading, handling, storing and insurance of the delivery and for the payment of statutory charges must be clearly defined in the Specification.

Installation, erection, construction Although these three terms may be considered to be synonymous, engineering convention has ascribed to them specific implications.

Installation is taken to refer to the setting up of prefabricated plant or equipment (including a complete system) in a building or a structure or on a previously prepared site. It usually refers to mechanical or electrical equipment and can involve a single item such as a pump or a motor or a combination of elements such as a complete air conditioning system.

Erection, on the other hand, is used to refer to the assembly on-site of a structure comprising a number of prefabricated elements such as the structural steel framework for a building or a large piece of equipment such as a crane or a loader.

Construction implies a more widespread activity and can incorporate both installation and erection. A complete building, a power station, or a dam is 'constructed'.

Procurement Obtaining goods and services required for the work. This is normally the responsibility of the Contractor as part of the work under the Contract, and there are three activities comprised under this term – purchasing, expediting and inspection.

Purchasing is the location of sources of supply, the obtaining of prices and the placing of purchase orders for the required quantities of materials, plant and equipment, consumables, services and the like at confirmed prices compatible with the specified requirements for quantity, quality, delivery, reliability of supply and other requirements.

Expediting comprises the monitoring of the progress of the supply of all goods and services covered by purchase orders to ensure that the specified delivery times will be met.

Inspection is the examination of the materials used and the standards and procedures adopted in the manufacture and fabrication of goods covered by the purchase orders. It includes a review of the work in progress, so that the finished products will comply with the specified requirements.

Supervision This is undertaken by both the Contractor and the Principal (or by the Superintendent on behalf of the Principal) for the purpose of ensuring that the work is being carried out in accordance with the provisions of the Contract. Supervision by or on behalf of the Principal can be carried out at two levels. The first level involves periodic inspection of the work and is usually carried out by the in-house staff of the Principal or by a Consulting Engineer engaged by the Principal.

The second level includes continuous and detailed inspection and is provided by a resident engineer, a clerk of works or an appropriately qualified inspector who is employed by or on behalf of the Principal.

Commissioning When the installation or erection of a piece of equipment is completed, it has to be 'commissioned'. That is, it has to be operated and tested to ensure compliance with the requirements of the Contract. This work is usually, but not always, carried out by the Contractor under supervision by the Principal or Owner. In some cases, the Principal or, possibly, the Owner may prefer to undertake the task. The responsibility for commissioning the work must be clearly specified.

Maintenance This must not be confused with making-good defects revealed before final acceptance of the Works. The liability for making-good defects for a nominated period after practical completion or until the completion of a nominated activity, or until certain specified conditions are met, must be clearly specified in the Contract. The Contractor is not normally required to make good *wear and tear* during the defects liability period unless this is specifically required. The term 'wear and tear' means the anticipated wearing of parts and the use of consumable items during the normal working of the equipment. Sometimes the Principal requires the Contractor to undertake, for a specified period, the replacement of parts or consumables covered by normal wear and tear. This is 'maintenance'.

Manuals and training Where the Contract provides for design by the Contractor, particularly where the supply of mechanical or electrical equipment is involved, the Contractor may be required to supply Operating and Maintenance Manuals and possibly to provide initial training of the personnel who will operate the completed plant on behalf of the Principal or Owner.

Part B – General Requirements

As the title implies, this part of the Specification provides general information and directions relating to the work under the Contract, both on-Site and off-Site. As pointed out in Sec. 8.1 – 'Location of Subject Matter' – the clauses in this part can be:

● Secondary statements supplementing primary statements in the Conditions of Contract (General Conditions and Supplementary Conditions).
● Primary statements relating to the performance of the work generally.
● Primary statements supplemented by secondary statements in two or more sections of the Detailed Requirements part of the Specification. (This is usually done to avoid unnecessary repetition of material in each section.)

In Table 11.4 (pages 192–193), the General Requirements clauses have been grouped under three headings:

- Clauses applicable to contracts generally
- Clauses applicable to contracts involving design by the Contractor
- Clauses applicable to contracts involving installation, erection or construction

This schedule can be used as a Check List when preparing this part of the Specification.

Part C – Particular Requirements

This part of the Specification is where the detailed technical requirements for the work are prescribed. The manner in which the material is arranged and presented will depend largely upon the type of contract and the nature of the work to be done.

It is extremely difficult to lay down firm guidelines to be followed in every instance. The Engineer will have to exercise skill and judgment, based on experience, on how best to set out the requirements in the most logical and systematic manner. It is of overriding importance to ensure that the provisions are easy to find and clearly expressed so as to be readily understood.

The most common arrangement is for the Specification to be broken up into one or more *Job Specifications* each of which defines the requirements for a particular activity or element specified under the Contract. The job specifications are then ordered in a logical sequence.

An alternative arrangement is to divide the work into sections, each representing a stage of manufacture or construction. These sections are then presented in chronological order. Which method to use will depend upon the nature of the work under the Contract. In both methods, the individual clauses in each job specification should be arranged in such a manner as to indicate the general flow of the work.

In preparing the job specifications there are three matters to be considered:

- The number of job specifications required and the scope of work covered by each
- The arrangement of the individual clauses within each Job Specification
- The order in which the job specifications are presented

The following configurations based on the first arrangement are provided as examples of common practice and may be used as guidelines. They may not be suitable for some contracts.

Civil and structural engineering work For contracts involving principally civil and structural work, such as required in buildings, bridges and similar structures, each job specification usually covers the work associated with an individual trade or skill – demolition, excavation, concretework, structural steelwork and the like.

A practical way of ordering the job specifications in a logical sequence is to present them in the order in which they are set out in whichever method is adopted for measuring quantities and preparing schedules.

There are National Standards available which set out the principles and rules for preparing schedules of quantities for such work. They can be used as a guide when deciding how the work is to be broken up into job specifications and the order in which the job specifications are to be presented. If a Bill of Quantities accompanies the Enquiry Documents, the job specification should correspond with the classification and order in which the Bill has been prepared.

The following is a suggested manner in which civil and structural engineering work can be broken up into individual job specifications and the order in which they can be presented:

Demolition
Earthworks
Tunnels and Shafts
Dredging
Piling and Caissons
Roads and Paving
Railway Trackwork
Concretework
Brickwork and Blockwork
Structural Steelwork
Miscellaneous Metalwork
Carpentry, Joinery and Ironmongery
Roofing, Roof Sheeting and Wall Cladding
Sheet Metalwork
Sanitary Plumbing and Piped Services
Water Mains
Stormwater Drainage
Electrical Installation
Heating, Ventilating and Air Conditioning
Plastering
Glazing
Painting

Table 11.4 Schedule of clauses for general requirements

Clauses Applicable to Contracts Generally

General Requirements	– Items and Services provided by Others
Statutory Requirements	– Government Acts and Regulations
	– Industrial and Site Agreements
Drawings	– Schedule of Drawings
	Contract Drawings
	Reference Drawings
	– Work-as-Executed Drawings
	– Submittal and Approval of Drawings
Materials, Plant, and Equipment	– Function in Relation to Other Plant
	– Terminal Points of Supply
	– Commissioning and Starting Up
	– Approval of Substitutions
	– General Requirements for Testing
	– Test Certificates and Approvals
	– Warranties and Guarantees (General)
	– Delivery of Materials and Equipment
Progress of the Work	– Programming and Scheduling
	– Reporting Progress
	– Maintenance of Records

Additional Clauses – Contracts Involving Design by Contractor

General Design Criteria	– Function of the Plant
	– Design and Performance Parameters
	Essential features
	Desirable features
	Approved materials
	Fabrication and construction
	Fire resistance and safety
	– Properties of Materials Handled and Stored
	Chemical and Physical Properties
	Laboratory and Test Data
	– Design Methods
	– Load and Service Requirements
	Design loads
	Operating conditions
	Service factors
	Efficiency requirements
	– Energy Sources and Fuels
	– Corrosion Prevention and Painting
Plant and Equipment	– Operating and Maintenance Manuals
	– Training of Operating Personnel
	– Nameplates and Notices
	– Recommended Spare Parts
	– Special Tools
	– Crating and Shipping

Table 11.4 Continued

Additional Clauses – Contracts Involving Installation, Erection or Construction

The Works Generally	– Setting Out and Tolerances
	– Surveys and Survey Marks
	– Permits for Construction Equipment
	– Reinstatement of Damage
	– On-Site Testing
	– Hiring of Labour
Site Data and Conditions	– Meteorological
	– Geotechnical
	– Seismic
Use of Site by Contractor	– Access to Site
	– Contractor's Working Area
	– Fencing and Security
	– Deliveries to Site
	– Workshop and Storage Areas
	– Storage of Flammable Gases, Fuels, and Explosives
Site Facilities	– Contractor's Offices and Sheds
	– Engineer's Office and Equipment
	– Utility Service Connections: Telephone, Telex, Fax Electric Power supply Water supply Sewerage
	– Messing, Change Rooms, and Sanitary Facilities
On-Site Regulations	– Access and Permits for Visitors
	– Traffic Control and On-Site Parking
	– Use of Existing Roads
	– Safety and First Aid
	– Publicity including Notice Boards, Advertising, and Photography
Environmental Protection	– Maintaining Site Cleanliness
	– Control of Pollution
	– Noise Limitation and Control
	– Burning off
	– Disposal of Rubbish and Debris
	– Disposal of Effluents
	– Stormwater Discharge
	– Final Clean Up
Temporary Works	– Diversion of Roads and Services
	– Temporary Access Roads
	– Protection of Adjacent Structures
	– Dewatering
Off-Site Facilities	– Accommodation
	– Camps and Caravan Parks

The following is a suggested arrangement and order of presenting the clauses within each job specification. There may be a number of individual clauses under each heading:

Scope of Work
General Requirements – Applicable Documents
                      – Statutory Requirements
Materials and Combinations of Materials
Workmanship
Preliminary Work before Fabrication/Construction
Fabrication/Construction
Finishing
Inspection and Testing

Mechanical and electrical engineering work Owing to the wide variety in the types of mechanical and electrical engineering work, there are many possible arrangements for compiling and presenting the job specifications. One practical method is to group the various elements in accordance with their principal function and prepare a job specification for each such group.

    The following schedules indicate such a grouping of elements. In practice, it may be necessary to agglomerate or further subdivide the groups nominated.

Mechanical systems and equipment
- Environmental Control Systems – Air Conditioning
  - – Dust Control
  - – Emission Control
  - – Fire Protection
  - – Heating, Ventilation, and Cooling
  - – Noise Control
- Heat Transfer Equipment – Boilers
  - – Fired Heaters
  - – Heat Exchangers
  - – Cooling Towers
- Materials Handling Equipment – Chutes and Hoppers
  - – Cranes and Hoists
  - – Conveyors
  - – Elevators
  - – Mining Equipment
  - – Loaders and Unloaders
- Miscellaneous Equipment – Driers
  - – Filters
  - – Mixers

- Access Facilities
  - Platforms and Walkways
  - Stairways and Ladders
- Pipework
  - Materials and Fabrication
  - Supports and Installation
  - Testing
- Rotating Equipment
  - Compressors
  - Engines
  - Fans and Blowers
  - Pumps
  - Turbines
- Vessels
  - Pressure Vessels
  - Storage Bins
  - Tanks

Electrical equipment
- Installation
  - Wiring and Conduits
  - Testing and Approval
- Motors
  - Low/Medium Voltage
  - High Voltage
- Generators
- Transformers
- Switchgear
  - Low/Medium Voltage
  - High Voltage
- Lighting
  Instrumentation and Controls   – Control Centre

The arrangement of the clauses within each job specification for mechanical and electrical work can, with minor differences, be similar to that suggested for civil or structural engineering work. Again, there can be a number of individual clauses under each heading:

- Scope of Work (Job Specification)
- General Requirements
  - Applicable Documents
  - Statutory Requirements
  - Specific Warranties and Guarantees
- Specific Design Criteria
- Materials
- Fabrication
  - Components
  - Sub-assemblies
    Painting and Protective Coatings
- Workmanship

- Inspection and Testing
- Packing and Shipping

Supplementing a Job Specification with Data Schedules

Where the work under the Contract includes the supply, and possibly the installation, of items of mechanical and electrical equipment, the use of *Equipment Design Data Schedules* (usually abbreviated to *Data Schedules*) can be an effective way of supplementing a Job Specification.

They can be particularly useful where there are a number of similar items (such as electric motors, pumps, fans and the like), each with different characteristics, to be specified. Where this situation occurs, a widely adopted practice is for the Job Specification to detail those particular requirements common to all items in the group covered by the Job Specification, while a Data Schedule is provided for each item detailing the remaining requirements for that item.

Where these items are individually identified as the particular products of nominated manufacturers or suppliers, the Contractor's prime responsibility is to obtain and if necessary install the specified items.

In such a situation, a single Data Schedule can be prepared for inclusion in the Specification, tabulating details such as reference number, location, manufacturer's catalogue number and other data to clearly identify and locate each item. Alternatively, this Schedule can be placed on an appropriate drawing.

However, it may be left to the Contractor to select suitable equipment on the open market or to have the items specially designed and made to meet the specified requirements. In this situation, particularly for major or key items, it is important to specify the requirements in detail so that the Engineer knows, when evaluating tenders, exactly what equipment is being offered. As already pointed out in Sec. 3.3 – 'Requirements for Tendering', tenderers are often reluctant to provide any information not specifically requested. It may therefore be necessary to ask tenderers to provide in their tenders specific details of key items of equipment being offered. This can be achieved by providing a suitably designed Data Schedule.

During the tendering stage, Data Schedules will serve a number of functions. They will:

- Ensure that tenderers are provided with all the specific requirements for the plant or equipment to be supplied.
- Help tenderers to understand the requirements.
- Enable tenderers to describe the plant or equipment they are offering.
- Act as a check list when evaluating and comparing equipment being

offered by tenderers.

- Save time in evaluating tenders and in selecting the appropriate equipment.

During the implementation stage they will:

- Provide a ready reference to all the technical features of the equipment.
- Provide a basis for standardization with other similar equipment.

Data Schedules can be prepared independently for each new contract but organizations which frequently invite tenders for such equipment usually have standard pre-printed Data Schedules for basic items of equipment.

The information provided on a Data Schedule can be considered as comprising two parts. The first part enables the Engineer to specify details of all the functions and technical features of the required equipment including design criteria, performance requirements, materials and fabrication, extent of testing required, and details of accessories to be supplied. It would also cover such matters as location, site conditions, service and operating parameters, information regarding utility services available to operate the equipment, details of the materials to be handled or processed by the equipment, and requirements for testing. The relevant Job Specification and Drawings should also be referenced.

The second part of the Data Schedule provides blank spaces to be completed by the tenderers. Here tenderers are asked to supply details of the equipment being offered in sufficient detail to show that they will comply with the Specification and Drawings. The questions must be carefully prepared so that all the relevant information is obtained to enable tenders to be evaluated and compared.

Some engineers prefer to tabulate the information contained in the first part, as described above, on one of the drawings leaving the Data Schedule for information to be provided by tenderers. The Engineer should decide which method should be adopted

Each Data Schedule forms part of and is bound with the relevant Job Specification. A separate copy is included with the other schedules attached to the Tender Form and which are listed in the Content of Tender as being required to be completed and returned with tenders. When the Contract Documents are being assembled, following the award of the Contract, a copy of the completed Schedule returned with the accepted tender replaces the incompleted form attached to the Job Specification. It thus becomes part of the Contract.

11.4 THE DRAWINGS

The function of drawings is to present technical details in a graphical rather than a written form.

In many standard General Conditions of Contract the term *Drawings* is defined in general and somewhat ambiguous terms such as 'the drawings referred to in the Contract including such other drawings as may from time to time be supplied or approved by the Principal'. Unfortunately, none of the standard General Conditions precisely defines what constitutes a 'drawing', apparently working on the assumption that 'everbody knows what a drawing is'. The usually accepted definition is *a representation by lines; a delineation as distinct from a painting*. However, what engineers term a 'drawing' may contain as many dimensions, descriptions and notes as lines. In effect, the Drawings are really a part of the Specification expressed in a different form. It is important to appreciate this point and it is for this reason that the Specification and the Drawings are considered together in this book.

Drawings, however, are usually prepared and printed on much larger sheets than are used for the Specification, and are normally bound separately. Drawings issued with the Enquiry Documents should be clearly titled and numbered so that they may be readily identified as Drawings as defined in the Contract. Diagrams, sketches, and standard details are often printed on smaller sheets and bound with the Specification. Technically, as defined above, they are Drawings, but for practical reasons they are considered to be part of the Specification. To clarify this point, they should be identified and numbered as pages in the Specification and referenced accordingly in the text unless it is intended that they are 'Drawings' under the terms of the Contract.

Under the above definition of 'Drawings', the term refers to both the drawings supplied by the Principal to the Contractor and the drawings supplied by the Contractor to the Principal under the terms of the Contract. The 'drawings referred to in the Contract' may therefore be divided into two groups:

contract drawings Drawings prepared and exchanged by the parties *before* the acceptance of the Tender and which are incorporated in the Contract by specific reference.

working drawings Drawings prepared and exchanged by the parties *after* the acceptance of the Tender; they are required under the Contract for the complete and proper performance of the work.

The first group should be individually listed in the Contract by title and number. Those prepared and issued by the Principal with the Enquiry Documents should be scheduled in the Specification. Those submitted by the

Contractor with the Tender Documents should be listed either in a separate schedule to be included in the Contract Documents or added to the schedule in the Specification amended for incorporation in the Contract Documents.

For obvious reasons, the drawings in the second group cannot be individually listed in the Contract. However, the respective obligations of both parties to provide these drawings must be clearly set out in the Contract, usually in the Supplementary Conditions of Contract or the Specification.

Classification of Drawings

Engineering drawings for contract purposes show three levels of detail:

- General Arrangement Drawings
- Design Drawings
- Shop Drawings

General arrangement drawings These are the first level of detail and are usually small-to-medium-scale line diagrams showing details such as the number and arrangement of the various elements comprising a particular facility or piece of equipment. They show the relationship of the elements to each other, controlling dimensions, materials and basic sizes of members or components, and principal design features. Read in conjunction with the Specification, general arrangement drawings should reflect the function and purpose of the design and provide sufficient information to enable basic quantities to be calculated, cost estimates to be prepared, and an estimate made of the time required for the performance of the work under the Contract.

Design drawings These show the second level of detail. They are usually drawn to larger scales than the general arrangement drawings and show in greater detail additional dimensions, member and unit sizes, the character of connections between components, fabrication and construction details, and all the information necessary for the Contractor to undertake the work. Together with the general arrangement drawings and the Specification, design drawings enable tenderers to prepare firm lump sum prices.

Shop drawings Also known as *shop details*, these are at the third level of detail. They give the worker on the Site or in the workshop all the information necessary for purchasing all the materials and components and for preparing and shaping every piece of material required, including the dimensions, tolerances, and finish for all items, and the size and location of every bolt and weld and identifying mark or number for each component.

Shop drawings also include marking plans and layout drawings, indicating the position and assembly of every part identified by mark or number, and assembly drawings which show how and what pieces are assembled in the workshop before delivery. Special layout drawings are sometimes required to determine clearances for installation and erection.

Shop drawings may include layouts for electrical conduits, pipework and ducts, reinforcement bending schedules, and details of prefabricated elements such as structural steelwork, timber, and precast concrete units.

General Provisions for the Supply of Documents

Primary statements regarding the respective obligations of the parties for the supply and review of documents, including the Drawings, are laid down in most General Conditions. These will usually require amplification or qualification in secondary statements in the Supplementary Conditions or, preferably, in the Specification.

Where the Contractor is responsible for the design of all or part of the Works, precise details of the Drawings and other data to be submitted to the Principal for review must be clearly specified. These submissions are required to allow the Principal to check the Contractor's design for compliance with the Contract and to provide information to enable the Principal to coordinate the interfaces with other equipment and with terminal points of supply being provided by others.

Although some General Conditions use the word 'approval' to describe the Principal's acceptance of documents submitted by the Contractor, it is recommended that the word 'review' be used instead; 'approval' may be taken to infer that the Principal accepts responsibility for all or part of the details submitted.

Unfortunately, in many Contracts, the term 'Drawings' is used somewhat casually to encompass all the documents and drawings required to be submitted by the Contractor. Examination of Table 11.5 will show that the dividing line between drawings and some related documents can indeed be very fine.

The preparation of drawings should conform with the recommendations outlined in 'General Requirements for the preparation of Drawings'.

General Requirements for the Preparation of Drawings

All drawings prepared for the work, whether by the Principal or by the Contractor, should comply with the following requirements:

1. Each drawing should be identified by a title block in which is stated:

Table 11.5 Checklist of documents to be submitted by the contractor

1. Project Programme	
2. Drawings	– Drawing list and issue dates
	– General arrangement drawings
	– Detail drawings with certified dimensions
	– Marking plans
	– Footing datails and anchor bolt layout
	– Pipework layout
	– Electrical schematic and wiring diagrams
	– Conduit layouts
	– Instrumentation diagrams
	– Logic diagrams
	– Plan of terminal points of supply
	– Work-as-executed drawings
3. Design Data	– Dead and working loads of equipment
	– Performance data
	– Details of instrumentation and controls
	– Calculation and data sheets
	– Fabrication details
	– Welding procedures and qualification
4. Production Data	– Production schedule
	– Shipping schedule
	– Installation instructions
	– Certificates: Statutory approvals: Material tests: Performance tests
5. Other Data	– List of parts
	– Recommended spare parts list and prices
	– Operating and Maintenance Manuals

- The name of the Principal/Contractor as appropriate
- Project identification
- Drawing title
- Drawing reference number and revision status with date
- Name of the person or corporation (if any) who has prepared the drawing on behalf of the Principal or Contractor

2. Drawings should be made to an appropriate scale and be as clear and accurate as possible. Explanatory notes must be concise, legible and easily understood. Abbreviations and contractions should be kept to a minimum and restricted to well-known forms. Dimensions should be adequate for thc purposc of thc drawing with well-defined arrowheads at the end of each dimension line.
3. The extent of the work under the Contract must be accurately defined and connections to existing work or work being undertaken by others must be clearly shown.

4. Terminology used on the drawings must be identical with that used in the text of the Specification.
5. Only nationally recognized materials and symbols must be used.

Additional Points to Watch in the Preparation of Drawings

Where the Principal is responsible for all or part of the design, the importance of coordination between the specification writer and the designer has already been pointed out. Between them, what information is to be shown on the Drawings issued with the Enquiry Documents and what is to be covered in the Specification should be determined at an early stage of the drafting procedure.

Each individual piece of information should be given once only in one place in the documents. Information contained in the Specification should not be repeated in the Drawings and vice versa. Unless it is essential, particular dimensions and other requirements should not be given on more than one drawing. Changes and additions inevitably occur during the design process and if a dimension or a note is given more than once there is a strong possibility that it will be overlooked in one of the places if it is amended.

There should be no overlaps between Drawings and the Specification, except that items on the Drawings should be labelled in such a manner as to clearly identify them with any written description in the Specification.

Care must be taken that unapproved drawings do not come into the possession of tenderers or the Contractor. It is recommended that the word 'Preliminary' should be printed (in pencil) on each sheet as soon as it is first fixed to the drawing board. If a CAD system is being used, the word should be placed above the title block when first laying out the drawing. If it is necessary to copy or make a print of the drawing for any purpose during the design phase, the date should be added under the word 'Preliminary' each time it is copied or printed. This will remove the necessity to formally revise the drawing each time it is issued during the design phase. This word should not be removed until the drawing is ready to be issued with the Enquiry Documents. It should then be replaced by 'For Tender Purposes Only' and the drawing again dated.

When a tender is accepted and the drawings issued for fabrication or construction purposes, the note can be replaced by 'Issued for Construction/ Fabrication'. Only after this status has been reached will it be necessary to note each amendment.

Principal's Obligations

Contract drawings

Design by the Principal The extent of detail on drawings relating to designs prepared by the Principal and issued with the Enquiry Documents, with the intent that they will form part of the Contract, will depend largely upon the type of contract.

Drawings for Lump Sum contracts should comprise such general arrangement and detail drawings as are required to allow the quantities of the work to be accurately estimated and a lump sum price determined. Provided that they comply with this requirement, they need not include all the detail drawings required for actually undertaking the work under the Contract. These can be supplied after the Contract is signed provided that they are made available in enough time to cause no delay to the Contractor. However, if the additional details change the scope of the work, the Contractor may have a claim for a variation.

For Schedule of Rates contracts, the drawings should include such general arrangement and detail drawings required to define the precise form and physical constraints for each item in the Schedule so that Schedule Prices can be determined.

As far as quantities are concerned, only the general extent of the work need be indicated as the final quantities for payment purposes will be measured on completion of the work. However, where the final quantities are to be measured against an original datum, that datum must be clearly shown. For example, in a contract involving excavation, the existing as well as the required contour lines must be shown.

For Part Lump Sum/Part Schedule of Rates contracts, the details provided for each part must be in accordance with the respective requirements.

For Cost Plus contracts, only such general arrangement drawings are required which will enable such cost and time estimates to be made so that tenderers can determine overheads and related costs.

Design by the Contractor Where the Principal seeks tenders based on design being undertaken by the Contractor, the extent of detail required for drawings, if any, issued with the Enquiry Documents will depend principally on the nature of the work under the Contract. Tenderers must be provided with drawings covering such information as is available to the Principal and which is relevant to the design parameters within which the Contractor must work. Where the Principal has carried out the conceptual design, general arrangement drawings indicating the preferred concept should be included with the Enquiry Documents. When site work is involved, any available topographical or cadastral plans of the Site should be provided, together with details of the preferred location. The drawings must distinguish clearly the relationship of the proposed new work with existing work and other facilities.

Working drawings

Design by the Principal If the drawings prepared and issued for tender purposes on designs prepared by the Principal are not sufficiently complete for construction purposes, the Principal is obliged to provide the Contractor with the necessary additional details so as not to delay the progress of the work. As a general rule, responsibility for the preparation of shop drawings lies with the Contractor. However, under some circumstances, shop drawings for all or some of the work may be provided by the Principal. This situation would occur where the complete design of a particular piece of specialized plant or equipment is undertaken or commissioned by the Principal.

Design by the Contractor Where the Contractor is responsible for the design under the Contract, it is unlikely that any working drawings will be prepared by the Principal.

An exception to this may occur when the design, supply and installation of plant or equipment is undertaken by a number of different contractors. The coordination of their various activities may fall to the Principal. Based on information supplied to or provided by the contractors, the Principal may prepare and issue to all concerned a drawing showing details of the footing or support structure, the location of anchor bolts and the terminal points of supply of services (such as water, electric power, gas, steam, and compressed air), and, if necessary, clearance dimensions for hoisting and installation.

Contractor's Obligations

Contract drawings

Design by the Principal When the design is prepared by the Principal it is unlikely that tenderers will be required to submit any drawings as part of their tenders unless an alternative tender is offered which requires drawings for clarification. How these drawings are to be incorporated in the Contract will depend upon the circumstances.

Design by the Contractor When the Enquiry Documents provide for design by the Contractor, tenderers will need to submit such drawings as are necessary to define clearly the scope and the nature of the facility offered and to enable the Principal properly to evaluate and compare the tenders. The drawings related to the design offered with a tender do not need to be in such detail as is required for fabrication or construction, but the requirements must be clearly outlined in the Specification.

Working drawings

Design by the Principal In most cases when the design is provided by the Principal, the only drawings required to be prepared and submitted by the Contractor for review by the Principal are shop drawings. This review is usually confined to a general examination of the work to satisfy the Principal that the details are in compliance with the Specification and the Drawings. This review examines details such as connections for adequacy, but does not include a check of dimensions other than those on interfaces with work being undertaken by others.

Design by the Contractor The requirements to be met by the Contractor, with regard to the preparation and submission of Drawings and other design data for review by the Principal, must be clearly stated in the Specification.

It is important to specify in a schedule exactly what and when information is to be submitted. The schedule must specify details as to the nature and scope of the Drawings and documents submitted, the number of copies required and the dates by which the submissions must be made. The dates for submission must allow adequate time for the Principal's review. The timely supply of Drawings and other data in a specified sequence may be critical for the successful execution of the Contract and completion by the required date.

The requirements for each item in the schedule must be clearly stated. These will include:

- Number of copies required – for review
  - for resubmission
  - after endorsement
- Nature of copies – prints
  - transparencies
  - microfilm
- Submission Dates – number of days /weeks after the acceptance of the tender
- Review Procedure – method of review
  - period required for review
- Review Code I: for information only
  F: for review before fabrication
  S: for review before shipment

When preparing the list of drawings and other documents required to be submitted by the Contractor, the specification writer should consult the engineers responsible for the respective disciplines.

Work-as-Executed Drawings

Consideration should be given to requiring the Contractor to prepare *work-as-executed drawings* detailing adjustments made to the work on-Site or in the workshop during the performance of the Contract and not otherwise recorded on the Drawings. For this purpose, where the design is provided by the Principal, it is sometimes helpful for the Principal to provide the Contractor at the end of the work with copies of the latest issue of those drawings affected. The Contractor can then mark up the Drawings with any changes made. On completion of the work, the Contractor should be required to supply up-to-date copies of all drawings prepared by the Contractor on which all on-Site amendments have been made. These drawings can be specified as prints, as transparencies or as micofilm as required.

TWELVE

RECOMMENDATIONS FOR PRESENTATION OF DOCUMENTS

12.1 FORMAT AND LAYOUT

Presentation

Indifferent typing and careless binding can spoil the effect of an otherwise carefully and consistently composed document. Just as the writer should follow rules and conventions in the interest of uniformity of style, so should the typist conform to an agreed set of disciplines so as to convert a well-prepared draft into a presentable publication.

Most well-organized offices have established rules for setting out and typing so that documents will be presented to a uniformly high standard which will reflect credit on all those who had a part in their preparation. Where such procedures have not been established, the following suggestions are provided as a guide.

Format

In a strict sense, 'format' is the size and shape of a publication. It can also refer to its general style and appearance. Most documents used for contract purposes are made using xerographed or offset copies from a paper original prepared on a typewriter or word processor. The most common size paper used is A4 (297 × 210 mm), although in countries not yet fully metricated 'American quarto' (11 × 8 in) paper is widely used.

Line spacing on typewriters and most word processor printers is a standard six lines per inch while letter spacing is usually either 10 or 12 characters per inch.

Continuous-feed (ladder-fold) paper used in printers associated with word processors must have an exact number of lines of type between end-of-sheet perforations. The 11-inch length of American quarto paper is exactly equivalent to 66 lines of type but the 297 mm length of A4 paper does not fit an exact number of lines. For this reason, A4 ladder-fold paper is made with slightly smaller sheets equivalent to 70 lines of type.

The four margins around the printed page are referred to as the back (at the binding), head (top), foredge (opposite the binding), and tail (bottom).

For 'quality' presentation, the area available for typescript should be about 50 per cent of the total page area, centred on the sheet. The depth of the head and tail margins should be determined by the overall appearance but for the best effect, the head and tail margins should be a little larger than the back and foredge margins.

This can be achieved by having head and tail margins each equivalent to 8 lines of type (34 mm) and back and foredge margins equivalent to 12 characters (30 mm). The back margin may need to be increased to accommodate the binding process to be used.

Using margins approximating to those suggested above, an A4 page will have a maximum of 54 lines of type single-spaced. On an average there will be 10 words per line at 10 characters per inch and 12 words per line at 12 characters per inch. In practice, the average number of words per page is about 75 per cent of the maximum theoretical number as a result of paragraph spacing, short lines at the end of paragraphs and subheadings. On this basis there are about 400 words per page at 10 characters per inch and 500 at 12 characters per inch.

Reducing each of these margins by about 5 mm will still give an acceptable appearance, although increasing the print area ratio to about 60 per cent and the number of words per page by about 20 per cent.

Layout

Layout is the disposition of the typescript within the area of the page. The appearance of the finished document will depend upon the skill with which this is done. The makeup of the document should be consistent. Elements of the same kind should be spaced equally throughout, so that the main headings are all at the same distance from the top of the page, while the space above and below subheadings should be consistent throughout.

The decision about indenting paragraphs is a matter of personal choice but the tendency today is not to indent. In this style, which gives a neat and uncluttered appearance, it is necessary to leave a space between paragraphs. As a general rule, one blank line should be left between paragraphs.

Should paragraph indentation be adopted, the normal indent is eight character spaces although this can be reduced to four spaces if desired. It is not necessary to leave a line between paragraphs with this style, but the appearance of the page is enhanced if a blank line is left. Note that the first line of text after a main centred or left-justified heading is usually left without indent. Whichever style is adopted, it should remain consistent throughout the whole document.

Headings

The variations in style of headings which can be produced on a typewriter or a dot matrix word processor printer are limited. They can be typed all in capitals or in lower case with upper-case initial letters; they can be typed at the centre, either side or run on; and they can be underlined. Dot matrix word processor printers give a little more scope; many have bold or italic typefaces. Laser printers have many typefaces and the scope for variation in headings is extensive. For practical reasons it is best to limit headings to three types:

- Main headings
- Subheadings
- Secondary subheadings

Main headings should be centred on the text. They should be typed all in capital letters and underlined. It is advisable to start each section of the text under a main heading on a fresh page. If the headings are numbered, three character spaces should be left between the number and the heading. The subheading, or the first line of text if there is no subheading, should start leaving two blank lines after the main heading.

Subheadings can be either on the left or offset to the right. The latter arrangement can be particularly useful for documents which are printed single-sided and which are frequently consulted, such as specifications. Headings offset to the right can be found more easily when 'flicking' through the pages. Subheadings should also be typed all in capital letters and underlined.

If subheadings are to be offset to the right, each should be commenced on the centreline of the text. If subheadings are numbered, the number should commence on the centreline of the text, with three character spaces left before the actual heading commences. If more than half a line is required for a subheading, the second line should be commenced directly below the first letter (not the number) of the subheading.

If the subheading is to be kept to the left-hand side of the page, it should be confined to the left of the centreline of the text by using more than one line if necessary. The layout of the subheading should be the same as for the subheadings offset to the right. A blank line should be left between the subheading and the first line of text.

Secondary subheadings should commence on the left-hand side of the page, typed in upper and lower case and underlined. The text may be run on after a secondary subheading, or else a blank line left as for subheadings. This is a matter of personal choice. Note that full stops are not used at the end of headings.

Page and Part Numbering

All pages should be numbered consecutively at the bottom of the page on the centreline. Each document should comprise a separately numbered Part, particularly when two or more are bound in a single volume. Each part should be identified either by a single letter ('Part A', 'Part B', 'Part C', etc.), or by Roman numerals ('Part I', 'Part II', 'Part III', etc.), and the part number incorporated in the page number:

A-1, A-2, B-1, B-2　　　or　　　I-1, I-2, II-1, II-2, etc.

Checking Typescript

The importance of accurate checking of the typescript cannot be overemphasised. It is an arduous task relished by few, but an apparently minor typographical error can completely change the meaning of a sentence. In a contract document this can have catastrophic results. Checking the typescript should be carried out independently of the checking of the material content of the documents.

Effective checking requires concentration. This means working in a quiet and calm atmosphere without interruptions. This is difficult to achieve in a busy engineering office, but every effort should be made to do the task in the best conditions possible.

Checking is best considered as a two stage operation. The primary check is directed at achieving two basic aims:

• Ensuring that the original (manuscript) draft has been accurately followed
• Eliminating errors in spelling, typography, and set-out

The original draft (manuscript or paste-up) should be as complete and as accurate as possible. Having a rough typed draft prepared and then corrected in detail is a time-consuming and expensive procedure and should be avoided if possible. The apparent ease with which text produced on word processors can be corrected has led to a regrettable tendency to give ill-prepared drafts to the typist in the mistaken belief that errors or amendments can readily be corrected or inserted.

Changes at any stage involve time and expense and this applies to both typewriter and word processor work. Another unfortunate effect of the use of word processors is for the typist not to check the work before handing it back to the writer for approval. Typists must be trained to check the work properly on the screen before printing. The advent of the word processor has not removed the need for care.

In checking typescript, errors are more likely to be picked up if a white card is moved down the page, line by line, as it is read. It is also helpful, but not always practicable, to have someone else read aloud from the original draft while the writer checks the typescript. The reader should mention punctuation marks, capital letters, underlining, bold or italic characters if appropriate, paragraphs, and the like.

Corrections are best indicated using correction marks based on modified proof reader's symbols as shown in Appendix E.

The corrections required are shown by inserting a mark in the text at the appropriate point and writing an explanatory comment or other mark in the margin opposite. Neither the comment or the amendment should be written between the lines of the text itself. If the writer considers that such marks do not make the intention clear, the full explanation should be written in the margin.

The only marks made in the text proper should be those shown under the heading ' Mark in Text' in the correction mark table. When several corrections occur in the one line, they may be divided between the left hand and right hand margins, the order being from the left margin to the right and from left to right in each.

When the corrections have been made the final draft should again be checked. This final check should be aimed at ensuring that:

- Corrections marked on the first typescript draft have been made and that, in making them, the typist has not introduced new errors
- No lines have been transposed or omitted
- Running headings and subtitles and page numbers are in position and correct

This final check should not be used to make further corrections to the content, style, or arrangement unless absolutely necessary. If possible, confine the corrections to a single word or phrase, or as a last resort, keep them to a single paragraph or to a page by altering paragraphs.

If the document is to be typeset, there will, of course, be a further check when the proofs are received from the printer.

12.2 PRINTING AND BINDING

There are many methods available for printing and binding but only a few of these are likely to be suitable for contract documentation.

Printing

Because of the comparatively limited number of copies required, it is unlikely that the documents would be typeset and printed by one of the letterpress processes. In all probability, the documents would be printed by a copying process such as offset duplicating or xerography.

For small numbers of copies, either of these two processes can produce documents of adequate quality, conveniently and economically, often using readily available in-house facilities. Many large engineering offices have equipment for both these processes. For less than 10 copies xerography is most probably cheaper.

Since both these copying processes use paper masters prepared on a typewriter or from a word processor or computer printer, the final document will be presented exactly as typed on the master. Consequently, great care must be taken to ensure that the typist prepares the master so as to display the material to the best advantage and in a consistent style.

The text can be printed either single- or double-sided on single sheets of A4 paper. Alternatively, if the finished volume is to be casebound (i.e. inside a hard cover) they can be printed on each side of an A3 sheet, four pages to a sheet. These sheets are then folded and collated into sections, usually 16 or 32 pages to a section depending upon the thickness (weight) of the paper. If this latter form is used, great care must be taken in the design of the layout and the collation (collection in order).

Binding

Binding is the operation by which individual printed sheets are collated and secured between covers so that the finished volume can be read conveniently or placed on a bookshelf. There are many methods of binding available and the one chosen will depend upon factors such as cost, the time required, and the availability of materials and equipment.

Where the number of pages is large and the size and status of the project warrants the expenditure, the documents can be printed so that they can be assembled in sections and casebound. The pages in the individual sections are secured through the fold in the spine by wire staples or by thread stitching, assembled in order and glued to a backbinding of cloth and paper. The backbinding is wider than the spine so that it can be glued to the cover boards which are then covered by the endpapers.

Individual sheets can also be casebound in this manner by glueing them to a backbinding, but the end product is not particularly robust; the method is not recommended for documents liable to be referred to frequently.

Case binding is a complex and highly skilled operation and should only be undertaken by specialists in the trade. Because of the cost and time involved, it is rarely used for contract documents.

The method most frequently employed for binding contract documents is to place the collated individual sheets between covers and secure them together through the backedge by wire staples, patent fasteners, or post bolts and then cover the spine and fasteners with a glued-on cloth strip or a slide-on plastic cover strip. Alternatively, a thermoplastic comb binding strip can be used to secure the appropriately punched covers and pages. This latter method is easy to use and is comparatively inexpensive; it has the added advantage that the volume will lie flat when opened. However, it may not be sufficiently robust on a jobsite or in a workshop, particularly if the volume is more than 15 mm thick.

THIRTEEN

WRITING EFFECTIVE ENGLISH

13.1 DEVELOPING AN APPROPRIATE STYLE

The Writer

Writing the documents for an engineering contract takes skill, hard work and experience. An effective writer must have complete knowledge of what is required to be done under the Contract. Furthermore, the writer should be able to define the methods and materials to be used, and should be able to express all these needs in a way readily understood by those doing the actual work.

Effective writing requires the careful review of what one has written. The effectiveness may be improved by altering the order of the words, sentences, paragraphs, and even whole sections. Obscure, repetitious, or inappropriate words and phrases should be rejected with the object of conveying the meaning as clearly, briefly, and concisely as possible.

There are many other requirements. The writer must have skill in the use of language as well as technical knowledge. While formal legal training is not expected, some knowledge of relevant legal principles is required, as discussed in Sec. 2.2 – 'The Law of Contract'.

Attention paid to detail will be rewarded. The ideal writer should understand all the requirements for each element or section in turn, and convey these clearly and concisely. Points of conflict in the documents must be avoided. Ambiguity or inconsistency is a recipe for dispute or disagreement, and this can cost time and money.

Approaching the Task

The ability to write clearly and effectively is one of the most important skills needed by an engineer when writing documents for contract purposes.

The technical writing needed in contract documents aims not to parade knowledge or emotion, nor to initiate discussion, but to inform or direct. To achieve this, good technical writing is systematic, balanced, and appropriate in choice of words, selection of material, and overall approach.

All writing is, to a large extent, personal. A message is not effective just because the writer understands what is intended; the reader must also understand it. The purpose of technical writing is to inform particular readers in a precise way.

Written English should not be confused with spoken English. English spoken face to face is accompanied by 'body language' – facial expressions, gestures and stance. Even when spoken over telephone or radio, meaning can be modified by tone, volume, and accent. Written English must stand alone on the page; all meaning must be conveyed by proper use of the correct words, phrases, and punctuation.

It is important to keep in mind the people who will read the documents. Many of those who need to refer to them (the Specification in particular) may not be skilled in the use of English; it may not even be their mother tongue. Others may lack a high level of formal education.

When one is giving instructions the message must be precise. Complicated phrases should be avoided and short, simple words should be used as much as possible. Long sentences should be avoided by restricting each sentence to one idea.

Choosing the Style

A good style is a quality inherent in effective writing. This quality will be evident if the purpose of the writing is achieved by the use of clear words and concise syntax.

The huge vocabulary of modern English, both general and technical, can itself cause difficulties. English has many different words to express fine shades of meaning. To convey the exact shade of meaning intended, the writer should be aware of the associations of words, not just of their basic meanings. This awareness comes most of all from wide, observant reading and frequent consultation of good reference works.

The first of these is a good dictionary. The *Concise Oxford Dictionary* is adequate for most purposes. If a more detailed reference is required the *Shorter Oxford English Dictionary* (2 volumes) may be consulted. The complete unabridged reference is, of course, the *Oxford English Dictionary* (20 volumes). All are published by Oxford University Press.

In Australia and New Zealand the *Macquarie Dictionary* (published by The Macquarie Library) has become the accepted standard reference for Antipodean English. In the USA and Canada, *Webster's New Collegiate Dictionary* (published by Merriam-Webster) is widely accepted as the standard for American English, particularly pronunciation. For more detailed reference the unabridged *Webster's New International Dictionary* (Merriam-Webster) is used.

A book of synonyms and antonyms can also be useful. The most widely known of these is Roget's *Thesaurus of English Words and Phrases* (published by Longmans). In the USA Webster's *Dictionary of Synonyms* (Merriam-Webster) is popular while in Australia and New Zealand the *Macquarie Thesaurus* (Macquarie Library) is now widely used.

For answers to grammatical questions reference to Fowler's *Dictionary of Modern English Usage* (Oxford University Press), notwithstanding the idiosyncracies of its author, is often profitable.

To write technical documents clearly, it is vital to plan. Effective writing is organized and methodical; it must be arranged in a logical sequence and in due proportion. A logical sequence requires that the subject matter be treated in a suitable order. A uniform approach should be evident throughout. A good sense of proportion causes subjects of similar importance to receive similar treatment.

Consistency is important. Writing which exhibits a consistency in style, spelling, and punctuation is easier to read and absorb than one which does not. Although different styles and conventions are current and all may be acceptable, varying styles in the one document can produce incongruities which may irritate the reader.

Writing Plain English

It has often been said that the secret of effective technical writing is to 'put yourself in the place of the reader'. To follow this rule, the writer should carefully read what has been written and then ask, 'Does this text make its message clear to me, simply and precisely?' Unless the answer is 'yes', the purpose of the message is lost. Here, then, are some suggested rules to be followed in writing clear, concise English:

1. Do not use unnecessary words or phrases Unnecessary words hinder rather than help. Empty expressions merely distract. Eliminate words that add nothing to the sentence in which they occur. The following examples show how the impact of a sentence can be improved by following this rule:

It should be noted that the measurements of tidal velocity are likely to be subject to an error of approximately 10 per cent.	Tidal velocity measurements may have a 10-per-cent error.
Due to the unique design features of the proposed system, the pump for moving sewage can be in an operational mode for 50 000 hours without interruption.	The sewage pump can operate continuously for 50 000 hours

2. Do not use pompous or stilted terms Old-fashioned, 'dignified' language can often obscure the meaning. It has no place in modern technical writing. Unless both the reader and the writer are trained in legal work, the use of 'legalese' should also be avoided.

Be careful with the use of 'jargon' – that is, long or obscure technical words and phrases. Do not use such terms unless you are sure that all the readers will be familiar with the words in question. If in doubt, explain.

The same applies to obscure words – words which will send most readers to the dictionary. Repeated use of unfamiliar words may antagonize the reader and may prevent the subject matter from being fully understood. However, keep in mind that although a word may not be well known it may still be the correct one to use in the circumstances.

3. Do not use a long word when a short one will do In choosing words, strive to be definite and specific. Reject vague statements and generalizations. Be positive in the choice of words; prefer the simple to the complicated , the familiar to the unusual, and the concrete word to the abstract. For example:

Use	near	rather than	in the vicinity of
	now		at this point in time
	before		prior to
	after		subsequent to
	use		utilize

4. Do not use clichés, slang, or overstatement Clichés are words and phrases which once had meanings which were precise and sometimes colourful but which have now lost their impact through being overused and misused. They are inappropriate in a technical document.

Slang, though clear and forceful, is likewise out of place. A careful writer can usually express the required meaning in another way. The writer should be aware of the difference between spoken and written English.

Overstatement, by the use of adjectives excessive to their purpose, should be avoided. Adjectives should not be used in technical writing unless they make a positive contribution.

Colloquialisms are also out of place in a technical document. This is another place where the careful writer will distinguish between spoken and written English. For example, contracted expressions such as 'don't', 'won't', and 'can't' should be avoided.

5. Avoid tautology Tautology is the unnecessary repetition of the same statement or idea. Thus in the sentence, 'It shall revert back to the Contractor,' the word 'back' is redundant; in the above context, 'revert' means 'go back'.

Sentences and Paragraphs

Grammarians define a sentence in a number of ways, many of which are irreconcilable. The writer of a technical document must be precise and definite and the most appropriate definition is 'a combination of words which contains one subject and one predicate'. A sentence should preferably be restricted to one idea. A sentence should not be allowed to get out of hand, resulting in what Fowler calls 'hanging up'.

Long sentences should be avoided. Recent studies in the USA have indicated that a sentence with an average length of about 18 to 20 words is the most easily understood. Where possible, sentences should be limited to less than 25 words, but sentence length can be varied to add impact.

There is no problem with an occasional longer sentence, provided that it is clear and easy to follow. Any sentence with more than 25 words should be examined to see if it can be shortened. The words 'and' and 'also' often indicate suitable places to break a long sentence into two shorter ones. Conversely, a short sentence can be an effective means of emphasis, but too many consecutive short sentences may irritate.

Text can be broken up into paragraphs, each of which comprises one or more sentences. There is no general rule applying to the number of sentences in a paragraph or the length of a paragraph. Press journalists like to commence a new paragraph with each new sentence, but this is inappropriate in a technical document. Sentences contained in any one paragraph should be 'homogenous in subject matter and sequential in treatment'. However, if the grouping of the subject matter results in an unreasonably long paragraph, the text can be divided into more than one paragraph.

Deciding where to break for a new paragraph may sometimes be a matter of visual appearance. As with sentences, too many long paragraphs can be confusing and too many short paragraphs can irritate.

13.2 GRAMMAR, SPELLING AND PUNCTUATION

Incorrect or inconsistent grammar, spelling and punctuation not only irritates, but can be dangerous. Contract documents must be precise and accurate. They can be subject to detailed scrutiny, not only by contractors but by lawyers in the event of a dispute. Any material which is ambiguous, inaccurate or imprecise will be seized upon and used in evidence in any claim for additional payments or damages.

While many engineers have the ability and confidence to write clearly and well, there are many who are confused and uncertain in their knowledge of how to write good English. The following guidelines and recommendations are directed to those questions which are most likely to arise when preparing documents for contracts.

Grammar

This is not the place for a treatise on English grammar; there are other more appropriate books for reference. Even the simplest rules of grammar are too extensive and too complex to summarize in one chapter. For guidance on grammar, a suitable reference book should be consulted, for example *The Oxford Guide to English Usage* by Weiner (Oxford University Press).

Language Conventions

In writing contract documents, a number of conventions are in common use. These conventions apply particular meanings to words and phrases which may not be strictly in accordance with current idiom.

Many engineers have difficulty in the use of the auxiliary verbs 'shall', 'will', and 'must'. This is not really surprising, as reference to the *Concise Oxford English Dictionary* and to Fowler's *Dictionary of Modern English Usage* will show that the possible distinctions between these words are elaborate.

In traditional grammar, auxiliary verbs in the future tense change with person. In the first person, 'shall' is used (I shall, we shall), whereas in the second and third persons, 'will' is used (you will, he/she will, they will). For stress and emphasis, the use of these auxiliaries may be reversed. This variation does not apply to 'must', which is used to express a mandatory or imperative requirement.

Documents for contract purposes are usually written in the third person. They are prepared by, or on behalf of, the Principal and are naturally written from the Principal's point of view. By convention, in this context the words 'shall' and 'will' have acquired special functions.

This convention is that 'shall' indicates what is obligatory on the part of the Contractor (The Contractor shall . . .), whereas 'will' indicates an intention on the part of the Principal (The Principal will . . .).

There is no real justification for this. Current practice is to eliminate the distinction as being discriminatory and to use 'shall' for both purposes. Although the use of 'must' (instead of 'shall') is finding increasing favour in documents and legislation, it has not yet found its way into standard general conditions. Until the situation changes, the use of 'shall' is recommended.

Non-discriminatory Language

The prevention of discrimination based on sex, race, marital status, religion, or physical impairment is current government policy in most English-speaking countries. This policy is now generally accepted throughout the community and has sometimes been reinforced by legislation.

This attitude has resulted in the widespread adoption of language conventions which treat everyone equally. While this, for the most part, has had little effect on engineering contract documentation, there are two situations which may give concern to the engineer. These are:

- The use of the third person singular personal pronoun
- The use of words incorporating 'man' as a prefix or suffix.

The first situation arises from a feature of English in which the form of a third person singular pronoun varies according to the sex of the person to whom it refers. Hence for each grammatical case there are three forms, or genders, representing male, female, or neuter respectively:

he, she, it him, her, it
his, her(s), its himself, herself, itself

Perhaps it is because this variation is almost the last remnant of grammatical gender in modern English (unlike in many other modern European languages), that these forms cause so much irritation. There are several ways to overcome this problem.

The first and most obvious is to rephrase the sentence so as to eliminate the pronoun. Often this can be done without difficulty. Alternatively, the plural can be used since the third person plural pronouns lack gender:

they, them, their(s), themselves

The subject can often be made plural without affecting the meaning of the sentence. Where this is not practicable, the plural form of the pronoun can be used even if the subject is singular:

'It is enough to drive anyone out of their senses'.

G. B. Shaw

While this may be frowned upon by grammarians, there are many examples in literature; Shakespeare, Fielding, Shaw and other famous writers have all on occasion used this device. Whether or not to adopt this practice is a matter for personal preference.

The second situation also arises frequently. There are many words in the English language incorporating 'man' as a prefix or suffix. The word 'man' has long been used to mean not only 'male' but also 'humanity', and dictionaries still use both meanings of the word. However, with the increased number of women in the workforce, many feel that the use of the word 'man' to encompass all humanity gives unequal treatment to men and women. Whether the engineering writer accepts this view is again a matter of personal taste.

A frequently adopted ruse is to use the word 'person' as the prefix or suffix. This is untidy and somewhat pedantic and should be avoided if possible. English has a sufficiently extensive vocabulary to enable the writer to select an alternative word, as the following examples show:

manned	operated
workman	worker
workmanlike	skilful
man-hours	work hours
draughtsman/draftsman	draughter/drafter
manmade	handmade, artificial, synthetic, etc.
manpower	workforce
craftsman	skilled worker

However, some words have specific meanings in the engineering profession. Words such as access hole, overseer, and trade can be substituted for manhole, foreman, and tradesman, but the precise engineering meaning may be lost.

For example, an access hole may not necessarily be large enough to admit an adult human body (all manholes are indeed access holes, but not vice versa). Likewise, the word 'foreman' has particular connotations in the factory and on the job site. Suggested alternatives such as 'supervisor' or 'overseer' may not have the same industrial significance.

Common sense should be used in the choice of such words. If there is no other suitable word, the use of a word with 'man' as a prefix or suffix should be accepted. The main point is to make the meaning clear.

Spelling

Little annoys readers more than incorrect or inconsistent spelling. So, when in doubt, check! The spelling given in the latest edition of the dictionary selected as the prime reference should be followed. When the dictionary gives alternative spellings, a useful rule is to adopt the first spelling listed. However, there may be some instances where the second spelling should be used because it has wider currency in the local community. One group of words which fall into this category and with which some people have difficulty are those which end with -*ise*, -*ising*, -*isation* (rather than -*ize*, etc.) when these are suffixes. The -*ise* suffix is listed as the second option in the *Concise Oxford Dictionary* but many people prefer it:

realise	rather than	realize
realising		realizing
realisation		realization

Note that this does not apply to words ending in -ize when it is not a suffix:

size   seize   prize

There are many instances where American spelling differs from the conventional English form:

English	*American*
fulfil	fullfil
skilful	skillful
calibre	caliber
woollen	woolen
labour	labor
centre	center
colour	color
programme	program

With regard to the last word, in countries where the English form predominates, the spelling 'program' is now universal in computer terminology.

Plurals also give some people trouble, particularly if they derive from Latin or other languages. Many English words retain the plural forms of the original language from which they derive:

Singular	*Plural*
addendum	addenda
agendum	agenda
criterion	criteria
matrix	matrices
radius	radii
stratum	strata
axis	axes
medium	media

Other English words have an English plural which should be adopted where appropriate:

Singular	Plural		
apex	apexes	rather than	apices
appendix	appendixes		appendices
bureau	bureaus		bureaux
premium	premiums		premia

However, some words give different meanings to the two plurals:

indexes (in a book)	indices (in algebra)
vortexes (whirlpools)	vortices (in physics)
stadiums (sports grounds)	stadia (units of measurement)

For the spelling of place names, a recognized atlas such as the *Oxford Atlas* or the *Encyclopaedia Brittanica Atlas* should be consulted.

Punctuation

Punctuation is the practice of inserting marks or symbols in text for the purpose of clarifying the meaning of the statement. Punctuation marks should not be confused with accent (diacritical) marks placed over some vowels (and under some consonants) in many European languages (other than modern English) to indicate the nature and position of a spoken accent in a word.

Punctuation in written English serves the same function as voice inflexion and pauses do in spoken English. While its function is to make the meaning as clear as possible, the overuse of punctuation can have the opposite effect. A useful rule is to use punctuation marks only when needed to avoid ambiguity. A mark should not be used unless it has a definite purpose.

Punctuation is largely a matter of individual style. Many writers use punctuation marks only when needed to avoid ambiguity and obscurity; others use them more freely to simulate pauses in speech. Inadequate punctuation may lead to ambiguity; unnecessary punctuation may distract and confuse. The difficulty is to steer a safe course between these two extremes.

The engineer should adopt the policy that the prime function of punctuation is to make the meaning as clear as possible. The following notes are for general guidance only and are directed particularly to contract documentation.

Apostrophe (') This mark, which is strictly speaking not a punctuation mark, is possibly the most misunderstood and therefore misused symbol in written English. Originally it was a sign to indicate the omission of the letter 'e' from the suffix 'es' used to form the possessive case in some nouns. Its use was extended to indicate the omission of other letters particularly when imitating the verbal contractions in spoken English such as 'don't' (do not), 'can't' (cannot) and 'isn't' (is not). It is sometimes used in poetry to suit the metre ('o'er' instead of 'over'). Its use in this fashion is not appropriate in technical writing. As a general rule, apostrophes should not be used for abbreviations and contractions.

Its prime use is to indicate possession but only in the case of nouns. Apostrophes are not used for the possessive personal pronouns 'his', 'hers', 'its', 'theirs' and 'yours'. A frequent confusion is between 'its' and 'it's'; 'it's' is a contraction of 'it is' and is not appropriate in technical writing. There are three simple rules for using apostrophes to indicate the possessive case in nouns:

- For singular and plural nouns which do not end in an 's', an apostrophe is used followed by an 's'; e.g.

    the tunnel's portal

- For plural nouns which end in an 's', an apostrophe is used but without a following 's'; e.g.

    the tunnels' portals

- For singular nouns which end in an 's', an aspostrophe is used followed by an 's'; e.g.

    the witness's report

However, when a noun is used in an adjectival sense, the apostrophe is omitted; e.g.

    an operators manual

(in the sense that it is a manual *for* operators).

Colon (:) This mark is used to indicate a pause longer than that indicated by a semicolon but shorter than that indicated by a full stop. Colons are also used to:

- Introduce a statement which explains or amplifies the preceeding one.
- Introduce a list. (A dash or hyphen should not be put after a colon used in this way.)
- Indicate a ratio or scale (e.g. 1 : 100).

Comma (,) The comma indicates a pause or separation. It should be used only where it is essential for clarity or when its omission could cause ambiguity. The following are a few examples of situations where commas should be used:

- between two or more adjectives preceding and qualifying a noun; e.g.

  a two metre long, timber post

However, when the adjective next to the noun is closely related to the noun, the comma can be omitted; e.g.

  a galvanized steel plate

- To differentiate between defining and non-defining clauses and phrases. A defining clause is one which contains a statement which is essential to the meaning of the sentence. It should *not* be identified by commas; e.g.

  Tenderers who fail to submit schedules may have their tenders rejected.

In the above example, placing commas after *Tenderers* and after *schedules* changes the meaning of the sentence by implying that *all* tenderers fail to submit tenders and therefore may have their tenders rejected.

A non-defining clause is one which contains a statement not essential to the meaning of the sentence; e.g.

  The steelwork, which is to be supplied under another contract, will be delivered by road vehicle.

In the above example, the non-defining clause ('which is ... another contract') could be discarded without affecting the meaning of the sentence. In this example, the question should be asked 'Is this clause really necessary?'

- Between coordinate clauses linked by conjunctions (such as 'for', 'or', 'and'); e.g.

  All defective materials shall be removed from the Site, or disposed of as directed.

- To distinguish parenthetical phrases. They are then used in pairs in the same manner as parentheses; e.g.

  The Contractor, upon request by the Superintendent, shall make the necessary tests.

When in doubt, read the sentence aloud, noting where it is necessary to pause for clarity or emphasis. This usually indicates a place where a comma may be used effectively.

Exclamation Mark (!) This is emotive and therefore unnecessary in contract documents.

Full stop (.) This should be used:

- At the end of a sentence
- After an abbreviation
- As an acceptable alternative to a decimal point

It should *not* be used:

- After titles and headings in documents, tables, schedules or forms
- After contractions
- After symbols for units of measurement and currency

Hyphen (-) Generally, this is used to indicate the association of two ideas. As with the comma, hyphens should be used only where they are needed to avoid ambiguity; for example, the following is potentially ambiguous:

> three year old machines

Hyphens can be used to remove the ambiguity. However,

> three year-old machines

is not the same as

> three-year-old machines

Hyphens can be used:

- To join numbers and fractions; e.g.

  > twenty-nine   one-quarter

- To avoid awkward adjoining letters; e.g.

  > re-emphasize

- In such expressions as

  > V-belt   U-shaped   O-ring

Hyphens can be used to differentiate words with the 're'-prefix which can have two meanings:

recollect (recall)	re-collect (collect again)
represent (designate)	re-present (present again)
reform (change)	re-form (form again)
recover (regain)	re-cover (cover again)
remark (comment)	re-mark (mark again)
relay (transmit)	re-lay (lay again)

A hyphen should be used with such words only where it is necessary to distinguish two meanings. It would be preferable to use a different phrase altogether and avoid an ambiguous expression.

Parentheses ( ) and square brackets [ ] Parentheses are used to enclose expressions which are not essential to the meaning of the sentence but which expand or clarify its meaning. If possible, their use in this manner within a sentence in contract documents should be avoided because the matter within the parentheses may be interpreted as being less important than other material.

Square brackets should only be used in a quotation to indicate matter that is not original.

The main use of parentheses in contract documents is to enclose letters or numbers denoting items in a series or list; e.g.

(a) (b)   (i) (ii)

The initial parenthesis should *not* be omitted; e.g. do not write

a) b)   i) ii)

Semicolon (;) This is used to indicate a pause greater than would require a comma but less than would require a full stop. A common use is to separate clauses which already contain commas. It can also be used at the end of items in a list.

Question mark (?) This should not be required in contract documents since the purpose of the documents is to inform or instruct, not to ask questions.

Quotation marks (") These are used in technical writing to enclose:

- Direct quotations.
- Titles of chapters or sections referred to elsewhere in the document.
- Terms used in an unfamiliar context or in a colloquialism. In this instance, the quotation marks can be omitted from the second and subsequent use of the term or word.

13.3 RULES AND CONVENTIONS

Consistency of style is encouraged by following rules and conventions. Taking care and being consistent will save time and expense, not only for the engineer and the typist, but also for the reader. The following guidelines are based on experience. Where there are alternatives, an attempt has been made to give specific advice. It is not expected that such advice will be free from criticism, but in each case there has been a sound reason for the option selected.

Abbreviations, Contractions and Acronyms

Definitions and use The use of shortened forms of words and phrases is intended to save space and to avoid needless repetition. However, these shortened forms should be used only where appropriate. As a general rule, abbreviations and contractions should not be used in the written text (other than units of measurement or currency), but they may be used in addresses in correspondence. Three types may be distinguished.

An *abbreviation* is a shortened form of a word consisting either of the first letter alone, or of the first letter followed by one or more other letters of the word *except the final one:*

Hon. for Honourable   Oct. for October.

A *contraction* is a shortened form of a word containing two or more letters and ending with the final letter of the the word itself:

Dr   for Doctor   Mr for Mister   St for Street
phone for telephone   plane   for aeroplane

An *acronym* is an abbreviation formed from the initial letters of a title or a phrase and which, from use, has become a word in its own right. Acronyms are thus made from the initial letters of other words, without full stops; e.g.

UNESCO   NATO   GATT

It is also permissible to write some well-known acronyms in lower case; e.g.

radar   laser

Plurals of abbreviations and contractions are formed by adding an 's' without an apostrophe. An 's' is not added to the plural form of an abbreviation or contraction of a unit of measurement. Some of the more commonly used abbreviations are as follows:

1. Days of the week:

   Sun. Mon. Tues. Wed. Thurs. Fri. Sat.

2. Months of the year:

   Jan. Feb. Mar. Apr. Aug. Sept. Oct. Nov. Dec.

   May, June, and July are not normally abbreviated unless for space reasons in tables and schedules.

3. The names of the States and Territories in Australia should be abbreviated only in addresses (without full stops):

   NSW   Vic   WA   SA   Qld   NT   Tas

Punctuation Abbreviations are usually followed by a full stop, but it is becoming accepted to omit the full stops in abbreviations formed from the initial letters of the names of widely known organizations:

BBC   ICE   SAA   BSI

Contractions should *not* be followed by a full stop unless they end a sentence:

Dr   Mrs   St   Ave

Some postal authorities (such as Australia Post) discourage the use of *ALL* punctuation on envelopes because of the problems which have arisen with the use of computer controlled sorting machines.

An exception to this rule are abbreviations and contractions which are likely to be misunderstood unless a full stop is added to indicate that they are shortened forms. For instance, *No.* for number, which is actually a contraction of the Italian word *numero*, may need a full stop to distinguish it from the word 'no' (meaning negative); the plural *Nos.*, however, is usually given one.

The standard abbreviations and contractions for both metric and British–US units of measurement have no full stops.

cwt   kW   lb   oz   mm   yd

But to avoid ambiguity a full stop must sometimes be added to the abbreviation of inch(es) to distinguish it from the preposition 'in'.

The railway gauge is 3 ft 6 in. in Western Australia

It is preferable, however, to rearrange the wording to avoid this:

The railway gauge in Western Australia is 3 ft 6 in.

Apostrophes are not used in abbreviations and contractions:

Assn (for Association)   not   Ass'n.
phone (for telephone)   not   'phone

Ideally, abbreviations and contractions, except for units of measurement, should be avoided. However, the main point is consistency; it is important to ensure that the same form is used every time. Unusual shortened forms of words should be avoided; if unavoidable, they should be clearly defined on their first use or, if extensive use is made of them, a schedule of abbreviations and contractions used should be provided. Apart from the SI units of measurement, there is no generally recognized standard for abbreviations and contractions. Some of the more common abbreviations and contractions used on drawings are shown in Appendix F.

Spacing If inserting full stops between letters comprising abbreviations and contractions formed from initials, spaces should not be left between the individual letters:

U.S.A.   not   U. S. A.
B.M.A.   B. M. A.

However, spaces should be left between the initials of personal names:

G. B. Shaw   J. M. Barrie

Except in the case of currency amounts there should be one space between a number and its unit of measurement:

65 m   750 mm   240 V

Units of Measurement

Two systems of measurement are used in English-speaking countries – the British–US system (formerly referred to as the Imperial system) based on the yard and the pound and the ISO system based on the metre and the kilogram. The former still dominates the industrial scene in the USA while other English-speaking countries such as Australia and New Zealand are completely converted to the ISO system. In the British Isles the systems exist side by side, albeit somewhat uneasily at times.

Note that there is a difference between the US and the British gallons. The US gallon is the 'wine' gallon, which is smaller than the British 'imperial' gallon in the ratio of 5 : 6. When quoting this unit in a contract, it is important to make it clear which gallon is being used.

The introduction of the Systèm International (SI) brought about the formal standardization of the names and the corresponding abbreviations of the metric units. There does not appear to be any formal standardization of names for British–US units.

In the SI units there is one discrete name for each unit of physical quantity, with larger and smaller decimal magnitudes indicated by attachment of standard prefixes. This has resulted in a consistent and logical set of units, some of which have single names while others have compound names. In the SI system, abbreviation of the units is generally in lower case with the following exceptions:

1. Prefixes for magnitudes greater than one thousand; e.g.

   M   (mega)   one million
   G   (giga)   one thousand million

2. Units named after people; e.g.

   N   newton   H   hertz   Pa   pascal

3. The abbreviation for litre. Originally, the only one was a lower-case 'l'. However, to avoid confusion with (1) (unity), the upper-case 'L' has since been adopted also, and the two are interchangeable.

Writing the Date

The three most common ways of writing the date are:

Style	Format	Example
British	day/month/year	9 November 1990
American	month/day/year	November 9, 1990
International	year/month/day	1990 November 9

It is unnecessary to add suffixes to the number of the day (e.g. 1st, 2nd, 3rd, 4th).

To avoid confusion, the name of the month should not be referred to by number:

9 November 1990	*not*	9/11/1990
	or	9.11.1990
	or	9-11-1990

Owing to the widespread use of both the British and the American styles, using a fully numerical form can cause confusion. In the example above, 9/11/1990 would be interpreted in many countries as referring to 9 November 1990 whereas in others, the USA in particular, it would be understood to mean 11 September 1990. The potential for a misunderstanding is obvious.

In some countries the date is given numerically by using Roman numerals for the month:

9.xi.1990

Postal authorities often use this format for franking stamps. This overcomes the problem but is not recommended. To abbreviate the date, such as in a table or schedule, the month should be identified by writing the first three letters; if necessary for space reasons, only the last two digits of the year need be stated:

9 Nov 1990   *or*   9 Nov 90

A full stop after the abbreviation of the month (Nov.) and an apostrophe before the abbreviation of the year ('90) are unnecessary.

The British style is clear and unambiguous with the two groups of numerals being separated by the name of the month. It can easily be abbreviated.

The American style requires a comma after the day to separate the two groups of numerals. It does not lend itself to abbreviation as comfortably as does the British style.

The International style is a recent proposal by the International Standards Organisation and has not yet been widely adopted. Since there is little chance of misinterpretation, the International style can be used in the full numerical format. This has certain advantages in computer databases particularly where 'search' and 'order' commands are required. It is only recommended for use in such situations. Thus

1990 November 9   can be written as   19901109.

Note that where the number of the day or the month is less than 10, it is necessary to insert a zero before the single number.

The selection of the style for writing the date is a matter of personal preference, but the English style is recommended for the reasons stated above. The main point is to be consistent.

Numbers

Numbers can be expressed either in figures or words but in contract documentation, where numbers appear frequently, it is preferable to use numbers throughout. It is not necessary to give a number in both words and figures.

There are, however, a few situations where a number should always be expressed in words or where figures and words are required together:

- Where two series of adjacent numbers appear in a sentence, it is preferable to express one of them in words and one in figures for clarity; write:

  forty-seven 25 mm bars   or   47 twenty-five mm bars.

- Where it is not possible to avoid two sets of adjacent figures, they should be separated by a comma:

  On Floor 26, 12 more carpenters will be required.

- Where numbers open or close a sentence, they should be expressed in words:

  Twelve more carpenters will be required on Floor Twenty-six.

- As a general rule, words should be used for numbers up to and including nine; 'one' and 'zero' should always be written – numbers should not be used.
- Where numbers are very large, words can be used. Never use *billion* or *trillion* because meanings differ from country to country: write:

  two thousand million   rather than   2 000 000 000

- Where numbers are less than one and expressed as decimal numbers, a zero should always be placed before the decimal point:

  0.005   0.0005

Although the decimal point was originally placed at half the height of the figures, in the UK and the USA today it is generally placed on the line on which the figures stand. In most European countries and the whole of the former USSR the decimal sign is a comma.

There are two conventions for expressing numbers greater than 999. The first is to place a comma before each group of three figures:

  50,000   1,654,000

For numbers less than one, no comma is used:

0.005   0.0005

This convention can cause difficulties in countries where the comma is used as a decimal point.

The second convention is to insert a space instead of a comma:

50 000   1 645 000

This is the preferred option.

In this latter convention, for values less than one, a space is usually inserted after every three digits to the right of the decimal point:

0.000 55   rather than   0.00055

However, in text and in some tables and schedules, the use of the space in numbers with four digits unbroken by the decimal point is liable to cause confusion because the fourth digit tends to become isolated; it is recommended that such figures be set out without the space:

3542   rather than   3 542
0.3542   rather than   0.354 2

The exception to this rule occurs in any column where one or more numbers are present which have more than four digits unbroken by the decimal point. Then spaces should be inserted every three digits either side of the point in *every* number.

Currency

The conventions for expressing numbers representing currency values are the same as for numbers generally, with the second convention also being the preferred option. All English-speaking countries have now adopted decimal currency, although the names for the units of the currency may vary. In the following examples, the dollar is used as an example; the rules apply equally to pounds and pence. The convention for expressing monetary amounts may be summarized as follows:

Amounts in exact dollars $100   or $100.00
Amounts in cents only   10c   or $0.08
Amounts in dollars and cents $5 678.92

Note that:

- A full stop is not required after the abbreviation for cent (c) unless it occurs at the end of a sentence. There is no space left between the number and the symbol for cent:

9c   29c

- The decimal point must be preceded by the dollar sign and at least one figure; if the value is less than one dollar, this figure will be zero. The decimal point must be followed by at least two figures:

     $0.80   *not* $.8

In some jurisdictions, it is a legal requirement that monetary amounts stated in deeds and bills of exchange (e.g. cheques and receipts) should be expressed in words followed by the equivalent numerical value in parentheses. This is to make forgery or conversion more difficult. Other than to comply with such a requirement, it is not necessary, or even advisable, to express monetary sums in both words and figures.

If monetary amounts are expressed in both words and figures, great care must be taken to ensure accuracy. In a recent court ruling in Alabama, where a sum was expressed as

     'eight thousand six hundred dollars ($80 600–00)'

the amount in words was held to govern. The omission of a 'y' cost the Contractor $72 000.

Since some countries use similar symbols for the units of their currencies, it is necessary to add additional qualifying symbols or letters if the document is expected to have a circulation outside the country of origin. The following are examples of this convention:

Australian dollar	$A ....
Canadian dollar	$Can.......
Hong Kong dollar	$HK ....
New Zealand dollar	$NZ ....
Pounds sterling	£stg ....
Singapore dollar	$S ....
United States dollar	$US ....

Lists

The format and punctuation to be adopted when giving a list of items or presenting a number of options or a series of instructions can be confusing. The following simple guidelines can be used:

1. The sentence or clause introducing the list should end with a colon (without a dash).
2. The list should be indented, the amount of indentation being a matter of choice.
3. If there is a possibility that reference will need to be made to items in the list in future correspondence, the items in the list can be numbered or

lettered (a), (b), etc or numbered (i), (ii), etc. Otherwise, each item in the list can be preceded by a full stop (.) or a dash (-).

4. If the list comprises single words or simple statements, no punctuation mark is necessary at the end of each word.

5. If the list contains one or more statements comprising complete sentences (i.e. containing a verb in each case) then every item should be ended with a full stop or other appropriate punctuation mark.

6. If the list is a series of clauses or statements without verbs, each item may be ended with a semi-colon or left without a punctuation mark.

7. If the list is a series of requirements or options, the word "and" or 'or' as appropriate may be added at the end of the penultimate (i.e. second last) item.

Points of the Compass

The points of the compass should be spelt out in lower-case letters. Where any of the four cardinal points occur together they should be hyphenated:

> north   north-east   east-north-east

Where the word 'by' occurs it should not be hyphenated:

> north by east   north-east by north

Where compass points are included in capitalized place names, they should also be capitalized:

> South-East Asia   New South Wales

Compass points can be abbreviated to single-letter format. In this form the initial letters are capitalized without full stops:

> N   NE   ENE   N by E

Capitals

Apart from being applied to the first letter in a sentence, initial capital letters are used to avoid misunderstanding between common names and specific names. Capitals should always be used for:

- Names of specific persons or institutions
- Nationalities
- Place names
- Proper or specific names
- Trade and proprietary names
- Days of the week and special days
- Months of the year
- Honorifics and titles

When in doubt, the selected reference dictionary should be consulted.

Time

There are two ways of writing the time:

| 12-hour notation: | 9.30 a.m. | 9.30 p.m. |
| 24-hour notation: | 09.30 | 21.30 |

Care should be taken when designating noon and midnight, particularly when using the 12-hour notation. To avoid ambiguity, the following nomenclature should be used when using this notation:

12 noon 9 November 1990
12 midnight 9–10 November 1990

The mean solar time centred on the Prime meridian at Greenwich is the datum for all time zones. Previously called Greenwich Mean Time, this is now referred to as Universal Time (UT).

The world is basically divided into 24 mean solar time zones at one-hour intervals, each covering 15 degrees of longitude. There are some cases where an intermediate time zone has been adopted, one half-hour different. For example, the time zone for South Australia is nine and a half hours ahead of Universal Time.

The International Date Line (IDL) runs more or less along the meridian 180 degrees east of Greenwich. When crossing the IDL when travelling from east to west, a day is added; crossing west to east, a day is dropped.

Most countries adopt some form of daylight saving in summer, when the clocks are advanced one hour. Some European countries have adopted this extra hour on a permanent basis. When quoting times in contract documents, it is important to make it clear what time zone is being referred to.

This is particularly important in countries which cover more than one time zone (such as Australia, Canada and USA). The simplest way is to have a general note somewhere in the contract to the effect that all times quoted are current local zone times at the site of the Works.

Foreign Words

The origins of the English language lie in the Germanic language (now referred to as Anglo-Saxon) introduced into Britain by the invading Angles, Saxons and Jutes beginning in the fifth century. It was only influenced to a minor degree by the Gaelic of the original Celtic inhabitants and the Latin introduced by the earlier Roman invasion. Such influence was mainly confined to the adoption of place names and words for physical features unknown in the invader's homelands.

Table 13.1 Foreign words usually written in abbreviated forms

i.e.	id est	that is
e.g.	exempli gratia	for example
viz.	videlicet	namely
a.m.	ante meridiem	before noon
p.m.	post meridiem	after noon
etc.	et cetera	and so on
q.v.	quod vide	which see
ibid. or ib.	ibidem	in the same place
AD	anno Domini	in the year of our Lord
inst.	instantem	of this month
loc. cit.	loco citato	in the place quoted
p.a.	per annum	by the year
p.d.	per diem	by the day
stet	stet	let it stand
ult.	ultimo	of the last month
vs.	versus	against

Note: Although the abbreviation 'etc.' is given above, it should never be used in a contract document. It is too imprecise, even vague. If it is necessary to give an incomplete list of examples it is preferable to use the words 'and the like' in the place of etc. An even better alternative is to introduce the incomplete list with the words 'including but not limited to'.

The Anglo-Saxon language was in turn radically altered as a result of the subsequent invasions of Britain by the Norsemen from Scandinavia and the French from Normandy. Again, during the Colonial era many words from Africa, Asia and the Pacific were absorbed into the vocabulary.

As a result of these influences, modern English has become a predatory language, readily adopting words from other languages. Most of these words have had their spelling 'anglicized' and are recognized now as English words.

There is one group of words and phrases, mainly of Latin origin, which are almost invariably given in an abbreviated or contracted form. Some of these are listed in Table 13.1.

A list of Latin words and phrases commonly used in the legal profession, and which the Engineer might encounter in dealing with legal documents, is given in Appendix G.

PART

FOUR

APPENDIXES

CERTIFICATES, FORMS, AND SCHEDULES

Most engineering organizations involved in the contract-by-tender system have developed *pro-formas* for certificates, forms, and schedules used in their operations. The following examples are given to illustrate the various points made in the book regarding the use of schedules and forms. They are not definitive but are suggested as guidelines:

- Notice to Tenderers
- Tender Form (Lump Sum Contracts)
- Tender Form (Schedule of Rates Contracts)
- Schedule of Rates
- Schedule of Prices for Tendering
- Tender Analysis Form
- Draft Form of Agreement
- Payment Certificate
- Valuation of Subcontract Work Completed
- Application for Payment
- Certificate of Practical Completion

DRAFT NOTICE TO TENDERERS

[*Headed by the name and address of the Principal or of the Principal's agent under whose name tenders are being invited with telephone, telex, and fax numbers*]

NOTICE TO TENDERERS No.:

Project:

Contract: Contract No.: ☐☐☐☐

Date:

Tenderers are required to confirm in their tenders receipt of this Notice.

....
(*Engineer*)

Date of issue ....

DRAFT TENDER FORM (LUMP SUM CONTRACTS)

....

(Name of Tenderer)

of ....

(Address of Tenderer)

hereby tenders to perform the work for

....

(Name and Number of Contract)

in accordance with the following documents:

[Here provide a full list of Tender Enquiry and Tender Documents, leaving room for the tenderer to list other supporting documents.]

for the Lump Sum of...

....($......................)

Dated this .... day of .... 19....

....

(Name of Tenderer)

....

(Signature of Tenderer or Authorized Person)

DRAFT TENDER FORM (SCHEDULE OF RATES CONTRACTS)

....

(Name of Tenderer)

of ....

(Address of Tenderer)

hereby tenders to perform the work for

....

(Name and Number of Contract)

in accordance with the following documents:

[Here provide a full list of Tender Enquiry and Tender Documents, leaving room for the tenderer to list other supporting documents.]

At the Rates in the Schedule of Rates (Schedule ....)

....($.........................)

Dated this .... day of .... 19....

....

(Name of Tenderer)

....

(Signature of Tenderer or Authorized Person)

SCHEDULE OF RATES

[Headed by the name and address of the Principal or of the Principal's agent under whose name tenders are being invited]

Contract: **No.:** ☐☐☐☐

This Schedule, when completed and signed by the tenderer, will form part of the Tender Documents.

SCHEDULE OF RATES

No.	Description	Unit	Quantity	Rate	$	¢

Total equals Tender Sum

Tenderer: .... Signed: ....

SCHEDULE OF PRICES FOR TENDERING

[*Headed by the name and address of the Principal or of the Principal's agent under whose name tenders are being invited*]

SCHEDULE OF PRICES FOR TENDERING

No.	Description	Unit	Quantity	Rate	$	¢

Total equals Tender Sum

Tenderer: .... Signed: ....

TENDER ANALYSIS FORM

Contract: Equipment: Contract No:		Tenderer	Tenderer	Tenderer	Tenderer
Item	Description				
	Remarks				
	Recommendation				

Date: ....

(Engineer)

DRAFT FORM OF AGREEMENT

AGREEMENT

By this Agreement made .... day of .... 19 ....
Between ....
of ....
called the Principal, of the first part
and ....
of ....
called the Contractor, of the second part

It is agreed that the annexed Documents marked .... to .... and the set
of Drawings numbered .... to .... inclusive shall together be deemed
to comprise the Contract between the parties.

In Witness whereof the parties hereto have executed this Agreement in
the manner required by their respective Articles of Association or Constitution and the laws of their respective countries.

Signed by the Principal ....

Signed by the Contractor ....

PAYMENT CERTIFICATE

[Headed by the name of the Superintendent or of the Superintendent's employer and the address for the service of notices to the Superintendent with telephone, telex, and fax numbers]

PAYMENT CERTIFICATE

Certificate No.:   INTERIM/FINAL

Project:

Principal:

Contractor:

Contract: CONTRACT No.: ☐☐☐☐

This is to certify that the Contractor is entitled to receive from the Principal the sum of

on account of work completed to .... *(date)* under the above named Contract.

Value of Work Completed	$
less Retention Money	$
Total Amount Payable	$
less Previous Payments	$
Amount Now Payable	$

....
(Superintendent)

Date of Issue ....

VALUATION OF SUBCONTRACT WORK COMPLETED

[Headed by the name of Superintendent or Superintendent's employer and address for the service of notices to the Superintendent with telephone, telex, and fax numbers]

VALUATION OF SUBCONTRACT WORK COMPLETED

Valuation No.: Interim/Final

Project: Reference No.: ☐☐☐☐

Contractor:

Contract: Contract No.: ☐☐☐☐

Subcontract:

Subcontractor: Subcontract No.: ☐☐☐☐

With reference to the Subcontractor's .... * dated ....
(copy attached), this is to certify that, for interim payment purposes, the
value of work completed to .... (*date*) and the amount now
payable in respect of the above Subcontract has been estimated as follows:

Value of Work Completed $

less Retention Money $ _____

Total Amount Payable $

less Previous Valuations $ _____

This Valuation Amount Now $ _____

.... Date of Issue ....
(*Superintendent*)

*Claim or Invoice.

APPLICATION FOR PAYMENT

APPLICATION FOR PAYMENT

To:

From:

Contract: Date:

---

1. *Current Contract Value*:

(a) Contract Sum $

(b) *less* Prime Cost/Provisional Sums $_____

(c) Net Contract Sum [1(a) − 1(b)] $

(d) Approved Variations $_____
   (adjusted to Base Index Date)

(e) Current Contract Value [1(c) + 1(d)] $

---

2. *Current Work Value and Amount Claimed*

(Including payments to Nominated Subcontractors)

(a) Value of contract work completed to date $

(b) Value of Variations completed to date $_____

(c) Value of work completed to date [2(a) + 2(b)] $

(d) *less* Value of work completed last claim $_____

(e) Current Work Value [2(c) − 2(d)] $

(f) *less* Retention Money (as applicable) $_____

(g) [2(e) − 2(f)] $

(h) *less* Current Work Value last claim $_____

(i) Amount Claimed for Payment [2(g) − 2(h)] $_____

....

(Contractor's Representative)

CERTIFICATE OF PRACTICAL COMPLETION

[Headed by the name of the Superintendent or the Superintendent's employer and address for the service of notices to the Superintendent, with telephone, telex and fax numbers]

CERTIFICATE OF PRACTICAL COMPLETION

Project:

Principal:

Contractor:

Contract: Contract No.: ☐☐☐☐

Portion:

I hereby certify that the Date of Practical Completion for /this portion of/* the work under the Contract as defined above is the .... day of .... 19.......

The following unfinished items of work under /this portion of/* the Contract shall be completed within .... of this date; otherwise the date for the measurement of the commencement of the Defects Liability Period is deferred:

....
(Superintendent)

Date of Issue ....

*/Delete/ if appropriate.

ASSOCIATIONS OF CONSULTING ENGINEERS AFFILIATED UNDER THE FÉDÉRATION INTERNATIONALE DES INGÉNIEURS-CONSEILS (FIDIC)

Most independent professional engineers in private practice are members of a national consulting engineering association. These associations have strict requirements for membership based on recognized qualifications and sufficient practical experience to ensure that their members are equipped to give independent professional engineering advice to their clients.

Most of these associations are, in turn, affiliated at an international level with the Fédération Internationale des Ingénieurs-Conseils (FIDIC) with headquarters in Lausanne, Switzerland. In 1991, FIDIC comprised 54 member associations. The following is a list of these associations:

Australia	The Association of Consulting Engineers Australia (ACEA)
Austria	Verband Beratender Ingenieure Österreich (VBIO)
Bangladesh	Bangladesh Association of Consulting Engineers (BACE)
Belgium	Chambre des Ingénieurs-Conseils de Belgique (CICB)
	Kamer van Raadgevende Ingenieurs van België (KRIB)

Botswana	Association of Consulting Engineers Botswana
Brazil	Associação Brasileira de Consultores de Engenharia (ABCE)
Canada	Association of Consulting Engineers of Canada (ACEC) Association des Ingénieurs-Conseils du Canada
Denmark	Foreningen af Raadgivende Ingeniører (FRI)
Egypt	The Egyptian Society of Consulting Engineers
Finland	The Finnish Association of Consulting Firms (SKOL)
France	Chambre des Ingénieurs-Conseils de France (CICF)
Germany	Verband Beratender Ingenieure (VBI)
Hong Kong	The Association of Consulting Engineers of Hong Kong (ACEHK)
Iceland	Félag Rádgjafarverkfraedinga (FRV)
India	The Association of Consulting Engineers (India) (ACE (India))
Indonesia	Inkindo-Teknik The National Association of Indonesian Consulting Engineers
Iran	Iranian Association of Consulting Engineers (IACE)
Ireland	Cumman Innealtóiri Comhairle na h-Eireann Association of Consulting Engineers of Ireland (ACEI)
Israel	The Israel Association of Consulting Engineers (IACE)
Italy	Associazione Ingegneri Consulenti Italiani (AICI)
Japan	Association of Japanese Consulting Engineers (AJCE)
Kenya	The Association of Consulting Engineers of Kenya (ACEK)
Korea	Korean Council of Consulting Engineers (KCCE)
Luxemburg	Chambre des Ingénieurs-Conseils du Grand-Duché de Luxemburg (CICL)
Malawi	Association of Consulting Engineers of Malawi (ACEM)
Malaysia	Association of Consulting Engineers of Malaysia (ACEM)
Namibia	The Association of Consulting Engineers of Namibia
Netherlands	Orde van Nederlandse Raadgevende Ingenieurs (ONRI)
Netherlands Antilles	Sociedat di Architekt i Ingenieur Antiyano (SAIA)
New Zealand	The Association of Consulting Engineers New Zealand (ACENZ)
Nigeria	Association of Consulting Engineers Nigeria (ACEN)
Norway	Radgivende Ingeniorers Forening (RIF)
Peru	Associacion Peruana de Consultoria (APC)

Philippines	Council of Engineering Consultants of the Philippines (CECOPHIL)
Poland	The Polish Consultants Society, Independent Consulting Engineers Section.
Portugal	Associação Portuguesa de Projectistas e Consultores
Senegal	Association Nationale des Ingénieurs-Conseils et Consultants du Senegal
Singapore	Association of Consulting Engineers Singapore (ACES)
South Africa	The South African Association of Consulting Engineers Suid-Afrikaanse Vereniging van Raadgewende (SAACE)
Spain	Associación Española de Consultores en Ingenieria (ASINCE)
Sri Lanka	The Association of Consulting Engineers Colombo, Sri Lanka (ACESL)
Surinam	Orde van Raadgevende Ingenieurs in Suriname (ORIS)
Sweden	Svenska Konsultforeningen (SKIF)
Switzerland	Association Suisse des Ingénieurs-Conseils Schweizerische Vereiningung Beratender Inenieure (AISC)
Taipei	The Chinese Association of Engineering Consultants
Tanzania	The Association of Consulting Engineers Tanzania (ACET)
Thailand	The Consulting Engineers Association of Thailand (CEAT)
Tunisia	Association Nationale des Bureaux d'Etudes et des Ingénieurs Conseils
Turkey	Association of Turkish Consulting Engineers and Architects
United Kingdom	The Association of Consulting Engineers (ACE)
United States of America	American Consulting Engineers Council (ACEC)
Yugoslavia	Zajednica Konzalting Organizacija Jugoslavije
Zambia	The Association of Consulting Engineers of Zambia (ACEZ)
Zimbabwe	Zimbabwe Association of Consulting Engineers (ZACE)

Addresses and other details of these organizations may be obtained from The Secretariat, Fédération Internationale des Ingénieurs-Conseils, PO Box 86, CH-1000 Lausanne 12, Switzerland.

TERMS FREQUENTLY USED TO QUALIFY CONDITIONS OF SALE

There are a number of terms used by tenderers and suppliers of materials and equipment to qualify their conditions of sale. These are often abbreviated to the initial letters of the term and can be confusing and ambiguous. When the Engineer encounters one of these terms, it is advisable to require the tenderers to specifically define the meaning of the term. The following is a list of such terms with their *most probable* meaning:

ex-factory; ex-store; ex-works These terms are synonymous and are not usually abbreviated. Their usual meaning is that the Tender Sum is the price at the vendor's premises and does not include delivery or insurance in transit. It normally includes packing and crating and loading aboard the carrier, and the vendor's responsibility ends when the goods are loaded. The Engineer should confirm these points.

COD Cash on Delivery ('Collect on Delivery' in USA). Payment for the goods is to be made at the time and at the place where the goods are handed over to the purchaser. The Engineer should confirm the precise manner in which paymernt is to be made. The vendor's responsibility ends when payment is made.

FAS [followed by name of ship and port of shipment] 'Free Alongside Ship [named]' at nominated shipment port. The Tender Sum includes all costs and charges until the goods are delivered alongside the named ship at the nominated port and within reach of the vessel's loading equipment. The Engineer should ensure that subsequent freight charges include loading aboard the ship. The term, as abbreviated, is ambiguous as it can be interpreted as 'Free Aboard Ship'. The vendor's responsibility ends when the goods are delivered to the nominated ship's side. The term does not make it clear who is to be responsible for any costs arising from delays in loading aboard the ship.

FOW [followed by name of shipment port] 'Free on Wharf' (at named shipment port). The Tender Sum includes all costs and charges until the goods are delivered to the wharf at the named shipment port. The meaning of this term must be clarified, as it does not make it clear who is to be responsible for unloading and possible temporary storage at the wharf and for subsequently moving the shipment to within reach of the vessel's loading equipment and loading thereon. The vendor's responsibility ends when the goods are delivered to the wharf.

FOB [followed by details of carrier] 'Free on Board [carrier]'. The Tender Sum includes all costs and charges applicable until the goods are loaded aboard the nominated carrier (aircraft, ship, rail wagon or road vehicle). The term should be clarified by defining the name of the carrier and the date and place of departure. The vendor's responsibility ends when the goods are loaded aboard the nominated carrier.

FIS [followed by named place] 'Free in Store [at a nominated place]'. The Tender Sum includes all costs and charges applicable until the goods are delivered to the purchaser at a nominated place. The Engineer should confirm arrangements for receiving, unloading and storing the shipment. The vendor's responsibility ends when the goods are delivered to the nominated place.

C & F 'Cost and Freight'.

CF & E 'Cost, Freight and Exchange'.

CIF 'Cost, Insurance and Freight'.

CIF & E 'Cost, Insurance, Freight and Exchange'. These terms are used to indicate the extent to which the Tender Sum covers the financial responsibility of the vendor for the supply and delivery of the goods. The usual meaning of the individual terms is as follows:

Cost The cost of the goods at the vendor's premises.

Freight The loading, transport and unloading of the shipment between the vendor's and the purchaser's premises.

Insurance The insurance of the goods in transit. As insurance is always a difficult subject, the Engineer should carefully examine the vendor's proposals in this matter.

Exchange Normally, bank and other charges and any variations in exchange rates where more than one currency is involved. The term can be interpreted in a number of ways and the Engineer should verify precisely what the vendor intends.

STANDARD CORRECTION MARKS FOR TYPESCRIPT (from British Standard 5261C)

Instruction	Mark in text	Direction	Mark in margin
Insert words indicated in margin	⋏		Words to be inserted followed by ⋏
Words of doubtful meaning to be checked	◯	Encircle words concerned	(?)
Delete	⊢────⊣ ╱	Draw line through words or characters to be deleted	ℰ
Leave as printed; stet	‒ ‒ ‒ ‒ ‒ ‒	under words or characters to remain	✓
Change to upper-case letters	≡	under words or characters to be changed	≡
Change to lower case letters	◯	Encircle words or characters to be changed	≢

Instruction	Mark in text	Direction	Mark in margin
Underline word or words to be italic or underlined	——	under words to be in italic or underlined	——
Close up (delete space between characters)	⌒	linking spaced characters	⌒
Insert space between letters or words	Y	between words or characters to be spaced	Y — Indicate amount of space required
Reduce space between letters or words	⋀	between words or characters to be closed up	⋀ — Indicate amount of space required
Insert space between lines or paragraphs	)—	The marginal mark extends between the lines or paragraphs to be spaced. Indicate amount of space required	
Reduce space between lines or paragraphs	⊂—	The marginal mark extends between the lines or paragraphs to be closed up. Indicate amount of space required	
Transpose words or characters	⎍	between words or characters to be transposed	⎍
Begin new paragraph	⌐	before first word of new paragraph	⌐
No new paragraph here	⊃	between paragraphs	⊃
Insert omitted copy as lettered in marked 'diamond'	⋋	followed by for example ⟨A⟩	⋋ — Supply the relevant copy, marked ⟨A⟩

ABBREVIATIONS AND CONTRACTIONS

There are no standards for abbreviations or contractions. However, the following are frequently used on drawings. The use of abbreviations and contractions within written documents should be kept to a minimum.

and	&
approximately	approx.
centreline	CL or ℄
centre of gravity	CG
centre to centre	c. to c.
centres	crs
degree (angular)	deg or °
degree Celsius	deg C or C
degree Fahrenheit	deg F or F
degree Kelvin	deg K or K
diameter	dia.
drawing	dwg
figure	fig.
galvanized	galv.
greater than	>
horizontal	horiz.

inside diameter	ID
less than	<
maximum	max.
minimum	min.
nominal	nom.
number	No. or #
outside diameter	O.D.
page	p.
pages	pp.
per cent	per cent or %
reference	ref.
vertical	vert.
volume	vol.

LATIN PHRASES FREQUENTLY USED IN LEGAL DOCUMENTS

ab initio	from the beginning
ad hoc	for this purpose
ad infinitum	without limit
ad interim	for the time being
ad nauseam	to the point of disgust
alias dictum	otherwise called (abbreviated as alias)
alibi	elsewhere
alter idem	another exactly the same
bona fide	in good faith
caveat emptor	let the buyer beware
compos mentis	of sound mind
corpus delicti	the evidence that a crime has been committed
corrigenda	items to be corrected (in a book)
cui bono?	who stands to gain?
cum privilegio	with privilege
curriculum vitae	an account of one's career
de facto	in reality
de jure	in law (as opposed to de facto)
dies irae	Judgement Day

ex contrario	on the contrary
ergo	therefore
exeat	grant of leave
ex gratia	as an act of grace
ex officio	by virtue of the office
ex parte	from one side only
ex tempore	without preparation
factotum	one who does all
flagrante delicto	in the very act
gratis	free of charge
honoris causa	for the sake of honour
idem	the same
impedimenta	things which impede progress; baggage
imprimatur	licence to publish
in camera	in secret
in esse	in fact
in re	in the matter of
inter alia	among other things
in toto	entirely
in terrorem	as a threat
ipse dixit	a dogmatic statement
ipso jure	by unquestioned right
lex scripta	statute law
locum tenens	a deputy
locus standi	the right to appear before a court
mandamus	a writ issued by a higher court to a lower one
mea culpa	by my own fault
minutae	trifles
modus operandi	the way of working
modus vivendi	the way of living
mutatis mutandis	after making the necessary changes
ne plus ultra	perfection
nihil ad rem	not to the point
nil desperandum	never despair
non compos mentis	of unsound mind
nulli secundus	second to none
obiter dictum	an opinion given by a judge in court and therefore not binding
onus probandi	the burden of proof
pace	by leave of
pari passu	with equal pace
passim	everywhere

per capita	each
per contra	contrariwise
per se	by itself
prima facie	at first sight
pro forma	as a matter of form
pro rata	in proportion
pro tempore	for the time being
quantum meruit	as the amount deserves
quid pro quo	tit for tat
quondam	former(ly)
seriatim	one by one
sine die	indefinitely
sine qua non	indispensible condition
status quo	as things were before
sub judice	under judicial consideration
sui generis	peculiar to itself
ubique	everywhere
ultra vires	beyond the powers possessed
ut infra	as below
ut supra	as above
vice	in place of
vice versa	the order being reversed
vide	see
viva voce	orally

GLOSSARY

addendum See appendix.

Agreement See Instrument of Agreement.

Alternative Tender A tender specifically nominated as containing one or more provisions contradicting or inconsistent with provisions of the Enquiry Documents.

Amendments to the Enquiry Documents Changes in details of the initial Enquiry Documents made during the tendering period. (*See also* Notices to Tenderers.)

annexure A supplement attached to a document.

Annexure The specific supplement to a General Conditions.

appendix An addition supplementary to a document having some contributory value but not essential to its completeness.

assignment When one of the parties to a contract substitutes another party in its place as a party to the contract for all or some of the purposes of the contract.

Bank Guarantee An unconditional undertaking by a bank to pay a sum or sums which may be demanded at any time by a party named in the Guarantee.

Bill of Quantities A document named as such in the Enquiry Documents and issued to tenderers by or on behalf of the Principal. It is a schedule detailing each item of work performed or equipment supplied under the Contract with a measured quantity for each item.

commissioning The operation and testing of plant and equipment supplied under the Contract to ensure that it functions satisfactorily and complies with the requirements of the Contract.

Competitively Tendered Contract A contract where agreement is reached between a Principal and a Contractor following a formal competitive tendering process.

Conceptual Design Preliminary design required to determine the feasibility and viability of a project.

condition A term in a contract which is of such basic importance that a breach goes to the root of the contract and gives the injured party the right to treat the contract as terminated.

Conditions of Contract The document containing all the provisions relating to the respective rights and obligations of the parties to the Contract.

consideration An inducement to enter into a legally enforceable agreement.

construction The combination of the various elements of the Works in a logical order and in their proper place. The act of assembling and putting together the parts of a structure.

Constructional Plant Items of plant or equipment used in the execution of the work under the Contract but not forming part of the Works.

Consulting Engineer A professional engineer consultant who may be engaged by the Principal to prepare the designs and documents and to invite tenders.

Content of Tender One of the Enquiry Documents which schedules all that is required to be included in the Tender Documents.

Contingency Sum A provisional sum in the Contract to enable the Superintendent to authorize minor variations without first seeking the approval of the Principal.

contract An agreement enforceable at law.

Contract Documents All the documents referred to in the Contract Agreement incorporating all amendments to the Enquiry Documents and Tender Documents arising from negotiations before the signing of the Contract.

Contract Documents for Tendering Documents issued with the Enquiry Documents which are intended to form the basis for the final Contract.

Contract Drawings Drawings prepared and exchanged by the parties before acceptance of a tender.

contract under seal See formal contract.

contractor Any firm or individual who supplies goods or services or who undertakes erection, installation or construction work as a commercial business.

Contractor The successful tenderer. The second party to the Contract who undertakes to perform the work or supply the goods or services under the Contract.

Contractor's Representative The person nominated to receive instructions and to act on behalf of the Contractor on the Site or in the workshop.

Contract Sum The amount stated in the Contract as consideration for performing the work under the Contract.

Contract Sum Adjustment A procedure whereby the Principal accepts responsibility for additional payments to the Contractor due to fluctuations in the cost of labour, materials and/or transport during the performance of the work.

Corporate Standards Standard specifications and codes issued by engineering corporations specifically for their own use.

corporation A legally created artificial body which has a legal existence quite apart from the individual persons who comprise it.

Cost Plus Contract A contract where the Contractor is reimbursed the actual cost incurred in carrying out the work under the Contract plus a fee determined on an agreed basis.

Cost Reimbursement Contract See Cost Plus Contract.

Data Schedule A statement and questionnaire form which supplements a job specification.

Date for Practical Completion The date nominated in the Contract Agreement by which the work under the Contract is to reach Practical Completion or the date resulting from an extension of time granted by the Principal.

Date of Practical Completion The date certified in the Certificate of Practical Completion to be the date upon which the Works reached Practical Completion.

deed An instrument in writing which must be signed 'under seal' by the party executing the deed and attested by a witness who is not a party to the contract.

Defects Correction Period See Defects Liability Period.

Defects Liability Period The period nominated in the Contract for which the Contractor is obligated to rectify omissions from, or defects in, the work revealed during that period.

delivery Specifically, the loading and transport of materials and components required for the work.

design The detailed formulation of the requirements for the execution of a proposed undertaking.

design drawings Drawings showing details of work under the Contract.

Designated Subcontractor A subcontractor named in the Enquiry Documents to carry out certain works or supply certain items or services.

Detailed Design The design of the components of a project to the extent of detail required for actual construction or fabrication.

determination The settlement of a contract by agreement or legal action.

discharge A contract is said to be discharged when it is completed or otherwise terminated.

documentation The preparation of documents required for tendering and implementation purposes.

drawing A representation by lines as distinct from a painting.

Drawings The drawings referred to in the Contract.

engineer An academically qualified person who uses professed knowledge and experience in the application of the art and science of engineering.

Engineer The professional engineer delegated to act in a technical capacity on behalf of the Principal during the Tender or Negotiating stage. The Engineer may be an employee of the Owner or of the Principal or any other party engaged to act on behalf of the Principal.

engineering The art and science of planning, designing and accomplishing the fabrication of machinery and the construction of works for use by and benefit of the community at large.

Engineering Contract A mutual agreement between a Principal and a Contractor to undertake certain defined engineering work.

engross To compile and express in legal form.

Enquiry Documents All the documents which are issued to Tenderers and which prescribe the Principal's requirements for the preparation and submission of bids.

Equipment Design Data Schedule See Data Schedule.

erection The assembly on-site of a structure comprising a number of pre-fabricated elements.

estoppel A rule of law which precludes a party from later claiming that a statement expressed in the Contract is incorrect.

excess A term used in insurance to describe the amount of cover which is to be the responsibility of the insured party.

expediting The activity of ensuring that the procedure of procurement is not delayed.

Extent of Work and General Description A statement outlining the nature and extent of the work under the Contract.

fabrication The manufacture of plant, equipment and elements or components.

fluctuation An increase or decrease in the value of the work under the Contract due to changes in the cost of labour, materials or services during the performance of the work.

force majeure See frustration.

form 1. A document with blank spaces to be filled in with particulars before it is executed.

2. A typical document to be used as a guide in framing others for like uses.

3. The manner in which an Instrument of Agreement is expressed.

formal contract A written agreement the validity of which depends solely on its form (*see* 3 above).

frustration A situation whereby a contractual obligation has become incapable of performance without default by either party to the contract.

fundamental breach A breach of a condition of the Contract of sufficient gravity to lead to the determination of the Contract.

general arrangement drawings Drawings showing the layout and arrangement of the various elements comprising a facility or piece of equipment.

General Conditions of Contract A standard form of Conditions of Contract comprising those conditions which may be regarded as applicable generally to contracts involving work in a particular engineering discipline or group of disciplines.

General Requirements Specification That part of the Specification containing information and directions relating generally to work under the Contract.

genuine consent The absence of duress or undue influence to either party when negotiating a contract.

Guideline Specification See Master Specification.

handling Activities, including preparation of documents, associated with the delivery of materials and equipment.

Head Contract See Main Contract.

inspection The examination to ensure that satisfactory standards and techniques of manufacture and fabrication are maintained during the production of goods and equipment for the Contract.

Instructions to Tenderers The document setting out all the requirements for the preparation and submission of tenders and included in the Requirements for Tendering.

installation The setting up of prefabricated plant or equipment at a previously prepared location.

Instrument of Agreement A written agreement or deed identifying the parties to the Contract by name and registered address, stating the date of the agreement and setting out the terms and conditions of the Contract.

intention The actions by which the parties to a contract demonstrate their wish to enter into a legally binding agreement.

International Standards Standard specifications and codes of practice prepared and issued by international bodies established for this purpose by international agreement.

Invitation to Tender A written or advertised invitation to submit an offer to undertake the work under the Contract and included in the Requirements for Tendering.

Job Specification That part of the Specification in which the requirements for a particular item of work or equipment are prescribed.

late tenders Tenders received after the time or date nominated for receiving tenders.

legal capacity The capacity of a person or persons or a corporation to enter into a legally binding agreement.

legality of purpose The state or quality by which the intention of the Contract is in conformity with Common Law or Statute.

Letter of Acceptence A formal notification by one party unconditionally accepting an offer by another party in order to form a legally binding contract.

Letter of Intent A letter notifying a tenderer that the Principal intends to accept the tenderer's offer and which may include authority to proceed with certain nominated preliminary work.

Liquidated Damages An agreed pre-estimate of damages for which the Contractor is liable in the event of failure to complete the work under the Contract by the agreed date.

Lump Sum Contract A contract where the Contractor is paid a fixed amount nominated in the Contract.

Main Contract The primary contract between a Principal and a Contractor for the execution of the whole or part of a project.

maintenance The operation of plant and equipment supplied under the Contract and the replacement of all consumable and worn items for a nominated period.

Manufacturer's Standards Standard specifications supplied by manufacturers relating to their own plant and equipment.

Master Specifications Source documents for standard specifications, usually comprising corporate standards.

merger A merger is effected if the parties to a simple contract later execute in its place a formal instrument of agreement covering the same matters and signed by the same parties.

National Standards Standard specifications and codes of practice prepared and issued by nationally recognized institutions, societies, and associations.

negotiations The spoken and written transactions between the Principal and the Contractor leading to an agreement to supply specified goods and services.

Negotiated Contract A contract agreement reached between a Principal and a Contractor by direct negotiations rather than through a formal competitive tendering process.

Nominated Subcontractor A particular subcontractor selected by the Principal without reference to the Main Contractor and nominated in the Enquiry Documents.

Nominated Tenderers Tenderers who are directly approached with a request to submit a tender.

Non-conforming Tender A tender which has been improperly completed or which does not comply with the Enquiry Documents.

Notice to Tenderers Written advice to Tenderers detailing Amendments to the Enquiry Documents.

Offer and Acceptance The process by which a contract is formed whereby an offer is made by one party and is unconditionally accepted by a second party.

Openly Invited Tenders Contractors who are publicly invited to submit tenders for work under a Contract.

Owner The party who ultimately pays for the work under the Contract and who will 'own' the Works. Usually the owner of the property on which the work under the contract is carried out.

Part Lump Sum Part Schedule of Rates Contract A contract where part of the work is covered by a Lump Sum and part is covered by a Schedule of Rates.

Particular Requirements Specification That part of the Specification wherein are detailed technical requirements of the work prescribed.

party An individual, a group of individuals, or a corporation who is a signatory to a legal agreement.

Payment Bond A surety bond provided as a guarantee that all subcontractors and suppliers who have a direct contract with the Contractor will be paid.

Performance Bond A surety bond deposited as a Security Deposit.

Practical Completion That stage in the execution of the work under the Contract when the Works are complete except for minor omissions and defects which will not prevent the convenient use of the Works.

Pre-Qualification Documents Documents completed and submitted by contractors when applying for pre-qualification.

Pre-qualified Tenderers Contractors who have been approved by the Principal as tenderers before being invited to submit a tender for an engineering contract.

Pre-registered Tenderers Contractors who have registered their interest in being invited to tender for an engineering contract.

Priced Bill of Quantities A Bill of Quantities priced and extended by the Contractor and lodged with the Principal under the terms of the Contract.

primary statement A contract condition or requirement covering generally applicable basic principles.

Principal The principal party to the Contract who invites tenders, negotiates the Contract and eventually signs the Agreement. The Principal may or may not also be the Owner.

privity The legal relationship and mutual interest that exists between the parties to a contract.

Process Design The design of a production process itself as opposed to the design of the components of the system.

procurement A composite term used to describe purchasing, expediting, inspection and quality control required for a project.

progress payment An instalment payment made to a contractor during the progress of the work.

Project Management The procedure for monitoring and controlling the expenditure of time and money during the execution of a project.

Project Plan The detailed programme for the transformation of the initial concepts for a project into practical and economic realities.

Provisional Sum Any monetary sum allowance in the Contract for work under the Contract not otherwise priced by the Contractor.

purchasing The activities associated with placing orders for materials and equipment for work under the Contract.

Requirements for Tendering Documents whose sole function is to inform tenderers of the Principal's requirements regarding the preparation and submission of tenders.

resumption The act by a public authority of repossessing, for the public good, privately owned property.

retainage See retention.

retention An amount stated in the Agreement to be withheld from moneys due to the Contractor when a progress payment is being made.

Risk Analysis The evaluation of the consequences of possible risks likely to arise during the performance of the Contract.

schedule A tabulated or classified compiliation of information or details.

Schedule of Daywork Rates A schedule of hourly rates or percentage on-costs for labour and equipment hire used to determine the cost of variations.

Schedule of Prices for Tendering A schedule included in the Enquiry Documents for Lump Sum tenders and to be completed by tenderers listing items, quantities, and provisional sums for the whole of the work under the Contract.

Schedule of Rates A schedule included in the Contract which shows the rates or respective rates of payment for the execution of work to be carried out under the Contract.

Schedule of Rates Contract A contract where the Contractor is paid for the work actually done at pre-agreed unit rates.

secondary statement A contract condition or requirement which supplements, amends a primary statement or adapts the principles outlined in a primary statement to the particular requirements of the Contract.

Section See Separable Portion.

Security Deposit A financial consideration lodged by the Contractor to indemnify the Principal in the event of default by the Contractor during the performance of the Contract.

Selected Subcontractor A subcontractor selected by the Contractor from a restricted list of selected subcontractors included in the Enquiry Documents.

Separable Portion A part of the Works which, on reaching Practical Completion, by agreement or by direction, is handed over to the Principal.

shop details See shop drawings.

shop drawings Drawings specifically prepared in sufficient detail to show everything that is required for purchasing, preparing and shaping every piece of material required for the work.

simple contract An agreement made verbally, in writing or partly in both.

Site Lands or other places used for the purpose of the Contract.

Specification The written description of the technical requirements of the work under the Contract.

Standard Conditions of Contract See General Conditions of Contract.

Stipulated Price Contract See Lump Sum Contract.

subcontract An agreement between the Contractor and another contractor to undertake part of the work under the Contract.

subcontractor A person, firm or corporation engaged to execute work under a subcontract.

Substantial Completion See Practical Completion.

Superintendent The individual delegated to act in a supervisory and administrative capacity on behalf of the Principal during the Contract or Implementation stage. The Superintendent may or may not be the Engineer depending upon circumstances.

Superintendent's Representative A person appointed by the Superintendent to carry out specific duties on behalf of the Superintendent.

supervision The examination of work in progress to ensure compliance with the requirements of the Contract.

Supplementary Conditions of Contract A document comprising additional conditions amending or supplementing those in the standard General Conditions of Contract.

Surety The party providing the guarantee in a Surety Bond.

Surety Bond An agreement between two parties to provide a financial guarantee to be paid by one party in the event of default of the other party.

Technical Requirements All the technical details of the work to be done under the Contract.

Temporary Works Facilities or things used in the execution of the work under the Contract but not forming part of the Works.

tender A formal offer made by a contractor in reponse to an invitation to submit a proposal to undertake specified work under nominated terms and conditions.

Tender Bond A surety bond deposited as a Tender Deposit.

Tender Deposit A financial consideration submitted by tenderers with their tenders as a guarantee of their good faith.

Tender Documents All the documents which comprise a Tenderer's offer and form the actual tender to be submitted.

Tender Enquiry Documents *See* Enquiry Documents.

Tender Form A document prepared or completed and signed by a tenderer as a legally binding offer to undertake work under a contract.

Tender Period The period between the issue of the Enquiry Documents and the receipt of tenders.

Tender Sum The amount nominated by a tenderer in a tender as consideration for performing the work under the Contract.

tenderer Any contractor who submits a tender.

tort An injury or breach of duty whereby a party acquires a right of action for damages arising from the alleged injury or breach.

Turnkey Contract A contract in which the Contractor assumes complete responsibility for the project.

Validity Period The period for which tenderers are required to guarantee their tenders.

valuable consideration *See* consideration.

variation An adjustment to the cost of the work arising from an increase, decrease, omission, change in character or quality, change in position or dimensions, or demolition of any part of the work under the Contract.

warranty A term in a contract which is subsidiary to the main purpose of the contract, a breach of which gives the right to sue for damages.

wear and tear The anticipated wearing or deterioration of elements or parts and the use of consumables during the normal use of the Works.

work-as-executed drawings Contract Drawings which have been amended at the conclusion of the work under the Contract to show all amendments and changes made during the Contract.

work under the Contract All work which the Contractor is, or may be, required to execute under the Contract; this includes all authorized variations, temporary work, making good defects, and the use of constructional plant and equipment.

Working Drawings Drawings prepared and exchanged by the parties after acceptance of the Tender.

Works The whole of the work to be performed in accordance with the Contract and which, on completion, is to be handed over to the Principal.

INDEX